Recipes

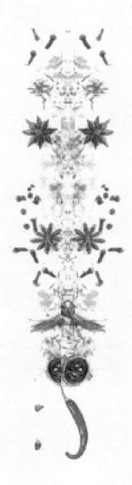

Richard Man

Welcome to the world of preserving and pickling! I am a culinary enthusiast and a lover of all things preserved. In this cookbook, we will take you on a delicious journey through the art of preserving and pickling foods in Ball Jars. These time-honored techniques have been passed down through generations and are a wonderful way to extend the life of your seasonal produce.

From tangy pickled cucumbers and spicy pepperoncini to fragrant dill green beans and sweet cherry preserves, the recipes in this cookbook are sure to delight your taste buds and add a touch of homemade goodness to your meals. Whether you are a seasoned canning expert or a beginner looking to learn the art of preserving, this cookbook has something for everyone.

So, join me as we explore the delicious world of preserving and pickling in Ball Jars. Let's create tasty, homemade treats that will be enjoyed for months to come.

Happy preserving!

APPLE AND CINNAMON JAM

This sweet and spicy jam is a perfect addition to toast, pancakes, or even as a topping for ice cream.

---

2 cups apple cider
4 cups apples, peeled and chopped
2 cups granulated sugar
1 tablespoon cinnamon
1/2 teaspoon nutmeg
1 tablespoon lemon juice

1. In a medium saucepan, combine the apple cider, apples, sugar, cinnamon, and nutmeg. Bring to a boil over medium-high heat, stirring constantly.
2. Reduce heat to medium-low and let simmer for 20-25 minutes, stirring occasionally, until the apples are tender, and the mixture has thickened.
3. Stir in the lemon juice and continue to cook for an additional 5 minutes.
4. Remove from heat and let cool slightly before transferring to a jar or container. Store in the refrigerator for up to 1 month.

APPLE CHUTNEY

This tangy and savory chutney is a great accompaniment to roasted meats or as a condiment for sandwiches.

---

3 cups apples, peeled and chopped
1 cup onion, chopped
1/2 cup brown sugar
1/2 cup apple cider vinegar
1 tablespoon mustard seeds
1 teaspoon ground ginger
1 teaspoon salt
1/2 teaspoon ground black pepper
1/4 teaspoon red pepper flakes

APPLE CHUTNEY

This sweet and tangy apple chutney is the perfect accompaniment to a variety of dishes. The combination of apples, vinegar, sugar, and spices creates a delicious spread that is perfect for topping sandwiches, meats, and cheeses.

---

2 apples, peeled, cored, and diced

1 onion, diced

1/2 cup apple cider vinegar

1/2 cup brown sugar

1/2 teaspoon ground cinnamon

1/4 teaspoon ground ginger

1/4 teaspoon ground allspice

1/4 teaspoon ground cloves

1/4 teaspoon ground nutmeg

1. In a medium saucepan, combine the apples, onion, apple cider vinegar, brown sugar, cinnamon, ginger, allspice, cloves, and nutmeg.
2. Bring to a boil over medium heat, stirring occasionally.
3. Reduce heat to low and simmer for 30 minutes, or until the apples are soft and the chutney has thickened.
4. Let cool completely and transfer to a jar or airtight container.
5. Store in the refrigerator for up to 2 weeks. Serve cold or at room temperature.

APRICOT AND SAGE JAM

2 cups fresh apricots, pitted and diced
1 cup sugar
1/4 cup water
1/4 cup fresh sage leaves, chopped
2 tbsp lemon juice
1/2 tsp salt

1. In a medium saucepan, combine the apricots, sugar, water, and sage leaves. Bring to a boil over medium heat, stirring occasionally.
2. Reduce the heat to low and simmer for 20 minutes, or until the apricots are soft and the mixture has thickened slightly.
3. Stir in the lemon juice and salt and continue to cook for an additional 5 minutes.
4. Carefully ladle the hot jam into a clean, sterilized ball jar, leaving about 1/4 inch of space at the top.
5. Secure the lid and let the jam cool to room

APRICOT CHUTNEY RECIPE

2 cups apricots, chopped
1 cup onion, chopped
1 cup white vinegar
1/2 cup brown sugar
1/4 cup raisins
2 tablespoons
mustard seeds
1 teaspoon salt

1. In a large saucepan, combine the apricots, onion, vinegar, brown sugar, raisins, mustard seeds, and salt.
2. Bring to a boil over medium-high heat, then reduce the heat to low and simmer for 45 minutes, stirring occasionally.
3. Ladle the chutney into sterilized ball jars, making sure to leave about 1/4 inch of headspace at the top of the jar.
4. Place the lids on the jars and screw on the bands until they are fingertip tight.
5. Process the jars in a boiling water canner for 15 minutes, then remove and let cool completely.

ASIAN PEAR KIMCHI

As a child, I remember my grandmother making kimchi in her kitchen. She would spend hours preparing the vegetables, mixing them with spices and fermenting them in large ceramic pots. Now, I continue her tradition by making my own kimchi, but with a twist. I use Asian pears to add a sweet and juicy element to the traditional spicy and tangy dish. And instead of a ceramic pot, I use a ball jar to ferment the

1 large napa cabbage
1 cup of Korean red pepper flakes
1 cup of water
1/4 cup of salt
4 cloves of garlic, minced
1 tablespoon of ginger, grated
1/2 cup of green onions, chopped
2 Asian pears, peeled and diced
1/4 cup of fish sauce

1. Cut the napa cabbage into small pieces and place in a large bowl.
2. In a small bowl, mix together the Korean red pepper flakes, water, and salt to create a paste.
3. Add the garlic, ginger, green onions, and Asian pears to the paste and mix well.
4. Pour the paste over the cabbage and mix until the cabbage is evenly coated.
5. Transfer the mixture to a ball jar and press down firmly to remove any air bubbles.
6. Seal the jar and let it ferment at room temperature for 3-5 days, depending on desired level of fermentation.
7. After the kimchi has fermented, transfer it to the refrigerator to slow down the fermentation process.
8. Enjoy the kimchi as a side dish or use it to add flavor to soups and stews.

BEET AND ONION RELISH

This tangy and sweet relish is a perfect accompaniment to any grilled meat or veggie burger. The deep red color of the beet's pairs beautifully with the bright yellow onion, creating a colorful and flavorful condiment that will elevate any dish. Plus, it's easy to make and can be canned and preserved in a ball jar for future use.

2 cups diced cooked beets
1 cup diced yellow onion
1/2 cup apple cider vinegar
1/4 cup sugar
1 tablespoon mustard seeds
1/2 teaspoon salt

1. In a medium saucepan, combine the beets, onion, vinegar, sugar, mustard seeds, and salt.
2. Bring the mixture to a boil over medium-high heat, then reduce the heat to low and simmer for 10 minutes, stirring occasionally.
3. Using a slotted spoon, transfer the relish to a ball jar, making sure to leave about 1/2 inch of headspace at the top.
4. Seal the jar tightly and process in a boiling water bath for 10 minutes.
5. Allow the jar to cool completely before storing in the refrigerator for up to 1 month. Enjoy on sandwiches, burgers, or as a topping for grilled meats.

BLACKBERRY AND LEMON JAM

The first time I made this blackberry and lemon jam, I was pleasantly surprised by the tangy and sweet flavors that were perfectly balanced in each bite. It was the perfect addition to my morning toast, and I knew I had to share the recipe with others.

3 cups blackberries
1 lemon, zested and juiced
1 cup sugar
1 tablespoon lemon juice
1 teaspoon vanilla extract
2 tablespoons butter

1. In a large saucepan, combine the blackberries, lemon zest and juice, sugar, and lemon juice. Cook over medium heat, stirring occasionally, until the sugar has dissolved, and the berries have started to release their juices.

2. Once the sugar has dissolved, add the vanilla extract and butter, stirring until the butter has melted.

3. Increase the heat to medium-high and bring the mixture to a boil. Boil for 10-15 minutes, stirring occasionally, until the jam has thickened, and a spoon dragged across the bottom of the pan leaves a clear trail.

4. Carefully spoon the hot jam into a clean ball jar, making sure to leave a 1/4-inch headspace at the top. Wipe the rim of the jar clean and apply the lid and band,

BLUEBERRY AND LAVENDER JAM

This recipe for blueberry and lavender jam is perfect for those who love the sweet and floral flavors of lavender. It's easy to make and can be preserved in a ball jar for enjoying throughout the year.

4 cups fresh blueberries

1/2 cup sugar

1/4 cup water

1 tablespoon lavender buds

1. In a saucepan, combine the blueberries, sugar, and water. Bring to a boil, stirring occasionally.

2. Reduce heat to a simmer and add the lavender buds. Simmer for 10 minutes, stirring occasionally.

3. Remove from heat and let cool for 5 minutes. Transfer the jam to a ball jar and let cool completely before storing in the refrigerator. Enjoy on toast, scones, or even ice cream.

BREAD AND BUTTER PICKLES

This recipe for bread and butter pickles comes from my grandmother's kitchen, where she used to make them every summer with cucumbers from her garden. She always used a ball jar to store them, and they were the perfect addition to any sandwich or burger.

---

4 cups sliced cucumbers
2 cups thinly sliced onions
1/2 cup kosher salt
2 cups white vinegar
1 1/2 cups sugar
1 tablespoon mustard seeds
1 teaspoon celery seeds
1/2 teaspoon turmeric
1/4 teaspoon ground cloves

1. In a large bowl, combine the cucumbers, onions, and salt. Let sit for 2 hours, then rinse and drain well.

2. In a large saucepan, combine the vinegar, sugar, mustard seeds, celery seeds, turmeric, and cloves. Bring to a boil over medium-high heat, then reduce heat to low and simmer for 10 minutes.

3. Add the cucumber and onion mixture to the saucepan and simmer for an additional 10 minutes.

4. Using a slotted spoon, transfer the pickles to a clean ball jar and let cool to room temperature.

5. Cover and refrigerate for at least 1 week before enjoying. The pickles will keep in the refrigerator for up to 6 months.

CARROT AND ONION RELISH

This tangy relish is a staple at summer barbecues and picnics. The sweet carrots and pungent onions are balanced perfectly with a mix of spices and vinegar. Once made, it can be canned and stored in a ball jar for months, allowing you to enjoy the taste of summer all year long.

---

2 cups carrots, grated

1 cup onion, diced

1/2 cup vinegar

1/4 cup sugar

1 tablespoon mustard seeds

1 teaspoon salt

1/2 teaspoon celery seeds

1/4 teaspoon ground turmeric

1. In a large saucepan, combine the carrots, onion, vinegar, sugar, mustard seeds, salt, celery seeds, and turmeric.
2. Bring the mixture to a boil over medium heat, stirring occasionally.
3. Reduce the heat to low and simmer for 15 minutes, or until the vegetables are tender.
4. Allow the relish to cool slightly, then transfer it to a ball jar.
5. Store the jar in the refrigerator for up to 2 weeks, or in the pantry for up to 3 months.
6. Serve the relish as a condiment on burgers, hot dogs, or sandwiches.

CAULIFLOWER AND ONION RELISH

This delicious relish is the perfect addition to any summer barbecue or picnic. The combination of sweet onions and tangy cauliflower is a match made in heaven, and the whole thing is preserved in a beautiful ball jar for easy transport and storage. Here's how to make it at home.

1 head of cauliflower, chopped into small florets

2 medium onions, finely chopped

1 cup of apple cider vinegar

1 cup of sugar

1 tablespoon of mustard seeds

1 teaspoon of celery seeds

1 teaspoon of salt

1. In a large saucepan, combine the cauliflower, onions, vinegar, sugar, mustard seeds, celery seeds, and salt.

2. Bring the mixture to a boil over medium-high heat, stirring occasionally.

3. Reduce the heat to low and simmer for 30 minutes, or until the cauliflower is tender and the liquid has thickened.

4. Let the mixture cool slightly, then transfer it to a clean ball jar.

5. Seal the jar and store in the refrigerator for up to 3 months.

6. Serve the relish chilled or at room temperature, as a condiment on sandwiches, hot dogs, or burgers. Enjoy!

CHERRY AND ALMOND JAM

This delicious cherry and almond jam are the perfect addition to your morning toast or as a topping for your favorite ice cream. The sweetness of the cherries is balanced out by the nutty flavor of the almonds, creating a unique and tasty spread. This recipe uses a ball jar for storage, ensuring that your jam stays fresh and tasty for months to come.

1 cup pitted cherries
1/2 cup almonds
1/2 cup sugar
1/4 cup water
1 tablespoon lemon juice

1. In a small saucepan, combine the cherries, almonds, sugar, and water. Bring to a boil over medium-high heat, stirring constantly.
2. Reduce the heat to low and simmer for 15 minutes, stirring occasionally.
3. Remove the saucepan from the heat and stir in the lemon juice.
4. Carefully pour the hot jam into a clean and sterilized ball jar. Seal the jar tightly and let cool to room temperature.
5. Store the jar in the refrigerator for up to 3 months. Enjoy!

CHERRY AND VANILLA JAM

This delicious jam is made with a combination of sweet cherries and rich vanilla flavor. The perfect spread for toast or a topping for ice cream.

2 cups pitted cherries
1/2 cup sugar
1/4 cup water
1/4 tsp vanilla extract
1 ball jar

1. In a small saucepan, combine the cherries, sugar, and water. Bring to a simmer over medium heat, stirring occasionally.
2. Once the cherries have softened and the sugar has dissolved, add the vanilla extract and stir to combine.
3. Carefully transfer the cherry mixture to the ball jar, making sure to leave about 1/4 inch of space at the top.
4. Place the lid on the jar and let it cool to room temperature. Once cooled, store in the refrigerator for up to 2 weeks.
5. Serve the cherry and vanilla jam on toast or as a topping for ice cream. Enjoy!

CHERRY CHUTNEY

This recipe is a delicious way to preserve fresh cherries and create a tasty condiment to add to sandwiches, salads, and more. Using a ball jar, you can easily store and enjoy this cherry chutney for months to come.

---

2 cups fresh cherries, pitted and chopped

1 cup apple cider vinegar

1 cup sugar

1 onion, minced

1 tablespoon ginger, minced

1 tablespoon mustard seeds

1 teaspoon salt

1. In a saucepan, combine the cherries, vinegar, sugar, onion, ginger, mustard seeds, and salt. Bring to a boil over medium heat, stirring frequently.
2. Reduce heat to low and simmer for about 30 minutes, until the mixture thickens and the cherries are soft.
3. Transfer the cherry chutney to a clean ball jar and let cool to room temperature.
4. Once cooled, seal the ball jar and store in the refrigerator for up to 3 months. Enjoy on sandwiches, salads, or as a condiment with your favorite dishes.

CORN AND ONION RELISH

This delicious jam is made with a combination of sweet cherries and rich vanilla flavor. The perfect spread for toast or a topping for ice cream.

---

2 cups corn kernels (fresh or frozen)

1 cup diced red onion

1/2 cup diced green bell pepper

1/2 cup apple cider vinegar

1/2 cup sugar

1 tablespoon mustard seeds

1 tablespoon celery seeds

1 tablespoon ground turmeric

1 teaspoon salt

1. In a large saucepan, combine the corn, onion, bell pepper, vinegar, sugar, mustard seeds, celery seeds, turmeric, and salt.
2. Bring to a boil over high heat, then reduce the heat to low and simmer for 10 minutes, stirring occasionally.
3. Let the relish cool to room temperature, then transfer to a clean ball jar and seal with a lid.
4. Store in the refrigerator for up to a month, or in the freezer for up to 6 months.
5. Serve as a condiment with grilled meats, hot dogs, or as a topping for sandwiches. Enjoy!

CRANBERRY AND ORANGE JAM

This recipe is the perfect addition to your fall and holiday spreads. The combination of tart cranberries and sweet oranges creates a delicious and unique jam that is sure to impress your guests. Plus, it's easy to make and can be canned and preserved in a ball jar for future use.

1-pound fresh cranberries
1 orange, peeled and chopped
1 cup granulated sugar
1/2 cup water

1. In a medium saucepan, combine cranberries, orange, sugar, and water.
2. Cook over medium heat, stirring occasionally, until cranberries have softened and mixture has thickened.
3. Remove from heat and let cool slightly.
4. Transfer jam to a clean ball jar and seal tightly.
5. Store in the refrigerator for up to 2 weeks, or process in a boiling water bath for longer shelf life.
6. Enjoy on toast, crackers, or as a topping for oatmeal or yogurt.

CRANBERRY CHUTNEY

This delicious cranberry chutney is a great way to preserve the flavors of the fall season. It's perfect for pairing with roasted meats or as a tangy addition to your Thanksgiving feast. And the best part? It's easy to make and can be stored in a ball jar for long-term preservation.

---

12 oz fresh cranberries
1 cup apple cider vinegar
1 cup sugar
1 medium onion, diced
1/2 cup raisins
1/2 cup chopped pecans
1/2 teaspoon ground ginger
1/4 teaspoon ground cinnamon
1/4 teaspoon ground cloves

1. In a medium saucepan, combine the cranberries, vinegar, sugar, onion, raisins, pecans, ginger, cinnamon, and cloves. Bring to a boil over medium-high heat, stirring occasionally.

2. Reduce heat to low and simmer for 20-25 minutes, until the cranberries are soft, and the mixture is thickened.

3. Remove from heat and let cool. Once cool, transfer the chutney to a sterilized ball jar and seal with a lid. Store in the refrigerator for up to 3 weeks or in the freezer for up to 6 months.

4. Serve as a condiment with roasted meats or as a tangy addition to your Thanksgiving feast. Enjoy!

CUCUMBER AND ONION RELISH

This refreshing and tangy relish is the perfect accompaniment to any summer meal. The crisp cucumbers and sharp onions are balanced out by the sweet and spicy flavors of the vinegar and sugar. This relish is easy to make and can be stored in a ball jar for up to 6 months, so you can enjoy its deliciousness all season long.

---

3 medium cucumbers, peeled and diced

1 medium onion, diced

1 cup white vinegar

1/2 cup sugar

1/4 cup water

1 teaspoon mustard seeds

1/2 teaspoon salt

1. In a medium saucepan, combine the cucumbers, onion, vinegar, sugar, water, mustard seeds, and salt. Bring to a boil over medium-high heat.

2. Reduce heat to low and simmer for 10 minutes, stirring occasionally, until the vegetables are tender, and the mixture is thickened.

3. Let the relish cool to room temperature, then transfer to a ball jar and store in the refrigerator until ready to use. Serve chilled as a condiment with grilled meats, sandwiches, or hot dogs.

EGGPLANT AND ONION RELISH

This delicious and tangy relish is the perfect addition to any summer BBQ. The eggplant and onion pair beautifully together and the added spices give it a unique and flavorful kick. It can easily be canned and preserved in a ball jar for later use.

2 eggplants, diced
2 onions, diced
1 red bell pepper, diced
1/2 cup apple cider vinegar
1/4 cup sugar
1 tsp salt
1/2 tsp black pepper
1/2 tsp cumin
1/2 tsp red pepper flakes

1. In a large saucepan, combine the diced eggplant, onion, and red pepper.
2. Pour in the apple cider vinegar and add the sugar, salt, black pepper, cumin, and red pepper flakes.
3. Bring the mixture to a boil, then reduce heat and simmer for about 30 minutes, stirring occasionally, until the vegetables are tender.
4. Ladle the relish into clean and sterilized ball jars, leaving about 1/2 inch of headspace.
5. Process the jars in a boiling water bath for 10 minutes to ensure proper preservation.
6. Allow the jars to cool and store in the pantry for up to one year.
7. Serve the relish as a condiment with grilled meats or on top of sandwiches and burgers. Enjoy!

FIG AND HONEY JAM

This sweet and delicious fig and honey jam is perfect for spreading on toast, muffins, or even as a topping for ice cream. The recipe uses fresh figs and honey, which are then preserved in a ball jar for a tasty treat any time of the year.

---

2 cups of fresh figs, chopped
1 cup of honey
1 tablespoon of lemon juice
1/2 teaspoon of vanilla extract

1. In a medium saucepan, combine the chopped figs, honey, and lemon juice. Bring to a boil over medium heat, stirring occasionally.
2. Once boiling, reduce the heat to low and let the mixture simmer for about 15 minutes, or until the figs have softened and the mixture has thickened.
3. Stir in the vanilla extract and let the mixture cool for about 10 minutes.
4. Using a funnel, carefully pour the fig and honey jam into a clean, sterilized ball jar. Secure the lid and let the jam cool completely before storing in the refrigerator for up to 2 weeks.
5. Enjoy your fig and honey jam on toast, muffins, or as a topping for ice cream. It's a tasty and sweet treat any time of the

GRAPE AND ROSEMARY JAM

This recipe is a delicious twist on a classic grape jam, with the addition of fragrant rosemary. It's perfect for spreading on toast, topping off your morning yogurt, or even as a glaze for roast pork. And it's super easy to make and can be preserved in a beautiful ball jar to enjoy all year long. Here's how

2 cups grapes
1/4 cup honey
2 tbsp lemon juice
1 tbsp chopped fresh rosemary
1/2 tsp salt

1. In a saucepan, combine grapes, honey, lemon juice, rosemary, and salt.
2. Bring to a boil over medium heat, stirring occasionally.
3. Reduce heat to low and simmer for 20 minutes, or until the grapes have softened and the mixture has thickened.
4. Carefully ladle the hot mixture into a sterilized ball jar, leaving about 1/4 inch of headspace.
5. Wipe the rim of the jar clean and seal with a lid.
6. Process the jar in a boiling water bath for 10 minutes.
7. Allow the jar to cool completely before storing in the pantry for up to a year.

Enjoy your homemade grape and rosemary jam on toast, yogurt, or as a glaze for roast pork. And don't forget to admire the beautiful ball jar it's preserved in!

GRAPE CHUTNEY

A symbol of preservation and home canning, the ball jar is a staple in any home cook's pantry. In this recipe, we will be using a ball jar to store our homemade grape chutney, a sweet and savory condiment perfect for any meal.

---

1 cup red grapes, chopped

1/2 cup white grapes, chopped

1/4 cup red onion, diced

1/4 cup raisins

1/4 cup apple cider vinegar

2 tbsp honey

1 tbsp mustard seeds

1 tbsp coriander seeds

1 tsp salt

1/2 tsp black pepper

1. In a medium saucepan, combine the grapes, onion, raisins, vinegar, honey, mustard seeds, coriander seeds, salt, and pepper.

2. Bring to a boil over medium-high heat, then reduce heat to low and simmer for 30 minutes, stirring occasionally.

3. Let the chutney cool slightly, then transfer to a clean ball jar and seal.

4. Store in the refrigerator for up to 2 weeks or freeze for longer storage.

5. Serve with sandwiches, cheese plates, or as a condiment for grilled meats. Enjoy!

GRAPEFRUIT AND GINGER JAM

This tangy and sweet grapefruit and ginger jam is the perfect addition to any breakfast or dessert spread. The zesty grapefruit pairs perfectly with the spicy kick of ginger, creating a unique and delicious flavor. The best part is that it can be easily made and stored in a Ball jar for future use.

4 cups of grapefruit segments, peeled and seeded
1 cup of sugar
1 tablespoon of grated ginger
1 tablespoon of lemon juice

1. In a medium saucepan, combine the grapefruit segments, sugar, ginger, and lemon juice. Cook over medium heat, stirring occasionally, until the sugar has dissolved and the grapefruit is soft.

2. Using a potato masher or fork, mash the grapefruit mixture until it is slightly chunky.

3. Increase the heat to medium-high and bring the mixture to a boil. Boil for 10 minutes, stirring occasionally, until the mixture thickens and becomes jam-like in consistency.

4. Remove the saucepan from the heat and let the jam cool to room temperature.

5. Once cooled, spoon the grapefruit and ginger jam into a clean and sterilized Ball jar. Secure the lid and store in the refrigerator for up to 1 week.

GRAPEFRUIT CHUTNEY

This tangy and sweet grapefruit chutney is the perfect addition to any meal. The combination of grapefruit, onions, and spices creates a unique and flavorful condiment that is sure to impress. To make this chutney, you will need a ball jar and the following ingredients

---

1 grapefruit

1 onion

1 cup of sugar

1 cup of vinegar

1 teaspoon of mustard seeds

1 teaspoon of ground ginger

1 teaspoon of ground cinnamon

1 teaspoon of ground cloves

1. Peel and dice the grapefruit and onion into small pieces.

2. In a medium saucepan, combine the diced grapefruit, onion, sugar, vinegar, mustard seeds, ginger, cinnamon, and cloves.

3. Bring the mixture to a boil over medium-high heat, then reduce the heat to low and simmer for about 30 minutes, stirring occasionally, until the chutney has thickened.

4. Allow the chutney to cool slightly, then transfer it to a ball jar.

5. Refrigerate the chutney until it is ready to serve. Enjoy!

GREEN TOMATO AND ONION RELISH

This tangy and delicious relish is the perfect accompaniment to any summer barbecue or picnic. It's easy to make and can be stored in a ball jar for up to a year, so you can enjoy the taste of summer all year round.

2 cups green tomatoes, diced
1 cup onion, diced
1 cup sugar
1 cup vinegar
1 tablespoon mustard seeds
1 tablespoon celery seeds
1 teaspoon salt

1. In a large saucepan, combine the tomatoes, onion, sugar, vinegar, mustard seeds, celery seeds, and salt.
2. Bring the mixture to a boil over medium-high heat, stirring occasionally to dissolve the sugar.
3. Reduce the heat to low and simmer the relish for about 45 minutes, or until it has thickened, and the vegetables are tender.
4. Let the relish cool to room temperature.
5. Transfer the relish to a clean ball jar and store it in the refrigerator until ready to use.

Enjoy your tangy green tomato and onion relish on hot dogs, burgers, or as a topping for grilled chicken or pork. It's also delicious served alongside a platter of cheese and crackers.

HOMEMADE KOMBUCHA

For those who are new to kombucha, it is a fermented tea that has been enjoyed for centuries for its refreshing and health-promoting properties. Making your own kombucha at home is a fun and rewarding process, and it allows you to experiment with different flavors and ingredients to create a unique and delicious beverage. In this recipe, we will show you how to make kombucha using a ball jar, black tea, and a SCOBY (symbiotic culture of bacteria and yeast).

1 ball jar
1 quart water
2-3 tea bags
1 cup sugar
1 SCOBY
1 cup kombucha (from a previous batch or store-bought)

1. In a small pot, bring the water to a boil.
2. Remove the pot from the heat and add the tea bags, allowing them to steep for 5 minutes.
3. Remove the tea bags and stir in the sugar until it is fully dissolved.
4. Let the tea cool to room temperature.
5. Transfer the tea to a clean ball jar and add the SCOBY and kombucha.
6. Cover the jar with a cloth and secure it with a rubber band.
7. Place the jar in a warm, dark place and let it ferment for 7-10 days.
8. After the desired fermentation time, carefully remove the SCOBY and strain the kombucha into a clean jar or bottles.
9. Enjoy your homemade kombucha, either plain or with added flavors of your choice. Be sure to save some of the kombucha and SCOBY for your next batch!

HOT AND SOUR PICKLED CUCUMBERS

These hot and sour pickled cucumbers are the perfect addition to any meal. The combination of vinegar, sugar, and red pepper flakes creates a tangy and spicy flavor that will make your taste buds dance. And the best part is that they're super easy to make! Just grab a few cucumbers, some vinegar, sugar, and red pepper flakes, and a couple of ball jars, and you're ready to go.

---

3 cucumbers, sliced into rounds

1 cup white vinegar

1/2 cup sugar

1 tablespoon red pepper flakes

1. Place the cucumber slices in a ball jar.
2. In a small saucepan, heat the vinegar, sugar, and red pepper flakes over medium heat until the sugar has dissolved.
3. Pour the hot liquid over the cucumbers, making sure to cover them completely.
4. Let the cucumbers cool to room temperature, then seal the jar and place it in the refrigerator for at least 24 hours before serving.
5. Enjoy your hot and sour pickled cucumbers as a tasty side dish or topping for sandwiches and salads.

LEMON AND MINT JAM

This refreshing jam is perfect for a summertime spread on toast or scones. The combination of tangy lemon and bright mint is sure to wake up your taste buds. To make this jam, you'll need a few basic ingredients and a ball jar to store it in. Here's what you'll need

1 cup sugar

1 cup water

2 lemons, zested and juiced

1/2 cup fresh mint leaves

1. In a small saucepan, combine the sugar and water. Bring the mixture to a boil, stirring to dissolve the sugar.

2. Add the lemon zest and juice, and the mint leaves. Stir to combine, and continue to cook over medium heat until the jam has thickened and reached the desired consistency. This should take about 10-15 minutes.

3. Remove the jam from the heat and let it cool to room temperature. Once it has cooled, transfer the jam to a ball jar and store it in the refrigerator for up to 2 weeks.

4. To serve, spread the jam on toast or scones for a refreshing breakfast or snack. Enjoy!

LEMON CHUTNEY

This tangy and slightly sweet lemon chutney is a perfect accompaniment to any meal. It's easy to make and can be preserved in a ball jar for future use.

2 cups fresh lemon juice
1 cup white sugar
1 cup diced onion
1 cup diced green bell pepper
1 cup diced red bell pepper
1 cup diced apple
1 cup raisins
1 cup white vinegar
1 tbsp salt
1 tbsp mustard seeds
1 tbsp ground cumin
1 tbsp ground ginger

1. In a large saucepan, combine the lemon juice, sugar, onion, bell peppers, apple, raisins, vinegar, salt, mustard seeds, cumin, and ginger. Bring to a boil over medium heat, stirring occasionally.

2. Reduce the heat to low and let the chutney simmer for 30 minutes, stirring occasionally, until the vegetables are tender, and the chutney has thickened slightly.

3. Let the chutney cool slightly and then transfer it to a ball jar. Seal the jar and store it in the refrigerator for up to 2 weeks. Serve the chutney with your favorite dishes, or use it as a condiment for sandwiches, burgers, or grilled meats.

LIME AND BASIL JAM

This delicious jam is perfect for adding a pop of flavor to your toast, sandwiches, and more. Made with fresh limes and fragrant basil, it's a unique and tasty treat that can be easily made at home using a few simple ingredients and a ball jar. Try it out and see for yourself!

1 cup sugar

1 cup lime juice

1 cup fresh basil leaves, chopped

2 tbsp lemon juice

1/2 cup water

1/4 cup pectin

1. In a small saucepan, combine the sugar, lime juice, basil leaves, lemon juice, and water. Bring to a boil over medium-high heat, stirring frequently to dissolve the sugar.

2. Add the pectin and stir until dissolved. Bring the mixture back to a boil and cook for 1 minute, stirring constantly.

3. Remove the saucepan from the heat and let the jam cool for about 10 minutes. Ladle the jam into a clean, sterilized ball jar and seal tightly.

4. Store the jam in the refrigerator for up to 3 weeks, or in the freezer for up to 3 months. Enjoy on toast, sandwiches, or as a topping for ice cream or yogurt.

LIME CHUTNEY

This delicious lime chutney is the perfect condiment for adding a tangy kick to your favorite dishes. It's so easy to make and can be canned in a ball jar for long-term storage. Simply combine fresh limes, vinegar, sugar, and spices in a saucepan and bring to a boil. Once the mixture has thickened, pour it into a sterilized ball jar and seal for a tasty condiment that will last for months in your pantry.

---

1 cup fresh lime juice
1/2 cup white vinegar
1/2 cup sugar
1 teaspoon mustard seeds
1/2 teaspoon ground ginger
1/2 teaspoon ground turmeric
1/2 teaspoon salt

1. In a saucepan, combine the lime juice, vinegar, sugar, mustard seeds, ginger, turmeric, and salt.
2. Bring the mixture to a boil over medium heat, stirring constantly.
3. Once the mixture has thickened, remove it from the heat and pour it into a sterilized ball jar.
4. Seal the jar and allow it to cool to room temperature before storing it in the pantry.
5. Enjoy your homemade lime chutney on sandwiches, wraps, or as a condiment for grilled meats and vegetables.

MANGO AND CHILI JAM

This spicy and sweet jam is the perfect accompaniment to any meal. The tangy flavor of the mango is balanced by the heat of the chili, creating a unique and delicious spread. We love to use this jam on toast, as a glaze for grilled chicken, or even as a topping for ice cream. To make this jam, you will need a ball jar to store it in and enjoy for months to come.

4 cups diced mango
1 cup white sugar
1/2 cup apple cider vinegar
2 tbsp minced chili peppers
1 tsp salt
1/2 tsp ground ginger

1. In a medium saucepan, combine the mango, sugar, vinegar, chili peppers, salt, and ginger.
2. Bring the mixture to a boil, stirring constantly.
3. Reduce the heat to low and simmer for 20-30 minutes, or until the jam has thickened and the fruit is soft.
4. Remove the pan from the heat and let the jam cool slightly.
5. Transfer the jam to a ball jar and seal tightly.
6. Store the jar in the refrigerator for up to 6 months. Enjoy!

MANGO CHUTNEY

This delicious mango chutney is a staple in many Indian households and is a perfect accompaniment to any savory meal. The tangy and sweet flavors of the mangoes are enhanced by the addition of spices and vinegar, and the resulting chutney is sure to be a hit with everyone. This recipe makes enough to fill a large ball jar, so you'll have plenty to enjoy for weeks to come.

3 cups mangoes, peeled and chopped
1 cup sugar
1/2 cup vinegar
1 tablespoon mustard seeds
1 tablespoon ground ginger
1 tablespoon ground cumin
1 teaspoon ground cinnamon
1/2 teaspoon ground cloves

1. In a large saucepan, combine the mangoes, sugar, vinegar, mustard seeds, ginger, cumin, cinnamon, and cloves. Bring to a boil over medium-high heat, stirring constantly.

2. Reduce the heat to low and simmer, stirring occasionally, for about 45 minutes, or until the chutney has thickened and the mangoes are very soft.

3. Let the chutney cool to room temperature, then transfer to a ball jar and store in the refrigerator until ready to use. Enjoy!

MUSHROOM AND ONION RELISH

This relish is a perfect addition to any summer barbecue or outdoor gathering. The earthy flavors of mushrooms and onions are enhanced by the tanginess of vinegar and the sweetness of sugar, creating a delicious condiment that pairs well with grilled meats and vegetables.

1 ball jar of canned mushrooms, drained and chopped

1 small onion, finely diced

1/4 cup white vinegar

1/4 cup sugar

1/2 teaspoon salt

1/2 teaspoon black pepper

1. In a medium saucepan, combine the mushrooms, onion, vinegar, sugar, salt, and pepper.

2. Cook over medium heat, stirring occasionally, until the onion is softened and the mixture is heated through.

3. Transfer the relish to a clean ball jar and seal with a lid.

4. Refrigerate until ready to serve. The relish will keep for up to one week in the refrigerator.

OKRA AND ONION RELISH

This okra and onion relish is a southern staple, perfect for adding a tangy, savory flavor to any dish. It's also easy to preserve in a ball jar, so you can enjoy it all year round.

2 cups okra, sliced
1 cup onion, diced
1/2 cup vinegar
1/4 cup sugar
1/4 cup water
1/4 cup olive oil
1/2 teaspoon salt
1/4 teaspoon black pepper

1. In a medium saucepan, combine the okra, onion, vinegar, sugar, water, olive oil, salt, and black pepper.
2. Bring to a boil over high heat, then reduce heat to medium-low and let simmer for 15 minutes.
3. Remove from heat and let cool to room temperature.
4. Transfer the relish to a ball jar, making sure to leave enough headspace for expansion during the canning process.
5. Process in a boiling water canner according to the manufacturer's instructions.
6. Once processed, let the jar cool completely before storing in a cool, dark place for up to a year.
7. To serve, simply spoon the relish over your favorite dish, or use as a topping for sandwiches and burgers.

ORANGE AND CARDAMOM JAM

This delicious orange and cardamom jam is the perfect addition to any morning toast or croissant. The sweet, tangy flavor of the orange pairs perfectly with the warm, spicy notes of the cardamom, creating a jam that is both unique and incredibly tasty. To make this jam, you will need a few simple ingredients, a pot, and a few clean ball jars to store the finished product in. Whether you're a seasoned canner or a beginner, this recipe is sure to become a staple in your home.

2 cups of freshly squeezed orange juice
2 cups of granulated sugar
1 tablespoon of ground cardamom
1 tablespoon of lemon juice
1/2 teaspoon of vanilla extract

1. In a medium-sized pot, combine the orange juice, sugar, and cardamom. Bring the mixture to a boil over medium heat, stirring occasionally to dissolve the sugar.
2. Once the mixture has reached a rolling boil, reduce the heat to low and let it simmer for about 15 minutes, or until it has thickened and reduced by half.
3. Stir in the lemon juice and vanilla extract and continue to simmer for another 5 minutes.
4. Carefully ladle the hot jam into clean ball jars, leaving about 1/2 inch of headspace at the top. Wipe the rims clean with a damp cloth, and then attach the lids and rings.
5. Process the filled jars in a boiling water bath for 10 minutes. Remove the jars from the water and let them cool completely on a wire rack.
6. Once the jars are cool, test the seals by pressing down on the center of the lid. If it doesn't pop back up, the seal is good. If it does, the jar will need to be refrigerated and used within a few weeks.
7. Store the sealed jars in a cool, dark place for up to a year. Enjoy your homemade orange and cardamom jam on toast, muffins, or whatever else your heart desires!

ORANGE CHUTNEY

This orange chutney recipe is a perfect addition to any meal that needs a tangy, sweet and spicy kick. The combination of orange and spices creates a delicious and unique flavor that will elevate any dish. This recipe makes enough to fill a quart-sized ball jar, perfect for storing in the pantry for later use.

2 cups peeled and diced oranges

1 cup diced onions

1 cup diced apples

1 cup diced mango

1 cup sugar

1 cup white vinegar

1 tablespoon grated ginger

1 tablespoon mustard seeds

1 teaspoon salt

1 teaspoon red pepper flakes

1. In a large saucepan, combine all ingredients and bring to a boil over medium-high heat.
2. Reduce heat to low and simmer for 30 minutes, stirring occasionally.
3. Using a ladle, carefully transfer the chutney to a sterilized ball jar.
4. Let the jar cool completely before sealing with a lid. Store in the pantry for up to 6 months.
5. Serve with your favorite meats, cheeses, or as a condiment for sandwiches and wraps. Enjoy!

PAPAYA AND GARLIC JAM

This delicious and unique jam is the perfect combination of sweet and savory. The papaya provides a tropical twist, while the garlic adds a subtle kick. It's the perfect addition to any sandwich or charcuterie board. Plus, it's easy to make and can be preserved in a ball jar for later use.

2 cups chopped papaya

2 cloves garlic, minced

1/2 cup sugar

1/4 cup apple cider vinegar

1/2 teaspoon salt

1. In a small saucepan, combine the papaya, garlic, sugar, vinegar, and salt.
2. Cook over medium heat, stirring occasionally, until the sugar has dissolved, and the mixture has thickened slightly, about 10 minutes.
3. Allow the jam to cool completely, then transfer to a clean ball jar and seal.
4. Store in the refrigerator for up to 2 weeks or freeze for longer storage.
5. Enjoy on toast, sandwiches, or as a condiment for grilled meats and vegetables.

PAPAYA CHUTNEY IN A BALL JAR

This tangy and sweet papaya chutney is the perfect accompaniment to any curry or grilled meat dish. The spicy kick of the ginger and chili peppers is balanced out by the sweet notes of the papaya and sugar, creating a flavor explosion in every bite. Plus, the convenience of a ball jar makes it easy to store and enjoy whenever the craving hits.

---

1 ripe papaya, peeled and diced

1 cup sugar

1/2 cup white vinegar

1/4 cup fresh ginger, grated

2 red chili peppers, minced

1 teaspoon salt

1/2 teaspoon ground cloves

1. In a medium saucepan, combine the diced papaya, sugar, vinegar, ginger, chili peppers, salt, and cloves.
2. Bring the mixture to a boil over medium heat, stirring constantly to dissolve the sugar.
3. Reduce the heat to low and simmer for 30 minutes, or until the papaya is softened and the chutney has thickened.
4. Carefully ladle the hot chutney into a sterilized ball jar, making sure to leave 1/2 inch of space at the top.
5. Seal the jar and let cool to room temperature. Store in the refrigerator for up to 1 month.

PARSNIP AND ONION RELISH

This tangy parsnip and onion relish is the perfect accompaniment to a summer barbecue. It's made with simple pantry ingredients and can be easily canned in a Ball jar for future use. The sweet and tangy flavors of the parsnip and onion pair perfectly with grilled meats or added to sandwiches for a unique twist. Try it out for your next cookout and see for yourself!

2 large parsnips, peeled and diced
1 medium onion, diced
1/2 cup white vinegar
1/2 cup sugar
1/4 cup water
1 tsp salt
1/2 tsp ground black pepper

1. In a medium saucepan, combine the parsnips, onion, vinegar, sugar, water, salt, and pepper.
2. Bring the mixture to a boil over medium heat, stirring occasionally.
3. Reduce the heat to low and let the relish simmer for 20 minutes, or until the parsnips are tender and the liquid has thickened.
4. Remove the relish from the heat and let it cool slightly.
5. Carefully spoon the relish into a sterilized Ball jar, making sure to leave about 1/2 inch of headspace at the top of the jar.
6. Wipe the rim of the jar with a clean cloth and seal it with a lid.
7. Process the jar in a boiling water canner for 10 minutes to ensure proper sealing.
8. Let the jar cool completely and store it in the pantry for up to one year. Enjoy the relish with grilled meats or added to sandwiches for a unique flavor.

PAPAYA AND GARLIC JAM

This delicious and unique jam is the perfect combination of sweet and savory. The papaya provides a tropical twist, while the garlic adds a subtle kick. It's the perfect addition to any sandwich or charcuterie board. Plus, it's easy to make and can be preserved in a ball jar for later use.

---

2 cups chopped papaya

2 cloves garlic, minced

1/2 cup sugar

1/4 cup apple cider vinegar

1/2 teaspoon salt

1. In a small saucepan, combine the papaya, garlic, sugar, vinegar, and salt.
2. Cook over medium heat, stirring occasionally, until the sugar has dissolved, and the mixture has thickened slightly, about 10 minutes.
3. Allow the jam to cool completely, then transfer to a clean ball jar and seal.
4. Store in the refrigerator for up to 2 weeks or freeze for longer storage.
5. Enjoy on toast, sandwiches, or as a condiment for grilled meats and vegetables.

PEACH AND THYME JAM

This jam is a delicious and unique twist on a classic fruit spread. The sweetness of the peaches is balanced by the earthy flavor of thyme, resulting in a spread that is perfect for toast, biscuits, or even as a glaze for meats. To make this jam, you will need a couple of ripe peaches, sugar, lemon juice, thyme, and a ball jar for canning. Here's how to make it

1. Start by sterilizing your ball jar by boiling it in water for 10 minutes.
2. Meanwhile, peel and dice your peaches, and place them in a saucepan with the sugar, lemon juice, and thyme.
3. Cook the mixture over medium heat, stirring frequently, until the peaches have broken down and the mixture has thickened into a jam consistency.
4. Once the jam has reached the desired consistency, carefully transfer it to the sterilized ball jar and allow it to cool.
5. Once the jam has cooled, seal the jar and store it in the refrigerator for up to a month, or in the pantry for up to a year.

Enjoy your delicious Peach and Thyme Jam!

PEACH CHUTNEY

This recipe for peach chutney is a sweet and tangy condiment that is perfect for adding a pop of flavor to sandwiches, grilled meats, and even crackers and cheese. It's easy to make and can be stored in a ball jar in the refrigerator for up to a month, making it a great option for preserving the summer bounty of peaches.

---

2 cups peeled and diced peaches
1/2 cup diced onion
1/4 cup apple cider vinegar
1/4 cup sugar
1 tablespoon grated ginger
1 teaspoon mustard seeds
1/2 teaspoon salt

1. In a medium saucepan, combine the peaches, onion, vinegar, sugar, ginger, mustard seeds, and salt.

2. Bring the mixture to a boil over medium-high heat, then reduce the heat to low and simmer, stirring occasionally, until the peaches are soft, and the mixture has thickened, about 20 minutes.

3. Let the chutney cool to room temperature, then transfer it to a clean ball jar and store it in the refrigerator until ready to use. Serve chilled or at room temperature.

PICKLED APPLE AND CINNAMON

This sweet and tangy pickled apple and cinnamon recipe is the perfect addition to your fall canning repertoire. The apples are sliced and packed into a sterilized ball jar along with cinnamon sticks, sugar, vinegar, and a few other spices. The jar is then sealed and processed in a hot water bath, creating a delicious and unique preserve that is perfect for enjoying throughout the colder months.

---

4 cups apples, sliced

2 cinnamon sticks

1 cup sugar

1 cup vinegar

1 teaspoon ground cinnamon

1/2 teaspoon ground cloves

1/2 teaspoon ground allspice

1. Sterilize a ball jar by washing it in hot, soapy water and then placing it in a pot of boiling water for 10 minutes.
2. In a large saucepan, combine the apples, cinnamon sticks, sugar, vinegar, cinnamon, cloves, and allspice. Bring to a boil, then reduce the heat and simmer for 10 minutes.
3. Carefully remove the ball jar from the boiling water and fill it with the hot apple mixture, leaving about 1/2 inch of headspace at the top.
4. Wipe the rim of the jar with a clean cloth, then place the lid on top and screw on the ring until it is finger tight.
5. Return the jar to the pot of boiling water and process for 10 minutes.
6. Remove the jar from the water and allow it to cool completely before storing in a cool, dark place. The pickled apples will be ready to enjoy in about a week.

PICKLED APPLE AND ONION RELISH

This tangy and sweet relish is the perfect addition to any sandwich or charcuterie board. The combination of crisp apples and tangy onions is brought together by the vinegar and sugar pickling liquid, resulting in a tasty condiment that will elevate any dish. To make this relish, you will need a ball jar and the following ingredients

2 apples, cored and diced
1 onion, diced
1 cup apple cider vinegar
1/2 cup sugar
1 tablespoon mustard seeds
1 tablespoon salt

1. In a small saucepan, combine the apple cider vinegar, sugar, mustard seeds, and salt. Bring to a boil over medium heat, stirring to dissolve the sugar.
2. Once the liquid is boiling, add the diced apples and onions. Reduce the heat to low and simmer for 10 minutes, or until the apples and onions are tender.
3. Using a slotted spoon, transfer the apple and onion mixture to a clean ball jar.
4. Pour the hot pickling liquid over the apples and onions, making sure to completely cover them.
5. Seal the jar and let it cool to room temperature. Once cool, store the jar in the refrigerator for at least 1 week to allow the flavors to develop.
6. Once the relish has pickled, it is ready to use. Enjoy it on sandwiches, burgers, or as part of a charcuterie board.

PICKLED APRICOT AND GINGER

As soon as the first apricots of the season start appearing at the farmer's market, I like to grab a few and turn them into a delicious pickle. The addition of ginger gives this recipe a nice kick and makes for the perfect condiment to serve alongside grilled meats or cheeses.

1-pound fresh apricots, pitted and quartered
1 cup white vinegar
1 cup water
1/2 cup sugar
1 tablespoon grated ginger
1 tablespoon mustard seeds
1/2 tablespoon salt
1/4 teaspoon red pepper flakes
1 ball jar

1. In a small saucepan, bring the vinegar, water, sugar, ginger, mustard seeds, salt, and red pepper flakes to a boil. Stir until the sugar has dissolved.
2. Place the apricots in the ball jar and pour the hot vinegar mixture over the top. Make sure the apricots are completely covered in the liquid.
3. Let the jar cool to room temperature, then cover and refrigerate for at least 24 hours before serving. The pickled apricots will last for up to 2 weeks in the refrigerator. Enjoy!

PICKLED APPLES

In the heart of fall, when apples are ripe and abundant, it is the perfect time to preserve them in a delicious pickling brine. This recipe for pickled apples uses a combination of apple cider vinegar and honey to create a sweet and tangy flavor. The apples are then sealed in a ball jar and left to pickle for several weeks to fully develop the flavor. Serve these pickled apples as a unique topping for salads or as a tangy accompaniment to cheese plates.

3 cups apple cider vinegar
1 cup honey
2 teaspoons salt
1 tablespoon whole cloves
1 tablespoon whole allspice berries
2 cinnamon sticks
4 medium apples, peeled and sliced

1. In a medium saucepan, combine the apple cider vinegar, honey, and salt. Bring to a boil over medium heat, stirring to dissolve the honey and salt.

2. Add the cloves, allspice berries, and cinnamon sticks to the saucepan and stir to combine. Reduce the heat to low and simmer for 10 minutes.

3. Meanwhile, peel and slice the apples and place them in a large heat-proof bowl.

4. Once the pickling brine has finished simmering, pour it over the sliced apples in the bowl. Stir to coat the apples evenly with the brine.

5. Transfer the apples and pickling brine to a large ball jar. Seal the jar with a lid and let the apples pickle at room temperature for at least 2 weeks before serving. The longer the apples pickle, the more flavorful they will become.

PICKLED APPLE AND CINNAMON

This sweet and tangy pickled apple and cinnamon recipe is the perfect addition to your fall canning repertoire. The apples are sliced and packed into a sterilized ball jar along with cinnamon sticks, sugar, vinegar, and a few other spices. The jar is then sealed and processed in a hot water bath, creating a delicious and unique preserve that is perfect for enjoying throughout the colder months.

---

4 cups apples, sliced
2 cinnamon sticks
1 cup sugar
1 cup vinegar
1 teaspoon ground cinnamon
1/2 teaspoon ground cloves
1/2 teaspoon ground allspice

1. Sterilize a ball jar by washing it in hot, soapy water and then placing it in a pot of boiling water for 10 minutes.
2. In a large saucepan, combine the apples, cinnamon sticks, sugar, vinegar, cinnamon, cloves, and allspice. Bring to a boil, then reduce the heat and simmer for 10 minutes.
3. Carefully remove the ball jar from the boiling water and fill it with the hot apple mixture, leaving about 1/2 inch of headspace at the top.
4. Wipe the rim of the jar with a clean cloth, then place the lid on top and screw on the ring until it is finger tight.
5. Return the jar to the pot of boiling water and process for 10 minutes.
6. Remove the jar from the water and allow it to cool completely before storing in a cool, dark place. The pickled apples will be ready to enjoy in about a week.

PICKLED APPLE AND ROSEMARY

This recipe is perfect for preserving the sweet and tart flavors of apples, enhanced with the fragrant aroma of rosemary. The pickling process transforms the apples into a delicious condiment that can be enjoyed on sandwiches, salads, or as a tasty snack.

3 apples, cored and sliced into thin wedges
1 cup apple cider vinegar
1 cup water
1/4 cup sugar
2 sprigs fresh rosemary
2 cloves garlic, peeled and minced
1 tablespoon salt
1/2 tablespoon black peppercorns
1/2 tablespoon mustard seeds

1. In a medium saucepan, combine the apple cider vinegar, water, sugar, rosemary, garlic, salt, peppercorns, and mustard seeds. Bring to a boil over medium-high heat, stirring until the sugar has dissolved.

2. Place the sliced apples in a clean, sterilized ball jar. Pour the hot vinegar mixture over the apples, making sure they are fully covered.

3. Let the jar cool to room temperature, then seal with a lid and store in the refrigerator for at least 24 hours to allow the flavors to develop.

4. The pickled apples will keep in the refrigerator for up to 2 weeks. Enjoy on sandwiches, salads, or as a tasty snack.

PICKLED APRICOT AND ONION RELISH

This unique and delicious relish is a perfect addition to any summer barbecue. The tangy sweetness of the apricots pairs beautifully with the sharpness of the onion, creating a mouthwatering condiment that will have your guests coming back for more. Plus, it's easy to make and store in a trusty ball jar.

1 cup diced apricots

1 cup diced red onion

1/2 cup white vinegar

1/2 cup sugar

1 tablespoon mustard seeds

1 tablespoon salt

1. In a small saucepan, combine the apricots, onion, vinegar, sugar, mustard seeds, and salt.
2. Bring the mixture to a boil, then reduce the heat and simmer for 10 minutes.
3. Let the mixture cool slightly, then transfer it to a ball jar and seal it tightly.
4. Store the jar in the refrigerator for at least 24 hours before serving, to allow the flavors to meld. Serve the relish alongside grilled meats, in sandwiches, or as a condiment.

PICKLED APRICOTS AND THYME

These sweet and tangy pickled apricots are the perfect addition to any charcuterie board or cheese platter. The addition of thyme adds a subtle herbal flavor that complements the fruit beautifully. Simply pack the apricots and thyme into a ball jar, cover with vinegar and sugar, and let the flavors mingle for a few days before serving.

1-pound apricots, pitted and quartered

4 sprigs fresh thyme

1 cup white vinegar

1 cup sugar

1 tablespoon salt

1 teaspoon whole peppercorns

1. Place the apricots and thyme in a ball jar.
2. In a small saucepan, combine the vinegar, sugar, salt, and peppercorns. Bring to a simmer over medium heat, stirring until the sugar is dissolved.
3. Pour the hot vinegar mixture over the apricots, making sure to completely cover the fruit.
4. Let the pickling liquid cool to room temperature, then seal the ball jar and store in the refrigerator for at least 3 days before serving.
5. Serve the pickled apricots on a cheese platter or charcuterie board, alongside your favorite cheeses and meats. Enjoy!

PICKLED ARTICHOKE AND OREGANO

These pickled artichokes are a delicious and tangy addition to any meal. The orega-no adds a lovely herbaceous flavor that pairs perfectly with the briny artichokes. These pickles are easy to make and are a great way to preserve the flavors of sum-mer. They are perfect for adding to salads, sandwiches, or even as a snack on their own. All you need is a ball jar and a few simple ingredients to make these delicious pickles.

cup white vinegar

1 cup water

1 tablespoon sugar

1 tablespoon salt

1 tablespoon dried oregano

2 cloves garlic, minced

1 teaspoon black peppercorns

1 lemon, sliced

1-pound fresh artichoke hearts

1. In a small saucepan, combine the vinegar, water, sugar, salt, oregano, garlic, and peppercorns. Bring to a boil over medium heat and stir until the sugar and salt have dissolved.

2. In a clean and sterilized ball jar, layer the lemon slices and artichoke hearts. Pour the hot pickling liquid over the artichokes, making sure they are completely covered.

3. Seal the jar with a lid and let it cool to room temperature. Once cooled, place the jar in the fridge and let it pickle for at least 24 hours before serving.

4. The pickled artichokes will keep in the fridge for up to 2 weeks. Enjoy them as a tasty addition to salads, sandwiches, or as a snack on their own.

PICKLED ASIAN PEAR AND GARLIC

Introducing our delicious Pickled Asian Pear and Garlic recipe! This mouthwatering dish is the perfect combination of sweet and tangy flavors and is a great addition to any meal. To make this dish, you will need a few simple ingredients and a ball jar to store the finished product. Follow our step-by-step instructions below to make this tasty treat in your own kitchen!

---

1 Asian pear, thinly sliced
1 clove of garlic, minced
1 tablespoon of sugar
1 tablespoon of rice vinegar
1 tablespoon of soy sauce
1/4 teaspoon of salt

1. In a small saucepan, combine the sugar, rice vinegar, soy sauce, and salt. Bring the mixture to a simmer over medium heat, stirring occasionally, until the sugar has dissolved.
2. Add the sliced Asian pear and minced garlic to the saucepan and stir to coat the fruit and garlic evenly with the pickling liquid.
3. Transfer the pickled Asian pear and garlic to a clean ball jar, and let it cool to room temperature. Once cooled, seal the jar and store it in the refrigerator for up to 1 week.
4. Serve the pickled Asian pear and garlic as a tasty side dish or topping for salads, sandwiches, or sushi rolls. Enjoy!

PICKLED ASIAN PEAR AND GINGER

This recipe is a delicious way to preserve the crisp, juicy flavor of Asian pears. The addition of ginger gives a spicy kick to this simple pickle.

---

2 large Asian pears, peeled and thinly sliced

1 cup apple cider vinegar

1 cup water

1/2 cup sugar

1 tablespoon fresh ginger, grated

1 teaspoon salt

1. In a large saucepan, combine the apple cider vinegar, water, sugar, ginger, and salt. Bring to a boil over medium heat, stirring until the sugar has dissolved.

2. Add the sliced Asian pears to the boiling liquid and reduce the heat to low. Simmer for 5 minutes, until the pears are tender but still firm.

3. Using a slotted spoon, transfer the pear slices to a clean ball jar. Pour the pickling liquid over the pears, making sure they are completely covered.

4. Cover the ball jar with a lid, and let it cool to room temperature. Refrigerate for at least 24 hours before serving. The pickled pears will keep for up to 2 weeks in the refrigerator.

PICKLED ASPARAGUS

This recipe for pickled asparagus is a delicious and easy way to preserve the bounty of springtime asparagus. Perfect for snacking on its own or adding a tangy twist to salads and sandwiches, this pickled asparagus is sure to be a hit. Simply place the asparagus in a sterilized ball jar and cover with a vinegar brine, then let it sit in the refrigerator for a few days to develop its tangy flavor. Once it's ready, the pickled asparagus will keep for several weeks in the fridge, so you can enjoy its tangy goodness all season long.

1 bunch asparagus
1 cup white vinegar
1 cup water
1 tablespoon sugar
1 tablespoon salt
1 teaspoon mustard seeds
1 teaspoon peppercorns
1 garlic clove, minced

1. Wash the asparagus and trim off the tough ends.
2. In a small saucepan, combine the vinegar, water, sugar, salt, mustard seeds, peppercorns, and garlic. Bring to a boil over high heat, then reduce the heat to medium and let simmer for 5 minutes.
3. Place the asparagus in a sterilized ball jar, then pour the hot vinegar brine over the asparagus, making sure to completely cover the asparagus.
4. Let the jar sit at room temperature for 30 minutes, then transfer it to the refrigerator to chill for at least 2 days before serving.
5. The pickled asparagus will keep in the refrigerator for several weeks. Enjoy as a snack or as a tangy addition to salads and sandwiches.

PICKLED ASPARAGUS AND GARLIC

This recipe is a delicious and tangy way to preserve the fresh flavors of asparagus and garlic. Perfect for snacking on or adding to salads, sandwiches, and more. Simply pack the asparagus and garlic into a ball jar, and let the vinegar and spices do their magic. The result is a tasty and tangy pickled treat that will keep for months in the fridge.

---

1 lb asparagus, trimmed and cut into 1-inch pieces

4 cloves garlic, peeled and sliced

1 cup white vinegar

1/2 cup water

1 tablespoon sugar

1 tablespoon salt

1/2 teaspoon black peppercorns

1/2 teaspoon mustard seeds

1. In a large saucepan, combine the vinegar, water, sugar, salt, peppercorns, and mustard seeds. Bring to a boil over medium-high heat, stirring to dissolve the sugar and salt.

2. Add the asparagus and garlic to the saucepan and reduce the heat to low. Simmer for 5 minutes, or until the asparagus is just tender.

3. Carefully transfer the asparagus and garlic to a ball jar, using a slotted spoon to remove any excess liquid.

4. Cover the jar with a lid and refrigerate for at least 24 hours before enjoying. The pickled asparagus and garlic will keep in the fridge for up to 2 months. Enjoy!

PICKLED ASPARAGUS AND LEMON

In the days of old, pickling was a way of preserving food for the long winter months. Nowadays, we can enjoy the tangy and refreshing flavors of pickled asparagus and lemon year-round thanks to the trusty Ball jar. This recipe is a twist on the traditional pickled asparagus, adding a zesty kick of lemon to the mix. It's the perfect addition to any charcuterie board or as a tangy snack on its own.

1-pound fresh asparagus, trimmed
1 lemon, sliced into thin rounds
1/2 cup white vinegar
1/4 cup water
1 tablespoon sugar
1 teaspoon salt
1/4 teaspoon black peppercorns
1/4 teaspoon mustard seeds
1/4 teaspoon red pepper flakes
1 Ball jar with lid

1. In a small saucepan, combine the vinegar, water, sugar, salt, peppercorns, mustard seeds, and red pepper flakes. Bring to a simmer over medium heat, stirring until the sugar and salt have dissolved.

2. In the meantime, wash and trim the asparagus, then slice the lemon into thin rounds.

3. Place the asparagus and lemon slices into the Ball jar, making sure to leave some room at the top.

4. Once the pickling liquid has come to a simmer, carefully pour it over the asparagus and lemon in the jar, making sure to fully submerge the vegetables.

5. Place the lid on the jar and let it cool to room temperature.

6. Once cool, transfer the jar to the refrigerator and let it pickle for at least 24 hours before enjoying. The asparagus and lemon will keep in the refrigerator for up to 2 weeks.

PICKLED ASPARAGUS AND ONION RELISH

This tangy and flavorful relish is the perfect addition to any summer barbecue or picnic. The combination of pickled asparagus and onions is a classic, and the added spices give it a unique twist. This recipe is simple to make and can be stored in a Ball jar for up to six months.

1 pound asparagus, trimmed and cut into 1-inch pieces

1 red onion, thinly sliced

1 cup white vinegar

1 tablespoon sugar

1 teaspoon salt

1/2 teaspoon mustard seeds

1/4 teaspoon red pepper flakes

1. In a large saucepan, bring the vinegar, sugar, salt, mustard seeds, and red pepper flakes to a boil.

2. Add the asparagus and onion to the boiling liquid and simmer for 5 minutes.

3. Remove the saucepan from the heat and let the asparagus and onion cool in the liquid.

4. Once cooled, transfer the asparagus and onion to a Ball jar and seal with a lid.

5. Store in the refrigerator for up to 6 months. Serve as a condiment on sandwiches or burgers, or as a garnish on salads and other dishes. Enjoy!

PICKLED AVOCADO AND ONION RELISH

This tangy and flavorful relish is the perfect addition to any sandwich or charcuterie board. Made with fresh avocados, onions, and a blend of spices, it's sure to become a new favorite condiment. Best of all, it's easy to make and can be stored in a ball jar for up to a month in the fridge.

---

2 ripe avocados, peeled and diced
1 medium red onion, sliced
1 cup white vinegar
1/2 cup sugar
1 tablespoon pickling spice
1 teaspoon salt
1/4 teaspoon black pepper

1. In a medium saucepan, combine the vinegar, sugar, pickling spice, salt, and pepper. Bring to a boil over medium heat, stirring to dissolve the sugar.
2. Add the avocado and onion slices to the saucepan and reduce the heat to a simmer. Cook for 5 minutes, stirring occasionally.
3. Using a slotted spoon, transfer the avocado and onion slices to a clean ball jar.
4. Pour the hot vinegar mixture over the avocado and onion slices, making sure to completely cover them.
5. Let the jar cool to room temperature, then seal with a lid and refrigerate for at least 24 hours before serving. The relish will last for up to 1 month in the fridge. Enjoy!

PICKLED BANANA AND CINNAMON IN A BALL JAR

In this unique and flavorful recipe, ripe bananas are sliced and pickled in a mixture of white vinegar, sugar, cinnamon, and allspice. The result is a sweet and tangy side dish that pairs perfectly with grilled meats or as a topping for ice cream.

4 green bananas, sliced into 1/4-inch rounds
1 cup white vinegar
1/2 cup sugar
1 cinnamon stick
1/4 teaspoon allspice
1/4 teaspoon salt

1. In a small saucepan, bring the vinegar, sugar, cinnamon stick, allspice, and salt to a boil.

2. Once the mixture has come to a boil, reduce the heat to a simmer and add the sliced bananas.

3. Simmer the bananas in the pickling liquid for 5 minutes, or until they are tender but not mushy.

4. Using a slotted spoon, carefully transfer the pickled bananas to a clean, sterile ball jar.

5. Pour the remaining pickling liquid over the bananas, making sure to completely cover the fruit.

6. Seal the jar tightly and store in the refrigerator for at least 24 hours before serving. The pickled bananas will keep in the refrigerator for up to 1 week.

PICKLED BANANA AND CLOVES

These pickled bananas are a unique and delicious treat that can be enjoyed as a snack or used as a topping for your favorite dishes. The addition of cloves adds a warm and spicy flavor, making these pickled bananas a perfect addition to your pantry.

---

4 medium ripe bananas

2 cups white vinegar

1 cup water

1/2 cup sugar

1/2 teaspoon whole cloves

1/2 teaspoon salt

1. Peel the bananas and cut them into 1/2-inch slices.
2. In a small saucepan, combine the vinegar, water, sugar, cloves, and salt. Bring to a boil over medium-high heat, stirring to dissolve the sugar.
3. Place the sliced bananas in a clean, sterilized ball jar.
4. Pour the hot vinegar mixture over the bananas, making sure they are completely covered.
5. Seal the jar with a lid and let it cool to room temperature.
6. Once cooled, refrigerate the pickled bananas for at least 24 hours before serving. The pickled bananas will keep for up to 2 weeks in the refrigerator.

PICKLED BANANA AND GARLIC

This unique pickling recipe combines the sweetness of bananas with the pungent flavor of garlic for a truly unique taste. Perfect for adding a tangy twist to sandwiches or salads, these pickled bananas are sure to become a new favorite.

---

3 ripe bananas
3 cloves of garlic, peeled
1 cup white vinegar
1 cup water
2 tbsp sugar
1 tsp salt
1 tsp peppercorns
1 ball jar with lid

1. Peel the bananas and cut into 1/2-inch slices. Peel the garlic cloves and slice into thin rounds.

2. In a small saucepan, combine the vinegar, water, sugar, salt, and peppercorns. Bring to a boil and stir until the sugar and salt have dissolved.

3. Place the sliced bananas and garlic into the ball jar. Pour the hot pickling liquid over the top, making sure to completely cover the bananas and garlic.

4. Seal the ball jar with the lid and let cool to room temperature. Once cooled, store in the refrigerator for at least 24 hours before enjoying.

5. Serve on sandwiches, salads, or as a tasty snack. Enjoy!

PICKLED BANANA AND HONEY

This sweet and tangy pickled banana and honey recipe is the perfect addition to any charcuterie board or as a unique topping for a salad. The honey balances out the vinegar in the pickling liquid, creating a complex flavor that is sure to impress. Simply place the sliced bananas in a ball jar and pour over the pickling liquid. Let sit in the refrigerator for at least 24 hours before enjoying.

2 ripe bananas, sliced
1 cup white vinegar
1/2 cup honey
1 tablespoon salt
1 teaspoon black peppercorns
1/2 teaspoon mustard seeds

1. In a small saucepan, combine the vinegar, honey, salt, peppercorns, and mustard seeds. Bring to a boil and stir until the salt and honey have dissolved.
2. Place the sliced bananas in a ball jar.
3. Pour the hot pickling liquid over the bananas, making sure they are completely covered.
4. Place the lid on the ball jar and refrigerate for at least 24 hours before enjoying.
5. Serve as a unique topping for a salad or as part of a charcuterie board.

PICKLED GREEN BANANA AND LEMON

In a small town nestled in the hills of rural Mexico, a local family has been preserving their green bananas and lemons for generations. Using a traditional recipe passed down through the generations, this dish has become a staple at family gatherings and celebrations. To begin, gather your ingredients and a clean ball jar.

4 green bananas, peeled and sliced into 1/4-inch rounds
1 lemon, sliced into thin rounds
1 cup white vinegar
1/2 cup water
1/2 cup sugar
1 tablespoon salt
1 tablespoon coriander seeds
1 tablespoon black peppercorns

1. Place the green banana slices and lemon slices in the bottom of the ball jar.
2. In a small saucepan, combine the vinegar, water, sugar, salt, coriander seeds, and black peppercorns. Bring the mixture to a boil and stir until the sugar has dissolved.
3. Pour the hot vinegar mixture over the green bananas and lemon slices, making sure to completely cover them.
4. Cover the jar with a lid and let it cool to room temperature. Once cool, transfer the jar to the refrigerator and let it sit for at least 24 hours before serving.
5. The pickled green bananas and lemon slices can be enjoyed as a side dish or added to salads and sandwiches for a tangy, tangy flavor.

PICKLED GREEN BANANA AND NUTMEG

This recipe for pickled green banana and nutmeg is a unique and flavorful way to preserve a surplus of ripe bananas. The combination of sweet and tangy pickling liquid, nutmeg, and crisp green bananas creates a delicious and unusual condiment.

2 cups white vinegar

1 cup water

1 cup sugar

2 tablespoons pickling salt

4 green bananas, peeled and sliced into 1/4-inch rounds

1 teaspoon ground nutmeg

1. In a large saucepan, combine the vinegar, water, sugar, and pickling salt. Bring to a boil over medium-high heat, stirring to dissolve the sugar and salt.

2. Add the sliced green bananas to the boiling liquid and reduce the heat to low. Simmer for 10 minutes, or until the bananas are tender but still firm.

3. Remove the saucepan from the heat and stir in the ground nutmeg. Let the pickled green bananas cool to room temperature.

4. Using a slotted spoon, transfer the pickled green bananas to a clean, sterilized ball jar. Pour the pickling liquid over the bananas, making sure they are completely covered.

5. Seal the ball jar with a lid and store in the refrigerator for up to 3 weeks. Serve the pickled green bananas as a condiment with sandwiches, burgers, or grilled meats. Enjoy!

PICKLED BANANA PEPPERS AND ONION RELISH

This relish is perfect for those who love a little heat and tang in their dishes. The combination of pickled banana peppers and sweet onion creates a flavorful and versatile condiment that can be used on sandwiches, burgers, and even as a topping for grilled meats and vegetables.

---

1 cup sliced banana peppers
1 cup sliced onion
1/2 cup white vinegar
1/4 cup sugar
1/4 cup water
1 teaspoon salt
1/2 teaspoon dried oregano
1/2 teaspoon dried thyme

1. In a small saucepan, combine the vinegar, sugar, water, salt, oregano, and thyme. Bring to a simmer over medium heat, stirring until the sugar has dissolved.

2. Add the sliced banana peppers and onion to a large ball jar. Pour the hot vinegar mixture over the top, making sure to cover the peppers and onion completely.

3. Let the jar cool to room temperature, then seal and store in the refrigerator for at least 24 hours before using. The relish will keep for up to 2 weeks in the refrigerator. Enjoy!

PICKLED BANANA PEPPERS AND ROSEMARY

This recipe is a delicious way to preserve the flavors of summer. The combination of pickled banana peppers and fresh rosemary creates a tasty, tangy condiment that can be enjoyed all year long. Simply fill a ball jar with sliced banana peppers and fresh rosemary sprigs, and cover with a vinegar and water mixture. Let the mixture sit for at least 24 hours before enjoying.

1 cup sliced banana peppers
2 sprigs fresh rosemary
1 cup white vinegar
1 cup water
2 teaspoons sugar
1 teaspoon salt

1. In a ball jar, combine sliced banana peppers and rosemary sprigs.
2. In a small saucepan, combine vinegar, water, sugar, and salt. Bring to a boil, then reduce heat and simmer for 5 minutes.
3. Pour vinegar mixture over the banana peppers and rosemary in the ball jar.
4. Seal the jar and let sit at room temperature for at least 24 hours.
5. Enjoy the pickled banana peppers and rosemary as a condiment on sandwiches or as a topping for salads.

PICKLED BEET AND BASIL RECIPE

This delicious, pickled beet and basil recipe is perfect for preserving the flavors of summer and enjoying them throughout the year. The sweet and tangy pickled beets are complemented by the fresh and herbaceous flavors of basil, creating a unique and tasty treat.

2 cups beetroots, peeled and sliced into rounds

1 cup white vinegar

1 cup water

1/4 cup sugar

1 tablespoon salt

1 tablespoon mustard seeds

1 tablespoon black peppercorns

1/4 cup fresh basil, chopped

1. In a medium saucepan, bring the vinegar, water, sugar, salt, mustard seeds, and peppercorns to a boil.

2. Reduce heat to low and add the beetroots. Simmer for 10 minutes, or until the beets are tender.

3. In a clean and sterilized ball jar, add the basil to the bottom of the jar.

4. Carefully transfer the cooked beetroots to the ball jar, using tongs to avoid burning your hands.

5. Pour the pickling liquid over the beets, making sure to cover them completely.

6. Seal the ball jar and let it cool to room temperature before storing it in the refrigerator.

7. The pickled beets will be ready to enjoy after at least 24 hours, but for the best flavor, let them pickle for at least a week.

8. Serve the pickled beets as a side dish or add them to salads and sandwiches for a tasty and unique flavor. Enjoy!

PICKLED BEET AND CLOVE RECIPE

In the heart of summer, when the garden is bursting with fresh beets, it's time to pre-serve the bounty in a tasty and tangy pickle. This recipe calls for whole beets, cloves, and a simple vinegar and sugar brine, all sealed in a beautiful ball jar. The resulting pickles are a delightful addition to any meal, adding a pop of color and a sharp, spicy flavor.

2 pounds fresh beets, washed and trimmed
1/4 cup whole cloves
1 cup white vinegar
1 cup water
1/2 cup sugar
1 tablespoon salt
1 teaspoon peppercorns

1. Bring a large pot of water to a boil and add the beets. Cook for 15-20 minutes, until the beets are tender but still firm.

2. Drain the beets and let them cool until they can be handled. Peel the beets and cut them into quarters.

3. In a small saucepan, combine the vinegar, water, sugar, salt, and peppercorns. Bring the mixture to a boil, stirring to dissolve the sugar and salt.

4. Pack the beets and cloves into a clean and sterilized ball jar. Pour the hot vinegar mixture over the beets, making sure they are completely covered.

5. Place the lid on the jar and let the beets cool to room temperature. Once cool, store the jar in the refrigerator for at least a week before enjoying the pickled beets. The pickles will keep in the refrigerator for up to 3 months.

BALL JAR PICKLED BEETS AND SAGE

This recipe is inspired by my grandma's classic pickling technique. She would always have a few ball jars filled with pickled beets and sage in her pantry, and I have fond memories of enjoying them as a snack or side dish. This recipe takes a bit of time to prepare, but the end result is well worth it. The combination of sweet, tangy beets and earthy sage is truly delicious.

4 cups water

1 cup vinegar

1/2 cup sugar

1 tablespoon salt

2 cloves garlic, minced

1 teaspoon mustard seeds

1 teaspoon coriander seeds

1/2 teaspoon black peppercorns

1 bunch fresh sage leaves

4 medium beets, peeled and sliced into

1. In a small saucepan, bring the water, vinegar, sugar, and salt to a boil over high heat. Stir until the sugar and salt have dissolved. Remove from heat and let cool to room temperature.

2. In a small bowl, combine the garlic, mustard seeds, coriander seeds, and peppercorns.

3. Divide the sage leaves evenly among four clean, sterilized ball jars.

4. Divide the beets evenly among the ball jars, packing them in tightly.

5. Pour the cooled brine over the beets, making sure to cover them completely.

6. Seal the jars and store in the refrigerator for at least 2 days before enjoying. The pickled beets will keep for up to 2 weeks in the refrigerator.

PICKLED BEETS IN A BALL JAR

These pickled beets are a delicious and easy way to preserve the bounty of the summer garden. The tangy vinegar and sweet sugar create a perfect balance of flavor, and the beets turn a beautiful pink color in the jar.

3 pounds fresh beets
1 cup white vinegar
1 cup water
1 cup sugar
2 teaspoons pickling spice
1 teaspoon salt
1 Ball jar with lid

1. Wash and trim the beets, leaving about 1 inch of the stem attached.
2. Bring a large pot of water to a boil and add the beets. Cook for about 20 minutes, or until the beets are tender when pierced with a knife.
3. Drain the beets and let them cool. Once they are cool enough to handle, peel the skins off and cut the beets into 1/4-inch slices.
4. In a small saucepan, combine the vinegar, water, sugar, pickling spice, and salt. Bring to a boil, stirring to dissolve the sugar.
5. Put the sliced beets into the Ball jar and pour the hot vinegar mixture over the beets. Make sure the beets are completely covered with the liquid.
6. Seal the jar with the lid and let it cool to room temperature. Once cooled, store the pickled beets in the refrigerator for up to 2 months. Serve as a delicious side dish or topping for salads

PICKLED BEETS AND BASIL

This recipe for pickled beets and basil is a delicious and unique way to preserve the fresh flavors of the summer. The bright red beets are pickled in a vinegar and sugar solution, and are then combined with fresh basil for a touch of herbaceous flavor. The finished product is perfect for adding to salads, sandwiches, or as a tangy and colorful side dish.

1-pound beets, peeled and sliced into 1/4-inch rounds

1 cup white vinegar

1/2 cup sugar

1 tablespoon kosher salt

1/2 cup fresh basil leaves, torn

1. In a medium saucepan, combine the vinegar, sugar, and salt and bring to a boil over high heat.

2. Once the mixture has come to a boil, add the sliced beets and reduce the heat to medium-low.

3. Simmer the beets for about 15 minutes, or until they are tender but still firm.

4. Remove the saucepan from the heat and add the torn basil leaves.

5. Transfer the beets and basil to a ball jar and let cool to room temperature.

6. Once the beets have cooled, cover the jar with a lid and store in the refrigerator for up to two weeks.

7. Serve the pickled beets and basil as a colorful and tangy side dish or as a flavorful addition to salads and sandwiches

PICKLED BEETS AND CLOVE

This recipe is a twist on traditional pickled beets, adding the spicy kick of cloves to create a unique and delicious flavor. Perfect for a quick and easy addition to any meal, these pickled beets can be stored in a ball jar in the refrigerator for up to a month.

2 cups beets, peeled and sliced
2 cups white vinegar
1 cup sugar
1 tablespoon whole cloves
1 teaspoon salt

1. In a medium saucepan, combine the vinegar, sugar, cloves, and salt over medium heat. Bring to a boil, stirring occasionally, until the sugar has dissolved.
2. Add the sliced beets to the saucepan and reduce the heat to low. Simmer for 10-15 minutes, until the beets are tender but still firm.
3. Carefully transfer the beets and liquid to a clean ball jar, making sure to leave about 1 inch of space at the top.
4. Seal the jar and place in the refrigerator to cool. The pickled beets will be ready to enjoy after 24 hours and can be stored in the refrigerator for up to a month.

PICKLED BEETS AND CLOVE

These pickled beets are a delicious and tangy addition to any meal. The clove adds a warm and spicy flavor that pairs perfectly with the sweetness of the beets. The recipe calls for a ball jar, which is a perfect vessel for preserving these tasty treats.

---

4 medium-sized beets, peeled and sliced into 1/4-inch rounds

1 cup white vinegar

1 cup water

1/2 cup sugar

1/2 teaspoon salt

4 cloves

1. In a medium-sized saucepan, bring the vinegar, water, sugar, and salt to a boil.
2. Add the sliced beets to the saucepan and let them cook for 5 minutes.
3. Remove the saucepan from the heat and let the beets cool in the liquid.
4. Once the beets are cool, transfer them to a ball jar, along with the cloves.
5. Seal the jar and let it sit in the refrigerator for at least 24 hours before serving.
6. Enjoy the pickled beets as a delicious addition to salads, sandwiches, or as a snack on their own.

PICKLED BELL PEPPER AND OREGANO

This tangy and flavorful pickle is a favorite in my family. The crisp bell peppers and fragrant oregano are preserved in a delicious vinegar brine, making them a perfect addition to any sandwich or charcuterie board. I love to use my Ball jar to store these pickled peppers, so they are always on hand for snacking or entertaining.

3 cups white vinegar
1/2 cup water
1/4 cup sugar
1/4 cup salt
1 tablespoon oregano leaves
1 teaspoon black peppercorns
4-5 large bell peppers, sliced into strips

1. In a medium saucepan, combine the vinegar, water, sugar, and salt. Bring to a boil over medium-high heat, stirring until the sugar and salt have dissolved.
2. Add the oregano and peppercorns to the saucepan and stir to combine.
3. Place the sliced bell peppers in a sterilized Ball jar and pour the hot vinegar mixture over the peppers.
4. Seal the jar tightly, and let the pickled peppers sit at room temperature for at least 24 hours before serving.
5. Once opened, store the pickled peppers in the refrigerator for up to 3 months. Enjoy as a tangy and flavorful addition to sandwiches, salads, and charcuterie boards.

PICKLED BELL PEPPER AND MINT

This recipe is inspired by my grandmother's signature dish that she would make every summer using fresh bell peppers and mint from her garden. She would carefully preserve the flavorful combination in a ball jar, allowing the flavors to marry and intensify over time. This dish is a tasty addition to any summer barbecue or as a tangy condiment on sandwiches and salads.

1 cup white vinegar

1 cup water

2 tbsp sugar

2 tbsp salt

1/2 tsp black peppercorns

1 bay leaf

2 cloves garlic, sliced

1 red bell pepper, julienned

1 yellow bell pepper, julienned

1 green bell pepper, julienned

1/4 cup chopped fresh

1. In a small saucepan, combine vinegar, water, sugar, salt, peppercorns, and bay leaf. Bring to a boil, stirring to dissolve the sugar and salt.

2. Meanwhile, divide the garlic, bell peppers, and mint evenly among 2 clean ball jars.

3. Once the vinegar mixture has come to a boil, carefully pour it over the vegetables in the jars, leaving about 1/2 inch of headspace.

4. Place the lids on the jars and gently screw on the rings to finger tight.

5. Process the jars in a boiling water bath for 15 minutes.

6. Remove the jars from the water bath and let cool completely on a towel-lined counter.

7. Once the jars have cooled, store in the refrigerator for up to 1 month.

PICKLED BEETS AND ONIONS

This recipe is a family favorite that has been passed down through generations. We always use fresh beets and onions from our garden and store them in a beautiful ball jar on our pantry shelf. The tangy vinegar and sweet sugar balance perfectly, making these pickled beets and onions a tasty addition to any meal.

---

2 lbs fresh beets, peeled and sliced into rounds
1 large onion, sliced into thin rounds
1 cup white vinegar
1 cup water
1/2 cup sugar
1 tablespoon salt
1 teaspoon peppercorns
1 bay leaf

1. In a medium saucepan, combine the vinegar, water, sugar, salt, peppercorns, and bay leaf. Bring to a boil over high heat, stirring until the sugar and salt are dissolved.
2. In a sterilized ball jar, layer the sliced beets and onions, making sure to evenly distribute them.
3. Carefully pour the hot vinegar mixture over the beets and onions, filling the jar to the top.
4. Place the lid on the jar and let it cool to room temperature. Once cool, transfer the jar to the refrigerator and let it sit for at least 24 hours before serving.
5. To serve, remove the jar from the refrigerator and open it carefully. Use a fork or tongs to remove the pickled beets and onions and enjoy!

PICKLED BEETS AND SAGE

This recipe is inspired by my grandmother's love for pickled beets. She used to make them every summer and preserve them in a ball jar to enjoy throughout the year. The addition of sage gives these pickled beets a unique flavor that pairs well with a variety of dishes.

2 pounds beets, peeled and sliced into 1/4-inch rounds
1 cup white vinegar
1 cup water
1/4 cup sugar
2 teaspoons salt
1 tablespoon fresh sage, chopped
1 tablespoon whole black peppercorns

1. In a medium saucepan, combine the vinegar, water, sugar, salt, and sage. Bring to a boil and stir until the sugar and salt are dissolved.

2. Place the sliced beets in a clean, sterilized ball jar and pour the hot vinegar mixture over the beets.

3. Add the black peppercorns to the jar and seal it with a lid.

4. Place the jar in the refrigerator and let it sit for at least 24 hours before opening. The beets will keep in the refrigerator for up to 2 weeks.

5. Serve the pickled beets as a side dish or use them to add flavor to salads, sandwiches, and other dishes.

PICKLED BELL PEPPER AND PAPRIKA

These pickled bell peppers and paprika are a tasty and colorful addition to any meal. The bell peppers are sliced and placed in a ball jar, along with paprika, vinegar, and spices. The jar is then sealed and left to pickle in the refrigerator for a few days. The result is a tangy and flavorful condiment that can be added to sandwiches, salads, or used as a garnish for soups and stews.

2 red bell peppers, sliced

1 tablespoon paprika

1 cup vinegar

1 tablespoon sugar

1 teaspoon salt

1/2 teaspoon black pepper

1/2 teaspoon garlic powder

1. Slice the red bell peppers into thin strips and place them in a ball jar.
2. Add the paprika, vinegar, sugar, salt, black pepper, and garlic powder to the jar, and stir to combine.
3. Seal the jar tightly and place it in the refrigerator for at least 3 days.
4. After 3 days, the pickled bell peppers and paprika are ready to enjoy. Use them as a condiment on sandwiches or salads, or as a garnish for soups and stews.

PICKLED BELL PEPPER AND PAPRIKA

This recipe is inspired by the traditional Hungarian dish, lecsó, which is a delicious mix of vegetables and spices pickled in a ball jar. The combination of sweet bell peppers and smoky paprika gives this dish a unique and flavorful taste. It's the perfect addition to any sandwich or salad and makes for a tasty snack on its own. Plus, it's super easy to make and can be stored in the fridge for up to a week.

2 red bell peppers, thinly sliced

1 yellow bell pepper, thinly sliced

1/2 onion, thinly sliced

1 tablespoon paprika

1 tablespoon sugar

1/2 cup vinegar

1/2 cup water

1 tablespoon salt

1 tablespoon olive oil

1. In a large saucepan, heat the olive oil over medium heat. Add the bell peppers, onion, and paprika, and cook for about 5 minutes, until the vegetables are softened.
2. In a small bowl, mix the sugar, vinegar, water, and salt. Pour the mixture over the vegetables and bring to a simmer.
3. Reduce the heat to low, and let the vegetables cook for about 10 minutes, until they are tender, and the liquid has reduced.
4. Transfer the vegetables to a clean ball jar and let them cool completely. Seal the jar, and store in the fridge for up to a week.
5. Serve the pickled bell peppers and paprika on sandwiches, salads, or as a tasty snack. Enjoy!

PICKLED BLACK OLIVES AND GARLIC IN A BALL JAR

Introducing our tasty pickled black olives and garlic in a convenient ball jar. These savory treats are perfect for adding a tangy and flavorful punch to any meal. The garlic adds a subtle kick, while the black olives provide a satisfying crunch. Simply open the jar and enjoy these pickled delights on their own or add them to your favorite dishes for a delicious twist. Here's how to make them at home

1 cup black olives

4 cloves garlic, sliced

1 cup white vinegar

1 cup water

1 tablespoon sugar

1 tablespoon salt

1 teaspoon black peppercorns

1 bay leaf

1 ball jar with lid

1. Begin by sterilizing your ball jar by boiling it in a pot of water for 10 minutes.
2. In a small saucepan, combine the vinegar, water, sugar, salt, peppercorns, and bay leaf. Bring the mixture to a boil over medium heat.
3. Once the mixture is boiling, add the sliced garlic and black olives. Stir to combine.
4. Carefully pour the hot pickling liquid over the olives and garlic in the ball jar, leaving a 1/2-inch headspace at the top of the jar.
5. Close the jar with the lid and let it cool to room temperature.
6. Once the jar has cooled, store it in the refrigerator for at least 24 hours before enjoying your pickled black olives and garlic. These pickles will last for up to 2 weeks in the fridge. Enjoy!

PICKLED BLACK OLIVE AND ONION RELISH

This tangy and flavorful relish is a perfect addition to any sandwich or charcuterie board. The salty brine of the black olives pairs perfectly with the sweet and tangy onions. It's easy to make and can be stored in a ball jar in the fridge for up to a month.

1 cup black olives, pitted and coarsely chopped
1 cup red onion, finely diced
1/2 cup red wine vinegar
1 tablespoon sugar
1 tablespoon mustard seeds
1/2 teaspoon salt

1. In a medium saucepan, combine the red onion, red wine vinegar, sugar, mustard seeds, and salt. Bring to a boil over medium-high heat, stirring occasionally.
2. Reduce heat to low and add the black olives. Simmer for 5 minutes, or until the onions are tender and the olives are plump.
3. Allow the relish to cool slightly before transferring to a ball jar. Seal the jar and store in the fridge for up to a month.
4. Serve the relish as a condiment for sandwiches, burgers, or with your favorite charcuterie board.

PICKLED BLACK OLIVE AND ROSEMARY

This recipe was inspired by a trip to the Mediterranean, where we sampled some delicious, pickled olives at a local market. We decided to recreate the flavors at home by using fresh rosemary and a ball jar to pickle our own black olives. The result is a tangy and fragrant treat that pairs perfectly with cheese and charcuterie.

1 cup black olives
1 sprig fresh rosemary
1/2 cup white vinegar
1/2 cup water
1 tablespoon sugar
1/2 teaspoon salt

1. Rinse the black olives and remove any stems or pits.
2. In a small saucepan, combine the vinegar, water, sugar, and salt. Bring to a simmer over medium heat, stirring to dissolve the sugar and salt.
3. Place the olives and rosemary sprig in a ball jar. Pour the hot vinegar mixture over the olives, making sure they are completely covered.
4. Let the jar cool to room temperature, then seal and refrigerate for at least 24 hours before serving. The pickled olives will keep for up to 1 month in the refrigerator.
5. To serve, remove the rosemary sprig and enjoy the olives as a snack or as part of a charcuterie board.

PICKLED BLACK OLIVES AND ROSEMARY

1 cup black olives
1 tablespoon rosemary
leaves
1 tablespoon vinegar
1/2 cup water
1 teaspoon sugar
1/2 teaspoon salt
1 ball jar

1. Start by rinsing the black olives and patting them dry with a paper towel.
2. In a small saucepan, combine the vinegar, water, sugar, and salt. Bring the mixture to a simmer over medium heat, stirring until the sugar and salt have dissolved.
3. Add the black olives and rosemary leaves to the ball jar. Pour the hot vinegar mixture over the olives, making sure they are completely submerged in the liquid.
4. Seal the jar tightly and let it cool to room temperature. Once cooled, transfer the jar to the refrigerator and let it pickle for at least 24 hours before serving.
5. Enjoy your pickled black olives and rosemary as a tasty snack or a flavorful addition to your favorite dishes.

PICKLED BLACK OLIVE AND THYME

This delicious and simple pickled black olive and thyme recipe is perfect for a quick and easy snack or appetizer. The thyme adds a fragrant and herbal touch, while the black olives provide a savory and slightly briny flavor. Simply pack the olives and thyme into a sterilized ball jar, and then cover with a vinegar and water mixture. Let the jar sit in the refrigerator for at least a day before enjoying the tasty and tangy results.

1 cup black olives, pitted

2 tbsp fresh thyme leaves

1 cup water

1 cup white vinegar

1 tbsp sugar

1 tsp salt

1. Begin by sterilizing your ball jar by washing it with hot soapy water and then rinsing it well. Let the jar dry completely.
2. In a small saucepan, combine the water, vinegar, sugar, and salt. Bring the mixture to a boil over medium heat, stirring occasionally, until the sugar and salt have dissolved.
3. Meanwhile, place the pitted black olives and thyme leaves in the sterilized ball jar.
4. Once the vinegar mixture has come to a boil, pour it over the olives and thyme in the jar. Be sure to fill the jar to the top, leaving about a half inch of space at the top of the jar.
5. Tightly seal the jar with a lid, and then let it cool to room temperature.
6. Place the jar in the refrigerator and let it sit for at least a day before enjoying the pickled black olives and thyme. The longer the olives and thyme sit in the vinegar mixture, the more flavorful they will become. Enjoy!

PICKLED BLACK OLIVES AND GARLIC

These pickled black olives and garlic are the perfect addition to any charcuterie board or antipasto platter. The tangy, briny flavor of the olives pairs perfectly with the spicy kick of the garlic, making for a delicious and unique snack. Best of all, they're easy to make and can be stored in a ball jar in the fridge for up to a month.

---

1 cup black olives, pitted
2 cloves garlic, sliced
1/2 cup white vinegar
1/2 cup water
1 tablespoon sugar
1 teaspoon salt
1 teaspoon dried oregano

1. In a small saucepan, combine the vinegar, water, sugar, salt, and oregano. Bring to a boil over medium-high heat.

2. Once boiling, add the sliced garlic and let simmer for 2 minutes.

3. Remove from heat and let the mixture cool for 5 minutes.

4. In a clean, sterilized ball jar, add the pitted olives and pour the cooled garlic and vinegar mixture over top.

5. Seal the jar and let it sit in the fridge for at least 24 hours before enjoying. The longer it sits, the more flavorful it will become.

6. Serve alongside other pickled or preserved snacks, or as a tasty addition to sandwiches and salads.

PICKLED BLACK OLIVES AND THYME

There's nothing quite like the tangy and herbaceous flavor of pickled black olives. This simple recipe is perfect for using up a jar of olives that have been sitting in the pantry for a while, and the addition of thyme adds a delightful depth of flavor. Simply pack the olives and thyme into a ball jar, cover with vinegar and a few spices, and let them sit for a few days to develop their flavor. Serve as a tasty snack or as part of a Mediterranean-inspired meal.

---

1 cup black olives, pitted
1 sprig fresh thyme
1 cup white vinegar
1 tablespoon sugar
1 teaspoon sea salt
1/2 teaspoon red pepper flakes

1. Rinse the olives and thyme under cold water, and pat dry.
2. In a small saucepan, combine the vinegar, sugar, salt, and red pepper flakes. Heat over medium heat until the sugar and salt are dissolved, then remove from the heat and let cool.
3. Place the olives and thyme in a ball jar and pour the cooled vinegar mixture over the top.
4. Cover the jar with a lid and let sit at room temperature for at least 2 days before serving. The olives will keep in the refrigerator for up to 2 weeks.

PICKLED BLACKBERRIES AND CINNAMON

There's nothing quite like the sweet and tangy flavor of pickled blackberries and cinnamon. This delicious treat is a perfect addition to any meal, whether it's served as a side dish or used as a topping for ice cream or yogurt. And because it's made in a ball jar, it's easy to store and enjoy anytime. Here's how to make it at home.

---

1 pint of fresh blackberries

1 cinnamon stick

1 cup of white vinegar

1 cup of water

1/2 cup of sugar

1 tablespoon of salt

1 tablespoon of whole cloves

1. Rinse the blackberries and remove any stems or leaves. Place them in a ball jar.
2. In a small saucepan, combine the vinegar, water, sugar, salt, and cloves. Bring to a boil over medium heat, stirring occasionally until the sugar and salt have dissolved.
3. Pour the hot liquid over the blackberries in the ball jar, making sure to cover them completely.
4. Add the cinnamon stick to the jar and screw on the lid.
5. Allow the jar to cool to room temperature, then transfer it to the refrigerator to chill for at least 24 hours before serving.
6. Enjoy the pickled blackberries and cinnamon as a side dish or topping for your favorite dishes.

PICKLED BLACKBERRY AND LAVENDER

As summer ends, we find ourselves with an abundance of blackberries from our backyard bushes. Rather than letting them go to waste, we decided to try our hand at pickling them with the added floral notes of lavender. The result is a unique and flavorful addition to any cheese board or charcuterie platter.

2 cups blackberries
1 cup apple cider vinegar
1/2 cup water
1/2 cup sugar
1 tablespoon dried lavender
1 teaspoon salt
1 teaspoon black peppercorns
1 ball jar with lid

1. In a medium saucepan, combine the vinegar, water, sugar, lavender, salt, and peppercorns. Bring to a boil over high heat, stirring occasionally to dissolve the sugar.

2. Once boiling, add the blackberries to the saucepan and reduce the heat to low. Simmer for 5 minutes, or until the blackberries are softened and the liquid has thickened slightly.

3. Remove the saucepan from the heat and let the mixture cool for 5 minutes.

4. Using a slotted spoon, carefully transfer the blackberries to the ball jar, making sure to pack them in tightly. Pour the pickling liquid over the blackberries, leaving about 1/2 inch of space at the top of the jar.

5. Secure the lid on the ball jar and let the pickled blackberries sit at room temperature for at least 1 hour before serving. The pickled blackberries will keep in the refrigerator for up to 2 weeks. Enjoy!

PICKLED BLACKBERRY AND ONION RELISH

This pickled blackberry and onion relish is the perfect accompaniment to grilled meats or as a tangy topping for sandwiches. The sweet and tart flavors of the blackberries are balanced by the sharpness of the onions, and the whole mixture is preserved in a beautiful ball jar to be enjoyed all year round.

2 cups fresh blackberries

1 large red onion, thinly sliced

1/2 cup white vinegar

1/2 cup sugar

1/2 cup water

1 tablespoon kosher salt

1/2 teaspoon black peppercorns

1. In a medium saucepan, combine the blackberries, onion, vinegar, sugar, water, salt, and peppercorns. Bring the mixture to a boil over high heat, stirring to dissolve the sugar.

2. Reduce the heat to medium-low and simmer for 15 minutes, stirring occasionally, until the onions are soft, and the liquid has thickened slightly.

3. Let the relish cool to room temperature, then transfer it to a clean ball jar and refrigerate for at least 24 hours before using. The relish will keep in the refrigerator for up to 1 week.

PICKLED BLACKBERRY AND THYME

This recipe is inspired by the lush blackberry bushes that grow wild in our backyard. We love to pick them in the summer and preserve them in a delicious pickling brine. The addition of thyme adds a lovely herbal flavor, and the resulting pickles are perfect for adding a tangy pop of flavor to sandwiches, salads, and charcuterie boards.

---

2 cups blackberries
1 cup white vinegar
1 cup water
1/4 cup sugar
2 tbsp pickling salt
2 sprigs thyme

1. In a medium saucepan, combine the vinegar, water, sugar, and pickling salt. Bring to a boil and stir until the sugar and salt are dissolved.
2. Place the blackberries and thyme sprigs in a sterilized ball jar.
3. Pour the hot brine over the blackberries, making sure they are completely covered.
4. Allow the jar to cool to room temperature and then place the lid on the jar.
5. Store in the refrigerator for at least 24 hours before serving. The pickles will keep for up to 1 month in the refrigerator. Enjoy!

PICKLED BLUEBERRIES

This recipe is perfect for those who love the tangy flavor of pickled fruits. The blueberries are preserved in a mixture of vinegar, sugar, and spices, and are perfect for adding a pop of flavor to salads, cheese plates, and cocktails.

2 cups fresh blueberries
1 cup white vinegar
1/2 cup sugar
1/2 teaspoon salt
1/2 teaspoon mustard seeds
1/2 teaspoon coriander seeds
1/4 teaspoon black peppercorns
1/4 teaspoon allspice berries

1. Rinse the blueberries and place them in a clean ball jar.
2. In a small saucepan, combine the vinegar, sugar, salt, mustard seeds, coriander seeds, peppercorns, and allspice berries. Bring to a boil and stir until the sugar has dissolved.
3. Carefully pour the hot liquid over the blueberries, making sure to completely cover them.
4. Place the lid on the jar and allow the pickled blueberries to cool to room temperature before transferring to the refrigerator.
5. The pickled blueberries will be ready to eat after 24 hours and will keep in the refrigerator for up to 2 weeks. Enjoy!

PICKLED BLUEBERRY AND LEMON CURD

This recipe is a unique twist on the traditional pickled fruit. The tartness of the blueberries is balanced by the rich and creamy lemon curd, creating a truly delicious and unexpected flavor.

1 pint of blueberries
1 cup of lemon curd
1 cup of white vinegar
1 cup of water
1/4 cup of sugar
1 tablespoon of pickling spice
1 tablespoon of salt

1. In a small saucepan, combine the vinegar, water, sugar, pickling spice, and salt. Bring to a boil and let simmer for 5 minutes.
2. While the pickling liquid is simmering, rinse and dry the blueberries.
3. In a clean and sterilized ball jar, layer the blueberries and lemon curd.
4. Once the pickling liquid has finished simmering, pour it over the blueberries and lemon curd, making sure they are completely covered.
5. Secure the lid on the ball jar and let cool to room temperature.
6. Once cooled, store in the refrigerator for at least 24 hours before enjoying. The pickled blueberries will last up to 2 weeks in the refrigerator.

TITLE PICKLED BLUEBERRY AND ONION RELISH

This tangy and sweet relish is perfect for adding a pop of flavor to any summer barbecue or grilled meal. The combination of sweet blueberries and tart onions is sure to delight the taste buds and make any dish stand out. Simply place the ingredients in a ball jar and let the pickling magic happen.

1 cup blueberries

1/2 cup red onion, thinly sliced

1/4 cup apple cider vinegar

1/4 cup sugar

1/2 teaspoon salt

1/2 teaspoon whole mustard seeds

1. In a small saucepan, combine the vinegar, sugar, and salt and heat over medium heat until the sugar and salt have dissolved.

2. Place the blueberries and onions in a ball jar and pour the vinegar mixture over the top. Add the mustard seeds and stir to combine.

3. Seal the jar and let it sit at room temperature for at least 24 hours before serving. The relish will keep in the refrigerator for up to a week.

4. Serve as a condiment with grilled meats, sandwiches, or as a topping for salads. Enjoy!

SUMMER IN A JAR PICKLED BLUEBERRIES AND LAVENDER

As the summer sun beats down, the blueberry bushes in my backyard are bursting with fruit. I love to pick and eat them fresh, but there's only so many I can eat before they start to go bad. That's why I love to preserve them in a ball jar, pickled with fragrant lavender and tangy vinegar. The result is a unique and delicious condiment that adds a pop of flavor to any dish. Plus, the beautiful purple hue makes for a pretty addition to any pantry. Give it a try and enjoy the taste of summer all year long.

2 cups fresh blueberries

1 cup white vinegar

1 cup water

1/2 cup sugar

1 tablespoon lavender buds

1 tablespoon salt

1. In a small saucepan, combine the vinegar, water, sugar, lavender, and salt. Bring to a boil over medium heat, stirring until the sugar and salt have dissolved.

2. Place the blueberries in a clean and sterilized ball jar. Pour the hot vinegar mixture over the blueberries, making sure to completely cover them.

3. Let the jar cool to room temperature, then seal with a lid and store in the refrigerator for at least 24 hours before using. The pickled blueberries will keep for up to 3 months in the refrigerator.

4. To use, simply spoon a few pickled blueberries over salads, grilled meats, or even ice cream for a unique and tangy flavor. Enjoy!

PICKLED BLUEBERRY AND THYME

A few summers ago, I stumbled upon a patch of wild blueberries in the woods near my house. I was amazed by their sweet, tangy flavor and knew I had to do something special with them. I decided to pickle them with some fresh thyme from my garden and the result was a delicious, tangy treat that I store in a ball jar in my pantry. This recipe is a great way to preserve the flavors of summer and enjoy them all year round.

---

1 pint of fresh blueberries

1/2 cup of white vinegar

1/2 cup of water

2 tablespoons of sugar

1 tablespoon of fresh thyme leaves

1 teaspoon of salt

1. Wash and dry the blueberries and place them in a sterilized ball jar.
2. In a small saucepan, combine the vinegar, water, sugar, thyme, and salt. Bring to a boil over medium heat and stir until the sugar and salt have dissolved.
3. Pour the hot vinegar mixture over the blueberries, making sure to cover them completely.
4. Let the jar cool to room temperature, then seal with a lid and store in the refrigerator for at least 24 hours before serving.
5. The pickled blueberries will keep in the refrigerator for up to 1 month. Serve as a tangy, refreshing snack or use as a condiment on sandwiches, salads, or other dishes.

PICKLED BLUEBERRY AND VANILLA BEAN JAM

This recipe was inspired by a trip to the farmer's market, where I discovered the most delicious blueberries I had ever tasted. I immediately knew I wanted to preserve them in a way that would allow me to enjoy their flavor all year round. So, I decided to pickle them and add a touch of vanilla bean for a unique and flavorful jam.

1 pint of fresh blueberries
1 cup of white vinegar
1 cup of sugar
1 vanilla bean, split and scraped
1 Ball jar

1. In a small saucepan, combine the blueberries, vinegar, sugar, and vanilla bean. Bring the mixture to a boil over medium heat, stirring occasionally.

2. Once boiling, reduce the heat to low and let the mixture simmer for about 20 minutes, or until the blueberries have softened and the liquid has thickened into a jam-like consistency.

3. Use a slotted spoon to transfer the blueberries into a clean Ball jar, making sure to include some of the vanilla bean scrapings.

4. Carefully pour the remaining liquid over the blueberries, filling the jar to the top.

5. Seal the jar and let it cool to room temperature before storing in the refrigerator for up to 2 weeks.

6. Enjoy the pickled blueberry and vanilla bean jam on toast, scones, or even as a topping for ice cream.

PICKLED BURDOCK AND MISO

This recipe is a twist on traditional Japanese pickles, using burdock root and miso paste to add depth and flavor. The pickles are perfect for serving alongside sushi or as a refreshing side dish.

---

1 large burdock root
1 cup white vinegar
1/2 cup water
1/4 cup white sugar
2 tablespoons miso paste
2 teaspoons salt
1 ball jar

1. Peel the burdock root and slice into thin matchsticks.
2. In a small saucepan, combine the vinegar, water, sugar, miso paste, and salt. Bring to a boil, stirring to dissolve the sugar and miso.
3. Place the burdock slices in a ball jar and pour the hot liquid over the top.
4. Let the pickles cool to room temperature, then seal the jar and place in the refrigerator for at least 24 hours before serving. The pickles will last for up to 1 month in the refrigerator.
5. Serve the pickled burdock and miso alongside sushi or as a refreshing side dish.

PICKLED BURDOCK AND SOY

This recipe for pickled burdock and soy is a delicious and unique way to enjoy the earthy flavor of burdock root. The addition of soy sauce adds a rich, salty depth to the pickling liquid, creating a savory and satisfying snack that can be enjoyed straight from the ball jar.

1 cup burdock root, sliced into thin rounds
1 cup soy sauce
1 cup rice vinegar
1 tablespoon sugar
1 tablespoon salt
1 teaspoon red pepper flakes (optional)

1. In a small saucepan, combine the soy sauce, rice vinegar, sugar, salt, and red pepper flakes (if using). Heat over medium heat, stirring occasionally, until the sugar and salt have dissolved.

2. Place the sliced burdock root into a clean and sterilized ball jar. Pour the hot pickling liquid over the burdock, making sure to completely cover the slices.

3. Allow the jar to cool to room temperature, then seal and store in the refrigerator for at least 24 hours before enjoying. The pickled burdock will keep for up to 2 weeks in the refrigerator.

4. Serve the pickled burdock as a snack on its own, or use it as a topping for salads, sandwiches, or sushi rolls.

STRAWBERRY AND VANILLA JAM

This sweet and fragrant jam is perfect for spreading on toast or spooning over your favorite ice cream. The combination of juicy strawberries and creamy vanilla creates a delicious and flavorful treat that is sure to become a family favorite.

3 cups strawberries, hulled and quartered
1 cup sugar
1 vanilla bean, split and seeds scraped
2 tablespoons lemon juice

1. In a medium saucepan, combine the strawberries, sugar, vanilla bean and seeds, and lemon juice. Stir to combine.

2. Bring the mixture to a boil over medium heat, stirring occasionally.

3. Once the mixture comes to a boil, reduce the heat to low and simmer for 15-20 minutes, or until the strawberries are soft and the mixture has thickened slightly.

4. Using a slotted spoon, carefully transfer the strawberry mixture to a sterilized ball jar.

5. Allow the jam to cool to room temperature before sealing the jar and storing in the refrigerator for up to 2 weeks.

6. Enjoy your delicious strawberry and vanilla jam on toast, ice cream, or any other way you please!

PICKLED CARROT AND BLACK PEPPER RECIPE

There's nothing like a tangy and spicy pickled carrot to add a punch of flavor to any dish. This recipe uses fresh carrots and black pepper to create a delicious and unique pickled treat. The best part? It's easy to make and can be stored in a ball jar for long-term preservation. So grab your ingredients and let's get started!

---

2 cups of sliced carrots

1 tablespoon of black peppercorns

1 cup of white vinegar

1 cup of water

1/2 cup of sugar

1 tablespoon of salt

1. Begin by sterilizing your ball jar by boiling it in water for 10 minutes.
2. In a small saucepan, combine the vinegar, water, sugar, and salt. Bring to a boil and stir until the sugar and salt have dissolved.
3. Place the sliced carrots and black peppercorns in the sterilized ball jar.
4. Once the vinegar mixture has come to a boil, pour it over the carrots and peppercorns in the jar.
5. Seal the jar tightly and let it cool to room temperature before storing it in the refrigerator.
6. The pickled carrots will be ready to eat after 24 hours and will keep for up to two weeks in the refrigerator. Enjoy!

PICKLED CARROT AND GARLIC

This recipe is a tasty and easy way to preserve carrots and garlic for a long time. The pickling process infuses the carrots with a tangy and flavorful brine, while the garlic adds a delicious and spicy kick. To make this recipe, you will need a ball jar and some basic pickling ingredients.

1-pound carrots, peeled and sliced into coins

6 cloves garlic, peeled and sliced

1 cup white vinegar

1 cup water

2 tablespoons sugar

1 tablespoon salt

1 teaspoon peppercorns

1 teaspoon dill seeds

1 teaspoon mustard seeds

1. Start by sterilizing your ball jar by boiling it in hot water for 5 minutes.
2. In a small saucepan, combine the vinegar, water, sugar, salt, peppercorns, dill seeds, and mustard seeds. Bring to a boil, stirring until the sugar and salt have dissolved.
3. Arrange the sliced carrots and garlic in the sterilized ball jar.
4. Pour the hot pickling liquid over the carrots and garlic, making sure to completely cover the vegetables with the liquid.
5. Seal the jar and let it cool to room temperature.
6. Once cool, store the jar in the refrigerator for at least 24 hours before serving. The pickled carrots and garlic will last for up to 2 weeks in the refrigerator. Enjoy them as a tasty and tangy snack, or use them as a flavorful addition to salads, sandwiches, or other dishes.

PICKLED CARROT AND MUSTARD RECIPE

This recipe is a delicious and tangy way to preserve carrots and enjoy them through-out the year. The combination of sweet carrots and tangy mustard creates a unique and flavorful pickle. All you need is a few simple ingredients and a trusty ball jar to store your pickles in.

1 lb carrots, peeled and sliced into thin rounds
1 cup white vinegar
1 cup water
1 tablespoon mustard seeds
2 cloves garlic, minced
1 tablespoon sugar
1 teaspoon salt
1/2 teaspoon black peppercorns

1. In a medium saucepan, bring the vinegar, water, mustard seeds, garlic, sugar, salt, and peppercorns to a boil over high heat.
2. Add the carrots to the boiling mixture and reduce the heat to medium-low. Simmer the carrots for 10 minutes, or until they are tender but still slightly crisp.
3. Using a slotted spoon, transfer the carrots to a clean ball jar.
4. Pour the boiling liquid over the carrots, making sure to completely cover them.
5. Close the ball jar with a lid and let it cool to room temperature. Once cooled, transfer the jar to the refrigerator to chill for at least 24 hours before serving.
6. Your pickled carrots and mustard are now ready to enjoy. Serve them as a side dish or as a tasty addition to sandwiches and salads. Enjoy!

PICKLED CARROT AND ONION RELISH

This delicious and tangy relish is the perfect addition to any sandwich or charcuterie board. It's easy to make and can be stored in a glass Ball jar for up to several months. The combination of sweet carrots and tangy onions is both refreshing and satisfying. Here's how to make it

2 cups grated carrots

1 cup sliced onions

1 cup vinegar

1/2 cup sugar

1 tablespoon mustard seeds

1 teaspoon salt

1/4 teaspoon black pepper

1. In a large bowl, combine the grated carrots and sliced onions.
2. In a small saucepan, bring the vinegar, sugar, mustard seeds, salt, and pepper to a boil over medium heat.
3. Pour the hot vinegar mixture over the carrots and onions and stir to combine.
4. Transfer the mixture to a clean glass Ball jar, making sure to leave about 1 inch of headspace at the top.
5. Let the jar cool to room temperature, then seal it and store it in the refrigerator for at least 24 hours before serving.
6. The relish will keep in the refrigerator for up to several months. Enjoy!

PICKLED CARROT AND PEANUT SALAD

This refreshing and tangy salad is the perfect side dish for any meal. It's easy to make and can be stored in a ball jar in the fridge for up to a week. The pickled carrots add a nice crunch, while the peanuts add a bit of heartiness and a delicious nutty flavor.

2 cups carrots, peeled and sliced into thin rounds
1/2 cup peanuts, roughly chopped
1/2 cup rice vinegar
1/4 cup sugar
1 tablespoon salt
1/2 teaspoon red pepper flakes

1. In a small saucepan, combine the rice vinegar, sugar, salt, and red pepper flakes. Bring to a boil, then reduce heat and simmer for 5 minutes.
2. Place the carrots and peanuts in a ball jar and pour the pickling liquid over top. Let cool to room temperature, then seal the jar and refrigerate for at least 4 hours before serving.
3. When ready to serve, drain the carrots and peanuts and place in a serving bowl. Enjoy!

PICKLED CARROT AND PARSLEY

A few years ago, I was given a beautiful ball jar filled with pickled carrots and parsley by a friend who had grown the vegetables in her garden. It was love at first bite, and I knew I had to recreate the recipe for myself. Here's how I do it.

4 cups of baby carrots

1 cup of fresh parsley leaves

1 cup of apple cider vinegar

1/2 cup of sugar

1 tablespoon of salt

1 teaspoon of black peppercorns

1 teaspoon of mustard seeds

1. Wash and scrub the carrots to remove any dirt. Trim the ends and slice them into thin coins.

2. In a small saucepan, combine the vinegar, sugar, salt, peppercorns, and mustard seeds. Heat over medium heat, stirring occasionally, until the sugar has dissolved.

3. Place the carrots and parsley leaves in a large ball jar. Pour the hot vinegar mixture over the top, making sure to cover the vegetables completely.

4. Let the jar cool to room temperature, then seal it with a lid and store in the refrigerator for at least 24 hours before serving. The pickled carrots and parsley will keep for up to 1 month in the refrigerator.

5. To serve, simply scoop out the desired amount of pickled carrots and parsley and enjoy as a tasty and tangy side dish or topping for sandwiches and salads.

SPICY PICKLED CAULIFLOWER

This delicious and spicy pickled cauliflower is the perfect addition to any meal. The heat from the red pepper flakes and jalapenos adds a nice kick, while the vinegar and sugar balance out the flavors. It's easy to make and can be stored in a ball jar in the fridge for up to a week.

---

1 head cauliflower, cut into small florets
1/4 cup red pepper flakes
1/4 cup jalapeno slices
1/2 cup apple cider vinegar
1/4 cup sugar
1 tablespoon salt

1. In a small saucepan, combine the apple cider vinegar, sugar, salt, red pepper flakes, and jalapeno slices. Bring to a boil, then reduce heat and simmer for 5 minutes.
2. Place the cauliflower florets in a ball jar and pour the pickling liquid over top. Let cool to room temperature, then seal the jar and refrigerate for at least 4 hours before serving.
3. When ready to serve, drain the cauliflower and place in a serving bowl. Enjoy!

PICKLED CARROTS AND SOY

A few years ago, I was given a beautiful ball jar filled with pickled carrots and parsley by a friend who had grown the vegetables in her garden. It was love at first bite, and I knew I had to recreate the recipe for myself. Here's how I do it.

2 cups of baby carrots, sliced into rounds
1/2 cup of soy sauce
1/4 cup of apple cider vinegar
1 tablespoon of honey
2 cloves of garlic, minced
1 teaspoon of grated ginger
1 teaspoon of red pepper flakes
2 Ball jars with lids

1. In a small saucepan, combine the soy sauce, vinegar, honey, garlic, ginger, and red pepper flakes. Bring to a boil over medium heat, stirring occasionally.
2. Once boiling, remove the saucepan from the heat and let the mixture cool for a few minutes.
3. Meanwhile, divide the sliced carrots evenly between the two Ball jars.
4. Pour the cooled sauce mixture over the carrots in the Ball jars, making sure the carrots are fully submerged in the liquid.
5. Tightly seal the Ball jars and store in the refrigerator for at least 24 hours before serving. The pickled carrots will keep in the refrigerator for up to 2 weeks.

Enjoy these tangy and spicy pickled carrots as a unique side dish or as a topping for sandwiches and salads. The soy sauce adds a depth of flavor, while the honey and vinegar give a balance of sweetness and acidity. The garlic and ginger add a pop of freshness, and the red pepper flakes give a slight kick. These pickled carrots are the perfect way to add a unique twist to any dish.

SPICY PICKLED CAULIFLOWER AND CUMIN

This pickled cauliflower and cumin recipe is a delicious twist on the classic pickled vegetables that my grandma used to make. She would always use a beautiful ball jar to store her pickles, and I like to do the same. The addition of cumin and red pepper flakes gives these pickles a nice kick that really sets them apart.

1 head of cauliflower, cut into small florets

1 cup of white vinegar

1/2 cup of water

1/4 cup of sugar

1 tablespoon of salt

1 tablespoon of cumin seeds

1 teaspoon of red pepper flakes

1. In a small saucepan, combine the vinegar, water, sugar, salt, cumin seeds, and red pepper flakes. Heat over medium heat, stirring occasionally, until the sugar has dissolved.

2. Place the cauliflower florets in a large ball jar. Pour the hot vinegar mixture over the top, making sure to cover the vegetables completely.

3. Let the jar cool to room temperature, then seal it with a lid and store in the refrigerator for at least 24 hours before serving. The spicy pickled cauliflower and cumin will keep for up to 1 month in the refrigerator.

4. To serve, simply scoop out the desired amount of pickled cauliflower and enjoy as a tasty and spicy side dish or topping for sandwiches and salads. You can also add a few of the cumin seeds and red pepper flakes to give it even more heat. Enjoy!

SPICY PICKLED CAULIFLOWER AND BLACK PEPPER RECIPE

This recipe is a flavorful and spicy twist on traditional pickled cauliflower. The combination of tangy pickling liquid and spicy black pepper adds depth and heat to the cauliflower, making it a delicious and unique pickle. All you need is a few simple ingredients and a ball jar to store your pickles in.

---

1 medium head of cauliflower, cut into florets

1 cup white vinegar

1 cup water

1 tablespoon black peppercorns, crushed

2 cloves garlic, minced

1 tablespoon sugar

1 teaspoon salt

1/4 teaspoon red pepper flakes

1. In a medium saucepan, bring the vinegar, water, black peppercorns, garlic, sugar, salt, and red pepper flakes to a boil over high heat.

2. Add the cauliflower to the boiling mixture and reduce the heat to medium-low. Simmer the cauliflower for 10 minutes, or until it is tender but still slightly crisp.

3. Using a slotted spoon, transfer the cauliflower to a clean ball jar.

4. Pour the boiling liquid over the cauliflower, making sure to completely cover it.

5. Close the ball jar with a lid and let it cool to room temperature. Once cooled, transfer the jar to the refrigerator to chill for at least 24 hours before serving.

6. Your spicy pickled cauliflower and black pepper is now ready to enjoy. Serve it as a side dish or as a tasty addition to sandwiches and salads. Enjoy!

SPICY PICKLED CAULIFLOWER AND MUSTARD SALAD

This bold and flavorful salad is perfect for adding some spice to your meals. It's easy to make and can be stored in a ball jar in the fridge for up to a week. The pickled cauliflower adds a nice crunch, while the mustard adds a tangy kick.

2 cups cauliflower florets
1/2 cup Dijon mustard
1/2 cup apple cider vinegar
1/4 cup sugar
1 tablespoon red pepper flakes
1 teaspoon salt

1. In a small saucepan, combine the apple cider vinegar, sugar, red pepper flakes, and salt. Bring to a boil, then reduce heat and simmer for 5 minutes.
2. Place the cauliflower florets and mustard in a ball jar and pour the pickling liquid over top. Let cool to room temperature, then seal the jar and refrigerate for at least 4 hours before serving.
3. When ready to serve, drain the cauliflower and mustard and place in a serving bowl. Enjoy!

SPICY PICKLED CAYENNE AND ONION RELISH

This tangy and spicy relish is the perfect condiment for any grilled meat or sandwich. The cayenne peppers add a kick of heat, while the pickled onions give a satisfying crunch and tang. The recipe is easy to make and can be stored in a beautiful ball jar for future use.

1 cup cayenne peppers, sliced

1 cup red onion, sliced

1 cup apple cider vinegar

1 cup water

1 tablespoon sugar

1 teaspoon salt

1 teaspoon mustard seeds

1. In a small saucepan, combine the cayenne peppers, red onion, apple cider vinegar, water, sugar, salt, and mustard seeds.
2. Bring the mixture to a boil, then reduce the heat and simmer for 10 minutes.
3. Remove the saucepan from the heat and let the relish cool to room temperature.
4. Transfer the relish to a ball jar and seal tightly.
5. Let the relish pickle in the refrigerator for at least 24 hours before serving.
6. Enjoy your spicy pickled cayenne and onion relish on grilled meats, sandwiches, or as a condiment for any dish that needs a little extra flavor and heat.

SPICY PICKLED CELERY AND LEMON

Pickled celery has become one of my favorite snacks lately. I love the tangy and slightly sweet flavor, and the crunchy texture is a nice change from the usual vegetables I eat. I decided to try a new twist on the classic pickled celery recipe by adding some spicy heat and lemon for a bright and flavorful variation. Here's how I made it.

---

4 cups of celery stalks, sliced into thin coins
1 lemon, thinly sliced
1 cup of white vinegar
1/2 cup of sugar
1 tablespoon of red pepper flakes
1 tablespoon of mustard seeds
1 tablespoon of salt

1. Wash and dry the celery stalks, then slice them into thin coins. Thinly slice the lemon as well.

2. In a small saucepan, combine the vinegar, sugar, red pepper flakes, mustard seeds, and salt. Heat over medium heat, stirring occasionally, until the sugar has dissolved.

3. Place the celery and lemon slices in a large ball jar. Pour the hot vinegar mixture over the top, making sure to cover the vegetables completely.

4. Let the jar cool to room temperature, then seal it with a lid and store in the refrigerator for at least 24 hours before serving. The spicy pickled celery and lemon will keep for up to 1 month in the refrigerator.

5. To serve, simply scoop out the desired amount of pickled celery and lemon and enjoy as a spicy and tangy snack or topping for sandwiches and salads. The heat from the red pepper flakes pairs perfectly with the bright and refreshing flavor of the lemon.

PICKLED CELERY AND SESAME RECIPE

This recipe is a delicious and flavorful way to preserve celery and enjoy it throughout the year. The combination of crisp celery and nutty sesame seeds creates a unique and tasty pickle. All you need is a few simple ingredients and a ball jar to store your pickles in.

---

1 lb celery, sliced into thin rounds
1 cup rice vinegar
1 cup water
1 tablespoon sesame seeds
2 cloves garlic, minced
1 tablespoon sugar
1 teaspoon salt
1/2 teaspoon black peppercorns

1. In a medium saucepan, bring the vinegar, water, sesame seeds, garlic, sugar, salt, and peppercorns to a boil over high heat.
2. Add the celery to the boiling mixture and reduce the heat to medium-low. Simmer the celery for 10 minutes, or until it is tender but still slightly crisp.
3. Using a slotted spoon, transfer the celery to a clean ball jar.
4. Pour the boiling liquid over the celery, making sure to completely cover it.
5. Close the ball jar with a lid and let it cool to room temperature. Once cooled, transfer the jar to the refrigerator to chill for at least 24 hours before serving.
6. Your pickled celery and sesame seeds are now ready to enjoy. Serve them as a side dish or as a tasty addition to sandwiches and salads. Enjoy!

SPICY PICKLED CELERY RECIPE

This recipe is a delicious and spicy twist on traditional pickled celery. The combination of tangy vinegar and fiery chili flakes creates a unique and flavorful pickle that is sure to spice up any dish. All you need is a few simple ingredients and a trusty ball jar to store your pickles in.

1 lb celery, washed and sliced into thin rounds
1 cup white vinegar
1 cup water
1 tablespoon sugar
1 tablespoon chili flakes
1 teaspoon salt
1/2 teaspoon black peppercorns

1. In a medium saucepan, bring the vinegar, water, sugar, chili flakes, salt, and peppercorns to a boil over high heat.
2. Add the celery to the boiling mixture and reduce the heat to medium-low. Simmer the celery for 10 minutes, or until it is tender but still slightly crisp.
3. Using a slotted spoon, transfer the celery to a clean ball jar.
4. Pour the boiling liquid over the celery, making sure to completely cover it.
5. Close the ball jar with a lid and let it cool to room temperature. Once cooled, transfer the jar to the refrigerator to chill for at least 24 hours before serving.
6. Your spicy pickled celery is now ready to enjoy. Serve it as a side dish or as a tasty addition to sandwiches and salads. Enjoy!

SPICY PICKLED CHERRIES AND ALMOND

Pickled cherries may sound like a strange combination but trust me when I say that the tangy sweetness of the cherries combined with the rich flavor of the almonds is truly something special. This recipe adds a kick of heat with red pepper flakes to make it even more delicious.

2 cups of fresh cherries, pitted and halved
1/2 cup of sliced almonds
1 cup of white vinegar
1/2 cup of sugar
1 tablespoon of salt
1 teaspoon of red pepper flakes

1. In a small saucepan, combine the vinegar, sugar, salt, and red pepper flakes. Heat over medium heat, stirring occasionally, until the sugar has dissolved.

2. Place the cherries and almonds in a large ball jar. Pour the hot vinegar mixture over the top, making sure to cover the fruit and nuts completely.

3. Let the jar cool to room temperature, then seal it with a lid and store in the refrigerator for at least 24 hours before serving. The pickled cherries and almonds will keep for up to 1 month in the refrigerator.

4. To serve, simply scoop out the desired amount of pickled cherries and almonds and enjoy as a unique and flavorful topping for salads, sandwiches, or even ice cream. The heat from the red pepper flakes adds a nice contrast to the sweetness of the cherries and the crunch of the almonds.

SWEET AND TANGY PICKLED CHERRY AND ONION RELISH

This sweet and tangy relish is the perfect addition to any summer barbecue. The combination of pickled cherries and onions gives it a unique flavor that is sure to impress your guests. And with the use of a beautiful ball jar, it makes for a gorgeous presentation on the table.

1 lb celery, washed and sliced into thin rounds
1 cup white vinegar
1 cup water
1 tablespoon sugar
1 tablespoon chili flakes
1 teaspoon salt
1/2 teaspoon black peppercorns

1. In a medium saucepan, combine the cherries, onion, vinegar, sugar, salt, pepper, and cloves.
2. Bring to a boil over high heat, then reduce the heat to low and simmer for 10 minutes.
3. Remove from the heat and let cool to room temperature.
4. Transfer the mixture to a clean and sterilized ball jar, making sure to leave about 1/2 inch of space at the top.
5. Seal the jar with a lid and refrigerate for at least 24 hours before serving.
6. Serve as a condiment with grilled meats or use as a topping for sandwiches and salads. Enjoy!

SPICY PICKLED CHERRY AND THYME SALSA

This salsa is a unique and tasty twist on traditional salsa. The pickled cherries add a nice tangy flavor, while the thyme brings a subtle herby depth. The spicy kick comes from the jalapeno peppers, which can be adjusted to your personal heat preference. This salsa is perfect for dipping with chips or topping on tacos and is great for storing in a ball jar in the fridge for up to a week.

---

1 cup fresh cherries, pitted and halved

1/4 cup red onion, diced

1 jalapeno pepper, minced

1 tablespoon thyme leaves

1/2 cup rice vinegar

1/4 cup sugar

1 tablespoon salt

1/2 teaspoon red pepper flakes

1. In a small saucepan, combine the rice vinegar, sugar, salt, and red pepper flakes. Bring to a boil, then reduce heat and simmer for 5 minutes.

2. Place the cherries, onion, jalapeno, and thyme in a ball jar and pour the pickling liquid over top. Let cool to room temperature, then seal the jar and refrigerate for at least 4 hours before serving.

3. When ready to serve, drain the salsa and place in a serving bowl. Enjoy!

VANILLA BEAN AND PICKLED CHERRY CHUTNEY

This sweet and tangy chutney is the perfect accompaniment to grilled chicken or pork. It's easy to make and can be stored in a ball jar in the fridge for up to a week. The pickled cherries add a nice tartness, while the vanilla bean adds a subtle sweetness and a delicious floral flavor.

---

1 cup cherries, pitted and quartered
1 vanilla bean, split lengthwise
1/2 cup red wine vinegar
1/4 cup sugar
1 tablespoon salt
1/2 teaspoon red pepper flakes

1. In a small saucepan, combine the red wine vinegar, sugar, salt, and red pepper flakes. Scrape the seeds from the vanilla bean and add them to the saucepan. Bring to a boil, then reduce heat and simmer for 5 minutes.

2. Place the cherries and vanilla bean in a ball jar and pour the pickling liquid over top. Let cool to room temperature, then seal the jar and refrigerate for at least 4 hours before serving.

3. When ready to serve, remove the vanilla bean and drain the cherries. Place in a serving bowl and enjoy!

PICKLED CHERRY PEPPERS

1 cup cherry peppers
1 cup white vinegar
1 tablespoon sugar
1 tablespoon salt
1 teaspoon black peppercorns
1 teaspoon red pepper flakes

1. Start by sterilizing a ball jar. Boil a pot of water and carefully place the jar and its lid in the boiling water for 10 minutes. Remove the jar and lid from the water and let them dry completely.
2. While the jar is sterilizing, rinse the cherry peppers and remove the stems. Place the peppers in the jar.
3. In a small saucepan, combine the vinegar, sugar, salt, peppercorns, and red pepper flakes. Bring the mixture to a boil, then reduce the heat to low and let it simmer for 5 minutes.
4. Carefully pour the vinegar mixture over the peppers in the jar, making sure to cover all of the peppers completely.
5. Place the lid on the jar and let it cool to room temperature before storing in the refrigerator for at least 24 hours.

These pickled cherry peppers are a delicious and spicy addition to any dish. Whether you slice them up and add them to a salad or serve them as a topping for sandwiches or burgers, they are sure to add a kick of flavor to any meal. The vinegar mixture preserves the peppers, ensuring they stay fresh and tasty for weeks to come. Enjoy!

SPICY PICKLED CHERRY PEPPER AND ONION RELISH

I love the tangy, spicy flavor of pickled cherry peppers, and I recently discovered that they make a delicious and unique addition to my favorite onion relish recipe. Here's how I make it.

1 cup of diced red onion

1 cup of diced yellow onion

1 cup of diced cherry peppers

1/2 cup of apple cider vinegar

1/4 cup of sugar

1 tablespoon of salt

1 teaspoon of crushed red pepper flakes

1. In a large ball jar, combine the diced onions, cherry peppers, vinegar, sugar, salt, and crushed red pepper flakes. Stir to combine.

2. Seal the jar with a lid and store in the refrigerator for at least 24 hours before serving. The relish will keep for up to 1 month in the refrigerator.

3. To serve, simply scoop out the desired amount of relish and enjoy as a tangy and spicy topping for sandwiches, burgers, hot dogs, and more. It's also delicious as a condiment for grilled meats and vegetables.

SPICY PICKLED CHERRY TOMATO AND GARLIC RECIPE

This recipe is a tasty and unique twist on classic pickled cherry tomatoes. The addition of spicy garlic and red pepper flakes gives these pickles a kick of heat, making them perfect for those who love a little spice in their life. All you need is a few simple ingredients and a trusty ball jar to store your pickles in.

---

1 lb cherry tomatoes, halved

1 cup white vinegar

1 cup water

1 tablespoon sugar

1 teaspoon salt

1/2 teaspoon red pepper flakes

2 cloves garlic, minced

1. In a medium saucepan, bring the vinegar, water, sugar, salt, red pepper flakes, and garlic to a boil over high heat.

2. Add the cherry tomatoes to the boiling mixture and reduce the heat to medium-low. Simmer the tomatoes for 10 minutes, or until they are tender but still slightly firm.

3. Using a slotted spoon, transfer the cherry tomatoes to a clean ball jar.

4. Pour the boiling liquid over the tomatoes, making sure to completely cover them.

5. Close the ball jar with a lid and let it cool to room temperature. Once cooled, transfer the jar to the refrigerator to chill for at least 24 hours before serving.

6. Your spicy pickled cherry tomatoes and garlic are now ready to enjoy. Serve them as a side dish or as a tasty addition to sandwiches and salads. Enjoy!

PICKLED CHERRY TOMATO AND ONION RELISH RECIPE

This recipe is a delicious and tangy way to preserve cherry tomatoes and onions and enjoy them throughout the year. The combination of sweet cherry tomatoes and tangy onions creates a unique and flavorful relish. All you need is a few simple ingredients and a trusty ball jar to store your relish in.

---

1 lb cherry tomatoes, halved

1 small onion, thinly sliced

1 cup white vinegar

1 cup water

1 tablespoon sugar

1 teaspoon salt

1/2 teaspoon dried oregano

1/2 teaspoon black peppercorns

1. In a medium saucepan, bring the vinegar, water, sugar, salt, oregano, and peppercorns to a boil over high heat.
2. Add the cherry tomatoes and onions to the boiling mixture and reduce the heat to medium-low. Simmer for 10 minutes, or until the tomatoes and onions are tender but still slightly crisp.
3. Using a slotted spoon, transfer the cherry tomatoes and onions to a clean ball jar.
4. Pour the boiling liquid over the cherry tomatoes and onions, making sure to completely cover them.
5. Close the ball jar with a lid and let it cool to room temperature. Once cooled, transfer the jar to the refrigerator to chill for at least 24 hours before serving.
6. Your pickled cherry tomato and onion relish is now ready to enjoy. Serve it as a condiment or as a tasty addition to sandwiches and salads. Enjoy!

PICKLED CHERRY TOMATOES WITH THYME

These delicious, pickled cherry tomatoes are a great addition to any meal. The thyme adds a unique flavor that pairs well with the tanginess of the tomatoes. These tomatoes are perfect for topping a salad, adding to a sandwich, or serving as a side dish.

To make these pickled cherry tomatoes, you will need a quart-sized ball jar and the following ingredients

---

1 pint cherry tomatoes

1 tablespoon fresh thyme leaves

1/4 cup white vinegar

1/4 cup water

1 tablespoon sugar

1 teaspoon salt

1. To begin, sterilize your ball jar by boiling it in a pot of water for 10 minutes. While the jar is sterilizing, combine the vinegar, water, sugar, and salt in a small saucepan and bring to a boil. Stir until the sugar and salt have dissolved.

2. Once the jar has been sterilized, carefully remove it from the pot of boiling water and place it on a clean, dry surface. Fill the jar with the cherry tomatoes, making sure to pack them in tightly. Add the fresh thyme leaves on top of the tomatoes.

3. Pour the vinegar mixture over the tomatoes, making sure to cover them completely. Seal the jar tightly and allow it to cool to room temperature. Once cool, place the jar in the refrigerator and let the tomatoes pickle for at least 24 hours before serving.

4. These pickled cherry tomatoes will last for up to a week in the refrigerator. Enjoy them as a tasty addition to your meals!

PICKLED CHERRY TOMATO AND GARLIC

1 cup cherry tomatoes
2 cloves garlic
1/4 cup white vinegar
1/4 cup water
1 tsp sugar
1 tsp salt

1. Rinse the cherry tomatoes and set aside. Peel the garlic cloves and thinly slice them.
2. In a small saucepan, combine the vinegar, water, sugar, and salt. Bring to a simmer over medium heat and stir until the sugar and salt dissolve.
3. Place the cherry tomatoes and garlic slices in a sterilized ball jar. Pour the vinegar mixture over the top, making sure to cover the tomatoes and garlic completely.
4. Let the jar cool to room temperature before sealing it and storing it in the refrigerator. The pickled cherry tomatoes and garlic will be ready to eat after 24 hours but will taste even better if allowed to pickle for a few days.

This tangy and savory pickled cherry tomato and garlic recipe is the perfect addition to any sandwich or salad. The bright and juicy cherry tomatoes are balanced by the spicy and pungent garlic, making for a truly delicious and unique flavor combination. Plus, the ease of storing the pickled vegetables in a ball jar means that you can always have a tasty and healthy snack on hand.

SPICY PICKLED CHILI AND CILANTRO SALSA

This spicy salsa is the perfect addition to any Mexican-inspired meal. The pickled chilis add a nice tanginess, while the cilantro gives the salsa a fresh and vibrant flavor. It's easy to make and can be stored in a ball jar in the fridge for up to a week.

1 cup pickled jalapeno slices

1/2 cup chopped cilantro

1/2 cup diced tomatoes

1/4 cup diced onion

1 tablespoon lime juice

1/2 teaspoon salt

1. In a medium bowl, combine the pickled jalapenos, cilantro, tomatoes, onion, lime juice, and salt. Mix well.

2. Transfer the salsa to a ball jar and seal the jar. Refrigerate for at least 4 hours before serving.

3. When ready to serve, drain the salsa and transfer to a serving bowl. Enjoy!

SPICY PICKLED CHILI AND LIME

This pickled chili and lime dish is the perfect addition to any meal that needs a little kick. The combination of spicy chilies and tangy lime is sure to wake up your taste buds. And since it's easy to make and can be stored in a ball jar in the fridge for up to a week, it's a great way to add some flavor to your meals throughout the week.

2 cups fresh chili peppers, sliced into thin rounds
2 limes, thinly sliced
1 cup rice vinegar
1/2 cup sugar
1 tablespoon salt
1/2 teaspoon red pepper flakes

1. In a small saucepan, combine the rice vinegar, sugar, salt, and red pepper flakes. Bring to a boil, then reduce heat and simmer for 5 minutes.
2. Place the chili peppers and lime slices in a ball jar and pour the pickling liquid over top. Let cool to room temperature, then seal the jar and refrigerate for at least 4 hours before serving.
3. When ready to serve, drain the chili peppers and lime slices and place in a serving bowl. Enjoy!

PICKLED COCONUT AND CARDAMOM IN A BALL JAR

This recipe is inspired by the flavors of South India, where coconut is a staple ingredient and cardamom is used to add a unique and fragrant touch to dishes. The combination of these two ingredients creates a tangy and slightly sweet, pickled treat that is perfect for enjoying on its own or as a condiment on top of rice or curry dishes.

1 cup of unsweetened coconut flakes
2 cups of white vinegar
1 tablespoon of cardamom pods
1 teaspoon of salt
1/2 cup of sugar

1. In a small saucepan, combine the vinegar, cardamom pods, salt, and sugar. Bring to a simmer over medium heat, stirring occasionally, until the sugar has dissolved.

2. In a medium-sized bowl, toss the coconut flakes with the vinegar mixture until well coated.

3. Transfer the coconut and vinegar mixture to a clean and sterilized ball jar. Make sure to leave about 1/2 inch of space at the top of the jar.

4. Seal the jar tightly and store in the refrigerator for at least 24 hours before serving. The pickled coconut will keep in the refrigerator for up to 1 month.

5. Serve the pickled coconut as a snack on its own or as a condiment on top of rice or curry dishes. Enjoy!

PICKLED COCONUT AND CURRY

1 cup fresh coconut, grated
1 tablespoon curry powder
1/4 cup vinegar
1/4 cup water
1 tablespoon sugar
1 teaspoon salt

1. In a small saucepan, combine the vinegar, water, sugar, and salt. Bring to a boil, stirring until the sugar and salt have dissolved.

2. In a small ball jar, place the grated coconut and curry powder. Pour the hot vinegar mixture over the coconut, making sure it is fully submerged.

3. Seal the jar and let it cool to room temperature. Then transfer it to the refrigerator to chill for at least 24 hours.

4. When ready to serve, spoon the pickled coconut and curry onto a plate and enjoy as a tangy and spicy condiment or side dish.

This recipe is inspired by the flavors of Southeast Asia, where pickled coconut is a popular condiment. The combination of fragrant curry powder and tangy vinegar creates a unique and delicious flavor that is perfect for adding a kick to your meals. Whether you serve it with grilled chicken, fish, or vegetables, this pickled coconut and curry is sure to be a hit at your next dinner party.

SPICY PICKLED COCONUT AND DILL RECIPE

This recipe adds a tropical twist to the classic pickling technique. The combination of tangy pickled coconut and fresh dill creates a unique and flavorful pickle that is perfect for adding a spicy kick to your meals. All you need is a few simple ingredients and a ball jar to store your pickles in.

---

1 cup coconut meat, cut into small cubes
1 cup white vinegar
1 cup water
1 tablespoon dill seeds
2 cloves garlic, minced
1 tablespoon sugar
1 teaspoon salt
1/2 teaspoon red pepper flakes

1. In a medium saucepan, bring the vinegar, water, dill seeds, garlic, sugar, salt, and red pepper flakes to a boil over high heat.

2. Add the coconut meat to the boiling mixture and reduce the heat to medium-low. Simmer the coconut for 10 minutes, or until it is tender but still slightly crunchy.

3. Using a slotted spoon, transfer the coconut to a clean ball jar.

4. Pour the boiling liquid over the coconut, making sure to completely cover it.

5. Close the ball jar with a lid and let it cool to room temperature. Once cooled, transfer the jar to the refrigerator to chill for at least 24 hours before serving.

6. Your spicy pickled coconut and dill is now ready to enjoy. Serve it as a side dish or as a tasty addition to sandwiches and salads. Enjoy!

PICKLED COCONUT AND GINGER RECIPE

This recipe is a unique and delicious twist on traditional pickling. The combination of sweet coconut and spicy ginger creates a flavor that is both exotic and familiar. All you need is a few simple ingredients and a trusty ball jar to store your pickles in.

1 cup grated coconut

1 cup white vinegar

1 cup water

1/4 cup sugar

1 tablespoon minced ginger

1/2 teaspoon salt

1. In a medium saucepan, bring the vinegar, water, sugar, ginger, and salt to a boil over high heat.

2. Add the coconut to the boiling mixture and reduce the heat to medium-low. Simmer the coconut for 5 minutes, or until it is softened.

3. Using a slotted spoon, transfer the coconut to a clean ball jar.

4. Pour the boiling liquid over the coconut, making sure to completely cover it.

5. Close the ball jar with a lid and let it cool to room temperature. Once cooled, transfer the jar to the refrigerator to chill for at least 24 hours before serving.

6. Your pickled coconut and ginger is now ready to enjoy. Serve it as a side dish or as a tasty addition to sandwiches and salads. Enjoy!

PICKLED COCONUT AND GINGER 2

1 cup coconut meat, grated
1/2 cup ginger, grated
1/2 cup rice vinegar
1/4 cup sugar
1/4 cup water
1 tablespoon salt
1/4 teaspoon red pepper flakes (optional)

1. In a small saucepan, combine the rice vinegar, sugar, water, salt, and red pepper flakes. Bring to a boil over medium heat, stirring until the sugar and salt are dissolved.

2. In a glass ball jar, layer the grated coconut and ginger. Pour the hot vinegar mixture over the top, making sure to completely cover the coconut and ginger.

3. Seal the jar and let it cool to room temperature. Store in the refrigerator for at least 24 hours before serving.

This pickled coconut and ginger is a delicious and unique twist on traditional pickled vegetables. The combination of sweet coconut and spicy ginger is a perfect balance of flavors that will complement any meal. The pickled coconut and ginger can be enjoyed as a side dish, condiment, or even as a topping for salads or sandwiches. Enjoy!

PICKLED COCONUT AND ONION RELISH

1 cup coconut flakes
1 onion, thinly sliced
1 cup white vinegar
1 tablespoon sugar
1 teaspoon salt

1. In a small saucepan, heat the vinegar, sugar, and salt over medium heat until the sugar and salt dissolve.
2. In a bowl, combine the coconut flakes and onion.
3. Pour the vinegar mixture over the coconut and onion and stir until well combined.
4. Transfer the mixture to a clean ball jar and let it sit at room temperature for at least 1 hour before serving.

This pickled coconut and onion relish is a delicious and unique way to add some tropical flair to your dishes. The sweet and tangy flavor of the coconut is balanced by the sharpness of the onion, creating a relish that is both tasty and versatile. Whether you're looking to add some zest to your sandwiches or want to elevate a simple salad, this relish is sure to become a new favorite.

SPICY PICKLED COCONUT AND RED PEPPER

This zesty and flavorful pickled coconut and red pepper dish is the perfect addition to any meal. The combination of sweet coconut and spicy red pepper is sure to delight your taste buds. And, since it's preserved in a ball jar, it's easy to store and enjoy for up to a week.

---

1 cup shredded coconut

1 red pepper, seeded and thinly sliced

1/2 cup vinegar

1/4 cup sugar

1 tablespoon salt

1 teaspoon red pepper flakes

1. In a small saucepan, combine the vinegar, sugar, salt, and red pepper flakes. Bring to a boil, then reduce heat and simmer for 5 minutes.

2. Place the coconut and red pepper slices in a ball jar and pour the pickling liquid over top. Let cool to room temperature, then seal the jar and refrigerate for at least 4 hours before serving.

3. When ready to serve, drain the coconut and red pepper and place in a serving bowl. Enjoy!

PICKLED COCONUT AND RED PEPPER

2 cups fresh coconut, grated

1 red bell pepper, sliced

1 cup white vinegar

1 tablespoon sugar

1 teaspoon salt

1/2 teaspoon black peppercorns

1/4 teaspoon red pepper flakes

2 cloves garlic, minced

1/4 cup water

1. In a medium saucepan, combine the vinegar, sugar, salt, peppercorns, red pepper flakes, garlic, and water. Bring to a boil over medium-high heat, stirring to dissolve the sugar and salt.

2. Add the coconut and red pepper to the saucepan and stir to combine.

3. Reduce the heat to low and simmer for 5 minutes, or until the peppers are tender.

4. Using a slotted spoon, transfer the coconut and red pepper to a clean ball jar.

5. Pour the hot pickling liquid over the coconut and red pepper, making sure to cover them completely.

6. Let the pickles cool to room temperature, then seal the jar with a lid and store in the refrigerator for at least 24 hours before serving.

This recipe for pickled coconut and red pepper is a delicious and unique twist on traditional pickled vegetables. The grated coconut adds a subtle sweetness to the tangy vinegar pickling liquid, and the red pepper adds a pop of color and a hint of heat. These pickles are the perfect addition to any sandwich, salad, or charcuterie board. Enjoy!

PICKLED COCONUT AND THYME

1 cup fresh coconut
meat, shredded
1 cup white vinegar
1/4 cup sugar
1 tablespoon dried
thyme leaves
1 teaspoon salt
1/2 teaspoon black
peppercorns
1 ball jar

1. In a small saucepan, combine the vinegar, sugar, thyme, salt, and peppercorns. Bring to a boil over medium heat, stirring until the sugar is dissolved.
2. In the meantime, pack the shredded coconut into the ball jar. Pour the hot vinegar mixture over the coconut, making sure to cover all the pieces.
3. Allow the jar to cool to room temperature, then seal with a lid and store in the refrigerator for at least 24 hours before serving.

This pickled coconut and thyme recipe is a delicious and unique twist on traditional pickles. The sweet and tangy vinegar mixture perfectly balances the earthy thyme and the creamy coconut. This dish is perfect as a side with grilled meats or even as a topping for salads. It is a must-try for anyone looking to add some new flavors to their pantry.

PICKLED CORIANDER AND ONION RELISH

1 cup chopped fresh coriander

1 cup chopped red onion

1/2 cup white vinegar

1/4 cup sugar

1/4 cup water

2 tsp salt

1/2 tsp black peppercorns

1/2 tsp mustard seeds

1/2 tsp celery seeds

1/2 tsp turmeric

1. In a small saucepan, combine the vinegar, sugar, water, salt, peppercorns, mustard seeds, celery seeds, and turmeric. Bring to a boil, then reduce heat and simmer for 5 minutes.

2. In a sterilized ball jar, layer the coriander and onion evenly.

3. Pour the hot vinegar mixture over the vegetables, making sure to cover them completely.

4. Let cool to room temperature, then seal the jar and store in the refrigerator for at least 24 hours before serving.

This pickled coriander and onion relish is a delicious and tangy addition to sandwiches, burgers, or even as a topping for grilled meats. The combination of fresh herbs and tangy vinegar creates a unique and flavorful condiment that will elevate any dish.

PICKLED CORN AND ONION RELISH

This delicious pickled corn and onion relish is the perfect accompaniment to any meal. The tangy, slightly sweet flavor of the corn is balanced perfectly by the sharp bite of the onions, creating a relish that is sure to be a hit with everyone. It's easy to make and can be enjoyed straight out of the jar or added to sandwiches and burgers to add a little extra zing.

1 cup corn kernels

1/2 cup diced onion

1/2 cup white vinegar

2 tbsp sugar

1/2 tsp salt

1/4 tsp black pepper

1. In a medium saucepan, combine the corn, onion, vinegar, sugar, salt, and black pepper.

2. Bring the mixture to a boil over medium heat, then reduce the heat to low and simmer for 5 minutes.

3. Using a slotted spoon, transfer the corn and onion mixture to a clean ball jar.

4. Let the relish cool to room temperature, then seal the jar and refrigerate for at least 24 hours to allow the flavors to meld.

5. Enjoy the relish straight from the jar or use it to add a tangy, sweet flavor to sandwiches and burgers.

PICKLED CORNICHON AND LEMON

1 cup cornichons, sliced into rounds

1 lemon, sliced into rounds

1 cup white vinegar

1 cup water

1 tablespoon sugar

1 teaspoon salt

1. In a small saucepan, combine the vinegar, water, sugar, and salt and bring to a boil.
2. Place the sliced cornichons and lemon rounds in a clean, sterilized ball jar.
3. Pour the hot vinegar mixture over the cornichon and lemon slices, making sure to cover them completely.
4. Allow the jar to cool to room temperature, then secure the lid and place in the refrigerator for at least 24 hours before serving.
5. The pickled cornichon and lemon will last for up to one month in the refrigerator. Enjoy as a tangy and refreshing addition to sandwiches, charcuterie boards, or as a simple snack on their own.

When it comes to making pickled vegetables, there are few combinations as delightful as cornichon and lemon. The tangy bite of the cornichon is perfectly balanced by the citrusy sweetness of the lemon, making for a snack that is both satisfying and refreshing. To create this recipe, I began by slicing the cornichon and lemon into thin rounds and placing them in a clean ball jar. I then heated a mixture of white vinegar, water, sugar, and salt until it reached

PICKLED CRANBERRIES

1 cup fresh cranberries
1 cup apple cider vinegar
1 cup water
1/2 cup sugar
1/2 tablespoon salt
1 cinnamon stick
1 star anise

1. In a medium saucepan, combine the apple cider vinegar, water, sugar, salt, cinnamon stick, and star anise. Bring to a boil over medium heat.
2. Once the mixture comes to a boil, add the cranberries and simmer for 5 minutes, until the cranberries begin to pop and soften.
3. Carefully transfer the cranberry mixture to a ball jar, making sure to include the cinnamon stick and star anise.
4. Let the jar cool to room temperature, then seal with a lid and store in the refrigerator for at least 2 hours before serving.
5. Serve the pickled cranberries as a tangy and flavorful accompaniment to cheese platters, pork dishes, or as a unique topping for salads.

As the leaves began to fall and the air turned crisp, I knew it was time to start preserving the abundance of cranberries from our family's farm. I decided to try my hand at pickling them, using a combination of sweet and spicy flavors. The result was a tangy and delicious condiment that added a unique twist to our holiday meals. I carefully sealed the pickled cranberries in a ball

PICKLED COCONUT AND THYME

1 cup fresh coconut
meat, shredded
1 cup white vinegar
1 tablespoon sugar
1 teaspoon salt
1 tablespoon fresh
thyme leaves

1. In a small saucepan, combine the vinegar, sugar, and salt. Bring to a boil and stir until the sugar and salt are dissolved.
2. Add the shredded coconut to a clean and sterilized ball jar. Pour the hot vinegar mixture over the coconut, making sure to completely cover it.
3. Top with the fresh thyme leaves and gently press down to submerge in the vinegar mixture.
4. Allow to cool to room temperature before sealing the jar and placing it in the fridge for at least 24 hours before enjoying.

This pickled coconut and thyme dish is a delicious and unique twist on traditional pickled vegetables. The fresh thyme adds a fragrant and earthy flavor, while the pickled coconut adds a tangy and crunchy texture. Enjoy as a tasty snack or as a flavorful addition to salads and sandwiches.

PICKLED CRANBERRY AND ONION RELISH

1 cup cranberries

1 red onion, thinly sliced

1/2 cup apple cider vinegar

1/4 cup sugar

1 teaspoon salt

1/2 teaspoon black peppercorns

1/2 teaspoon mustard seeds

1/4 teaspoon ground cinnamon

1. In a medium saucepan, combine the cranberries, onion, vinegar, sugar, salt, peppercorns, mustard seeds, and cinnamon. Bring to a boil over medium-high heat, then reduce the heat to low and simmer for 10 minutes.

2. Remove from the heat and let cool to room temperature.

3. Transfer the mixture to a sterilized ball jar and seal with a lid. Let the relish sit at room temperature for at least 1 hour before serving.

As the leaves start to change color and the air turns crisp, there's nothing like a homemade pickled cranberry and onion relish to add a tangy and sweet touch to your Thanksgiving feast. Made with simple ingredients and sealed in a beautiful ball jar, this relish is the perfect addition to your holiday table.

DELICIOUS DILL PICKLED CUCUMBERS

1 large cucumber
1 cup white vinegar
1 cup water
1 tablespoon sugar
1 tablespoon salt
1 tablespoon dill seeds
1 tablespoon mustard seeds
1 tablespoon peppercorns
2 cloves garlic, minced

1. Begin by slicing the cucumber into thin rounds.
2. In a small saucepan, combine the vinegar, water, sugar, and salt. Bring to a boil, then remove from heat.
3. In a clean and sterilized ball jar, place the cucumber slices, dill seeds, mustard seeds, peppercorns, and minced garlic.
4. Pour the vinegar mixture over the cucumber slices, making sure they are fully submerged.
5. Let the pickles cool to room temperature, then seal the jar and store in the refrigerator for at least 24 hours before enjoying.

The tartness of the vinegar and the sweetness of the sugar balance perfectly with the crunch of the cucumber and the earthy flavor of the dill. These pickled cucumbers make a delicious addition to sandwiches, salads, or as a simple snack on their own.

DELIGHTFULLY CRUNCHY MISO PICKLED CUCUMBERS

Have you ever tried pickling your own cucumbers? It's an easy and delicious way to preserve the fresh flavors of summer and enjoy them all year round. Our miso pickled cucumbers are a twist on the classic recipe, adding a tangy and savory miso flavor that pairs perfectly with the crisp cucumber. They're perfect for snacking on their own or adding to sandwiches and salads for a burst of flavor.

---

4 medium cucumbers

1 cup water

1 cup rice vinegar

1/4 cup miso paste

1/4 cup sugar

1 tablespoon salt

2 cloves garlic, minced

1 tablespoon grated ginger

1. Start by washing and drying the cucumbers. Cut them into 1/4 inch slices and set aside.

2. In a small saucepan, combine the water, rice vinegar, miso paste, sugar, salt, garlic, and ginger. Heat over medium heat until the sugar and salt have dissolved.

3. Place the cucumber slices in a sterilized ball jar. Pour the miso mixture over the cucumbers, making sure they are fully covered.

4. Let the jar sit at room temperature for at least 1 hour to let the flavors meld. Then, transfer the jar to the refrigerator and let it chill for at least 24 hours before enjoying.

5. The pickled cucumbers will keep in the refrigerator for up to 1 month. Serve them as a snack, or add them to sandwiches and salads for a burst of flavor. Enjoy!

TANGY PICKLED CUCUMBER AND ONION RELISH

This recipe is a staple in our family's summertime gatherings. It's the perfect accompaniment to any grilled meat or veggie burger. The tangy vinegar and spices give the cucumber and onion a delicious, pickled flavor, making it irresistible to even the pickiest eaters.

2 large cucumbers, sliced into thin rounds

1 large onion, sliced into thin half-moons

1 cup white vinegar

1/2 cup sugar

1 tablespoon mustard seeds

1 tablespoon dill seeds

1 teaspoon celery seeds

1 teaspoon salt

1/2 teaspoon black peppercorns

1. In a medium saucepan, combine the vinegar, sugar, mustard seeds, dill seeds, celery seeds, salt, and peppercorns. Bring to a boil over medium-high heat, stirring to dissolve the sugar.

2. Meanwhile, in a large bowl, combine the cucumber and onion slices. Pour the hot vinegar mixture over the cucumber and onion, stirring to evenly coat.

3. Transfer the pickled cucumber and onion to a clean ball jar, making sure to pack the vegetables tightly.

4. Let the pickled cucumber and onion sit at room temperature for at least 2 hours before serving or refrigerate for up to 3 weeks. Serve chilled or at room temperature as a tasty condiment or side dish. Enjoy!

CRISPY SESAME PICKLED CUCUMBERS

These crispy sesame pickled cucumbers are a refreshing and tangy side dish that will add a pop of flavor to any meal. Using a ball jar, these cucumbers are pickled in a mixture of vinegar, sugar, and sesame seeds for a unique twist on traditional pickled cucumbers.

1/2 cup white vinegar

1/4 cup sugar

1 tablespoon sesame seeds

1/2 teaspoon salt

2 medium cucumbers, sliced into 1/4-inch rounds

1. In a small saucepan, combine the vinegar, sugar, sesame seeds, and salt. Bring to a boil over medium heat, stirring occasionally, until the sugar has dissolved.

2. Place the sliced cucumbers in a ball jar and pour the hot vinegar mixture over the top.

3. Let the cucumbers cool to room temperature, then seal the jar and refrigerate for at least 2 hours before serving.

4. Serve the pickled cucumbers as a side dish or garnish for sandwiches and salads. Enjoy!

SPICY PICKLED DAIKON AND GINGER

Pickled daikon and ginger is a traditional Japanese condiment that adds a burst of flavor to any dish. It's easy to make at home and can be stored in the fridge for up to a month. The spicy kick from the chili flakes pairs perfectly with the sweet and tangy flavors of the daikon and ginger.

---

1 medium daikon radish, peeled and thinly sliced
1/4 cup ginger, thinly sliced
1/2 cup rice vinegar
1/2 cup water
1/4 cup sugar
1 teaspoon salt
1/2 teaspoon chili flakes (optional)

1. In a small saucepan, combine the rice vinegar, water, sugar, salt, and chili flakes (if using). Bring to a boil, stirring to dissolve the sugar and salt. Remove from heat and let cool.
2. Place the daikon and ginger slices in a clean ball jar.
3. Pour the pickling liquid over the daikon and ginger, making sure to fully submerge the vegetables.
4. Cover the jar with a lid and let it sit in the fridge for at least 24 hours before serving. The pickles will keep in the fridge for up to a month.
5. Serve the pickled daikon and ginger as a condiment for sushi, sandwiches, or as a topping for salads and bowls. Enjoy!

SPICY PICKLED CUMIN AND ONION RELISH

This pickled cumin and onion relish is a spicy and tangy condiment that pairs perfectly with grilled meats or as a topping for sandwiches and tacos. It's easy to make and will last for several weeks in the refrigerator.

1 large onion, thinly sliced

1 jalapeno pepper, seeded and thinly sliced

2 cloves garlic, minced

1 tsp cumin seeds

1 tsp coriander seeds

1 tsp mustard seeds

1/2 tsp red pepper flakes (optional for extra heat)

1/2 cup white vinegar

1/4 cup water

1 tbsp sugar

1 tsp salt

1 ball jar with a tight-

1. In a medium saucepan, combine the onion, jalapeno, garlic, cumin seeds, coriander seeds, mustard seeds, red pepper flakes (if using), vinegar, water, sugar, and salt.

2. Bring the mixture to a boil over medium heat, stirring occasionally.

3. Reduce the heat to low and simmer for 5 minutes, until the onions are tender.

4. Remove the saucepan from the heat and let the mixture cool slightly.

5. Transfer the mixture to the ball jar and close the lid tightly.

6. Place the jar in the refrigerator and let it sit for at least 24 hours before serving, to allow the flavors to meld. The relish will last for several weeks in the refrigerator.

ZESTY PICKLED CUCUMBERS

Pickling cucumbers is a great way to preserve them for later use and add a tasty tang to your dishes. These pickled cucumbers are made with vinegar and a blend of spices, giving them a zesty flavor that pairs well with a variety of dishes. Whether you're serving them as a snack or using them as a topping for sandwiches and salads, these pickled cucumbers are sure to be a hit.

---

3 medium cucumbers, thinly sliced
1 cup white vinegar
1 cup water
2 tablespoons sugar
1 tablespoon salt
1 teaspoon mustard seeds
1 teaspoon dill seeds
1/2 teaspoon celery seeds
1/2 teaspoon black peppercorns
4 cloves garlic, peeled and smashed
4 sprigs fresh dill

1. In a medium saucepan, combine the vinegar, water, sugar, salt, mustard seeds, dill seeds, celery seeds, and peppercorns. Bring the mixture to a boil, stirring until the sugar and salt have dissolved.

2. Place the sliced cucumbers in a large jar or multiple smaller jars. Add the smashed garlic cloves and fresh dill sprigs.

3. Pour the vinegar mixture over the cucumbers, making sure to completely cover them. Let the jars sit at room temperature for at least an hour to allow the flavors to meld.

4. Once the pickled cucumbers have cooled, seal the jars and store them in the refrigerator. The pickles will be ready to eat after 24 hours and will keep in the refrigerator for up to 1 month. Enjoy!

SESAME-INFUSED PICKLED CUCUMBERS

Pickling is a great way to preserve the crispness and flavor of cucumbers. These sesame-infused pickled cucumbers are a delicious and refreshing addition to any meal. They are easy to make and can be stored in the fridge for up to a month.

4 medium cucumbers, thinly sliced

1 cup rice vinegar

1/2 cup sugar

1/4 cup sesame seeds

1 tablespoon salt

1 teaspoon red pepper flakes (optional)

1. In a small saucepan, combine the vinegar, sugar, sesame seeds, salt, and red pepper flakes (if using). Bring to a boil, stirring until the sugar has dissolved.

2. Place the sliced cucumbers in a large bowl. Pour the hot vinegar mixture over the cucumbers and stir to coat.

3. Transfer the cucumbers and vinegar mixture to a large ball jar. Cover and refrigerate for at least 24 hours before serving.

4. Serve chilled as a side dish or garnish for sandwiches and salads. Enjoy!

ZESTY PICKLED DAIKON AND GINGER

This pickled daikon and ginger recipe is a perfect addition to any meal. The combination of the spicy ginger and the crisp, refreshing daikon creates a unique and flavorful condiment that is sure to impress. Whether you're looking for something to add to your sandwiches or just want to have a tasty snack on hand, these pickled daikon and ginger slices are sure to hit the spot.

1 large daikon radish, peeled and thinly sliced

1/4 cup fresh ginger, peeled and thinly sliced

1 cup white vinegar

1 cup water

2 tablespoons sugar

1 tablespoon salt

1. In a medium saucepan, bring the vinegar, water, sugar, and salt to a boil. Stir until the sugar and salt have dissolved.
2. Place the daikon and ginger slices in a clean and sterilized ball jar.
3. Pour the hot vinegar mixture over the daikon and ginger, making sure to fully submerge the slices.
4. Let the jar cool to room temperature before sealing with a lid.
5. Place the jar in the refrigerator for at least 24 hours before enjoying. These pickled daikon and ginger slices will last for up to a month in the refrigerator. Enjoy!

SALTY, CRUNCHY PICKLED DAIKON AND SESAME

This recipe is a twist on traditional pickled daikon and sesame seeds. The daikon is sliced thin and soaked in a salty, flavorful brine, making it the perfect addition to any sandwich or bowl. The sesame seeds add a crunchy texture and nutty flavor that pairs perfectly with the tangy daikon.

1 large daikon radish, peeled and sliced thin

1 cup white vinegar

1 cup water

1/4 cup sugar

1 tablespoon salt

1/4 cup sesame seeds

1. In a medium saucepan, combine the vinegar, water, sugar, and salt. Bring to a boil, stirring until the sugar and salt are dissolved.

2. Place the daikon slices in a clean, sterilized ball jar.

3. Pour the hot brine over the daikon, making sure to completely cover the slices.

4. Sprinkle the sesame seeds over the top of the daikon.

5. Place the lid on the ball jar and allow it to cool to room temperature.

6. Once cooled, store the jar in the refrigerator for at least 24 hours before enjoying. The pickled daikon and sesame will last for up to a month in the refrigerator.

7. Serve the pickled daikon and sesame on sandwiches, bowls, or as a tasty snack on its own. Enjoy!

DELICIOUSLY PICKLED DAIKON AND MUSTARD

As a child, my mom would always make a batch of pickled daikon and mustard to serve as a refreshing side dish at our family dinners. The crisp and slightly sweet daikon combined with the tangy mustard flavor was always a hit. Now, I continue the tradition and love to make a jar of these pickles to have on hand in the fridge. They're perfect for topping sandwiches or adding a burst of flavor to any dish.

1 large daikon radish, peeled and sliced into thin rounds

1 cup white vinegar

1 cup water

1/2 cup sugar

1 tablespoon mustard seeds

1 tablespoon salt

1 ball jar

1. Begin by sterilizing your ball jar. Wash it thoroughly with warm, soapy water and then place it in a pot of boiling water for 10 minutes. Remove from the water and let it cool.

2. In a small saucepan, combine the vinegar, water, sugar, mustard seeds, and salt. Bring to a boil and stir until the sugar and salt have dissolved.

3. Pack the sliced daikon into the ball jar. Pour the vinegar mixture over the top, making sure to fully cover the daikon.

4. Secure the lid on the ball jar and let it cool to room temperature. Once cooled, store the jar in the refrigerator for at least 24 hours before serving. The pickles will keep in the fridge for up to a month. Enjoy!

SPICY PICKLED DAIKON AND SESAME

Pickled daikon is a traditional Japanese condiment that is often served alongside sushi or other rice dishes. It is made by pickling thin slices of daikon radish in a mixture of vinegar, sugar, and spices. In this recipe, we will add some toasted sesame seeds to the pickling mixture for added flavor and crunch.

---

1 medium daikon radish, peeled and thinly sliced
1/2 cup rice vinegar
1/4 cup sugar
1 tablespoon salt
1 teaspoon red pepper flakes (optional)
1 tablespoon toasted sesame seeds

1. In a small saucepan, combine the vinegar, sugar, salt, and red pepper flakes (if using). Bring to a boil over medium heat, stirring to dissolve the sugar and salt. Remove from the heat and let cool.

2. In a clean and sterilized ball jar, layer the daikon slices and sesame seeds. Pour the cooled pickling liquid over the top, making sure to fully cover the daikon.

3. Secure the lid on the ball jar and let the pickles sit at room temperature for at least 24 hours before serving. The pickles will keep in the refrigerator for up to 1 month.

PICKLED DRAGON FRUIT AND LIME

Welcome to our recipe for pickled dragon fruit and lime! This unique and colorful recipe is a great way to preserve the flavors of dragon fruit, which is a tropical fruit that is native to Central and South America. It is known for its sweet and slightly tangy flavor, and its vibrant pink or yellow flesh. When pickled, the flavors of the dragon fruit become even more pronounced and delicious.

---

1 cup white vinegar

1 cup water

1/2 cup sugar

2 limes, thinly sliced

1 dragon fruit, peeled and thinly sliced

1 teaspoon mustard seeds

1 teaspoon coriander seeds

1 teaspoon peppercorns

1/2 teaspoon salt

1 small fresh chili pepper, thinly sliced (optional)

1. In a small saucepan, combine the vinegar, water, and sugar. Bring to a boil over high heat, stirring occasionally, until the sugar is dissolved.
2. Place the lime slices and dragon fruit slices in a sterilized ball jar.
3. In a small bowl, mix together the mustard seeds, coriander seeds, peppercorns, salt, and chili pepper (if using). Sprinkle the mixture over the lime and dragon fruit slices.
4. Pour the hot vinegar mixture over the top of the lime and dragon fruit slices, making sure to cover them completely.
5. Secure the lid on the ball jar and allow the pickles to cool to room temperature.
6. Once cooled, store the pickled dragon fruit and lime in the refrigerator for at least 24 hours before serving to allow the flavors to fully develop. Enjoy as a flavorful and unique addition to sandwiches, salads, or as a snack on their own.

PICKLED DURIAN AND LEMONGRASS DELIGHT

Have you ever tried durian? It's a tropical fruit known for its unique and strong flavor, which some people describe as a combination of sweet, savory, and slightly bitter. It's also known for its pungent aroma, which some people find unpleasant. If you're a fan of durian, you'll love this pickled version that's combined with the refreshing and citrusy flavor of lemongrass. This recipe is perfect for those who love to experiment with unique flavors and want to add a twist to their pickling game.

1 medium durian, peeled and cut into small pieces

1 cup white vinegar

1 cup water

1/4 cup sugar

2 stalks lemongrass, minced

2 cloves garlic, minced

1 teaspoon salt

1 Ball jar

1. In a small saucepan, combine the vinegar, water, sugar, lemongrass, garlic, and salt. Bring the mixture to a boil, stirring until the sugar has dissolved.
2. Place the durian pieces in the Ball jar.
3. Pour the hot vinegar mixture over the durian, making sure to cover all the pieces.
4. Seal the jar and let it cool to room temperature.
5. Once cooled, refrigerate the jar for at least 24 hours before serving.
6. The pickled durian and lemongrass will keep in the refrigerator for up to 1 month. Enjoy as a condiment or as a topping for salads, sandwiches, and more.

SPICY PICKLED EGGPLANT DELIGHT

Looking for a new twist on the classic pickled eggplant recipe? This spicy version is sure to satisfy your taste buds. Perfect as a topping for sandwiches or as a side dish, these pickled eggplants will add a burst of flavor to any meal.

2 medium eggplants, sliced into 1/4-inch rounds
1 cup white vinegar
1/2 cup water
1/4 cup sugar
2 tablespoons salt
1 tablespoon red pepper flakes
1 tablespoon mustard seeds
2 cloves garlic, minced

1. Begin by sterilizing a ball jar and its lid by boiling them in hot water for 10 minutes.
2. In a small saucepan, combine the vinegar, water, sugar, salt, red pepper flakes, mustard seeds, and garlic. Bring to a boil, stirring occasionally.
3. Place the sliced eggplant into the sterilized ball jar, packing them tightly.
4. Pour the hot vinegar mixture over the eggplant, making sure to cover all of the slices.
5. Secure the lid on the ball jar and allow the pickled eggplants to cool to room temperature.
6. Once cooled, place the ball jar in the refrigerator and allow the eggplants to pickle for at least 24 hours before serving. Enjoy!

PICKLED EGGPLANT AND CHILI

These pickled eggplants are the perfect combination of sweet, sour, and spicy flavors. They are a great addition to any meal, and they make a delicious snack on their own. The chili adds a nice kick to the eggplants, making them even more flavorful.

1 large eggplant, sliced into 1/4-inch rounds
1 red chili, sliced
1/2 cup white vinegar
1/4 cup water
2 tablespoons sugar
1 tablespoon salt

1. Place the eggplant slices in a large ball jar.
2. In a small saucepan, combine the vinegar, water, sugar, and salt. Bring to a boil and stir until the sugar and salt are dissolved.
3. Pour the hot vinegar mixture over the eggplant slices in the ball jar.
4. Add the sliced chili to the jar.
5. Close the jar tightly and let it sit at room temperature for at least 24 hours before serving.
6. Enjoy the pickled eggplants and chili as a snack or add them to your favorite dishes for extra flavor.

TANGY AND SPICY PICKLED EGGPLANT AND GARLIC

Growing up, my grandma always had a batch of pickled eggplant and garlic in her pantry. She would serve it as a side dish with almost every meal and it quickly became one of my favorite preserved foods. This recipe is a delicious variation on my grandma's classic pickle, with the addition of red pepper flakes for a spicy kick.

---

1 large eggplant, sliced into 1/4-inch rounds
1 head of garlic, cloves peeled
2 cups white vinegar
1 cup water
2 tablespoons sugar
1 tablespoon salt
1 teaspoon red pepper flakes

1. Begin by sterilizing your ball jars and lids. Wash the jars and lids in hot, soapy water and then place them in a large pot of boiling water for 10 minutes. Remove the jars and lids from the water and set aside.
2. In a small saucepan, combine the vinegar, water, sugar, salt, and red pepper flakes. Bring the mixture to a boil, stirring until the sugar and salt have dissolved.
3. Meanwhile, pack the eggplant and garlic cloves into the sterilized ball jars, leaving about 1/2 inch of headspace at the top of each jar.
4. Once the vinegar mixture has come to a boil, carefully pour it over the eggplant and garlic in the jars, making sure to cover the vegetables completely.
5. Wipe the rim of each jar with a clean, damp cloth and then place the lid on top, screwing on the band until it is finger tight.
6. Place the jars in a large pot of boiling water and process for 15 minutes. Remove the jars from the water and let them cool completely before storing in the pantry for up to 6 months. Enjoy your pickled eggplant and garlic as a side dish or add it to sandwiches and salads for a tangy and spicy flavor boost.

PICKLED EGGPLANT AND ONION RELISH

This pickled eggplant and onion relish is a tangy and flavorful accompaniment to any meal. It's perfect for topping sandwiches, burgers, or even just enjoying as a snack on its own. Plus, it's easy to make and can be stored in a ball jar for up to a few months in the refrigerator.

---

1 large eggplant, cut into small cubes
1 large onion, thinly sliced
1 cup apple cider vinegar
1/2 cup granulated sugar
1 tsp salt
1 tsp black peppercorns
1 tsp mustard seeds
1 tsp coriander seeds

1. In a large pot, bring the vinegar, sugar, salt, peppercorns, mustard seeds, and coriander seeds to a boil.

2. Add the eggplant and onion to the pot and reduce the heat to a simmer. Cook for about 10 minutes, or until the vegetables are tender.

3. Using a slotted spoon, transfer the vegetables to a sterilized ball jar.

4. Pour the remaining liquid from the pot over the vegetables in the jar, making sure to fully cover them.

5. Close the jar and let it sit at room temperature for about an hour to allow the flavors to meld.

6. Once cooled, store the jar in the refrigerator for up to a few months. Enjoy!

SPICY PICKLED EGGPLANT AND PAPRIKA

This recipe for pickled eggplant and paprika is a delicious and easy way to preserve your eggplants for the winter months. The combination of paprika and vinegar gives the eggplant a spicy and tangy flavor that pairs well with almost any dish. Whether you're looking to add some flavor to your sandwiches or want to mix up your pickle game, this recipe is sure to become a staple in your kitchen.

2 medium eggplants, sliced into 1/4-inch rounds
1 red bell pepper, thinly sliced
1 yellow bell pepper, thinly sliced
1 cup vinegar (white or apple cider vinegar both works well)
1/2 cup water
1 tablespoon paprika
1 tablespoon sugar
1 teaspoon salt
1/2 teaspoon black pepper

1. In a small saucepan, combine the vinegar, water, paprika, sugar, salt, and black pepper. Bring the mixture to a boil, then reduce the heat and simmer for 5 minutes.
2. Place the sliced eggplant, bell peppers, and minced garlic into the ball jars.
3. Pour the vinegar mixture over the top of the vegetables, making sure to cover them completely.
4. Close the ball jars and place them in the refrigerator. Allow the pickles to marinate for at least 24 hours before serving.
5. Enjoy your pickled eggplant and paprika as a tasty addition to sandwiches, salads, or as a snack on their own!

EGGPLANT BLISS IN A BALL JAR

Pickled eggplant is a tasty and unique way to preserve the bounty of your garden or farmer's market. This recipe combines eggplant with the fresh flavors of parsley, garlic, and lemon for a pickle that is sure to be a hit at any gathering.

2 lbs eggplant, cut into 1/2-inch slices
2 cups parsley leaves, chopped
6 cloves garlic, minced
2 cups white vinegar
1 cup water
1/4 cup sugar
2 tbsp salt
1 tbsp black peppercorns
1 tsp mustard seeds
2 lemon slices

1. In a large saucepan, bring the vinegar, water, sugar, salt, peppercorns, and mustard seeds to a boil.

2. Place the eggplant, parsley, garlic, and lemon slices in a sterilized ball jar.

3. Pour the hot vinegar mixture over the eggplant mixture, making sure to cover all of the vegetables.

4. Allow the jar to cool to room temperature before sealing and refrigerating.

5. The pickled eggplant will be ready to eat in about a week and will keep in the refrigerator for up to 2 months.

Enjoy your pickled eggplant and parsley as a side dish or use it to add flavor and crunch to sandwiches and salads.

CRISP AND REFRESHING PICKLED FENNEL

For this recipe, you'll need a few ball jars and some fresh fennel bulbs. If you've never worked with fennel before, it's a crunchy, licorice-flavored vegetable with a subtle sweetness. Pickling is the perfect way to preserve its crunch and flavor, and it's a great addition to a charcuterie board or as a topping for sandwiches and salads. Here's how to make it

---

2 medium fennel bulbs, thinly sliced
1 cup white vinegar
1 cup water
2 tablespoons sugar
2 teaspoons salt
1 teaspoon peppercorns
2 cloves garlic, thinly sliced
2 sprigs fresh dill

1. In a small saucepan, combine the vinegar, water, sugar, salt, and peppercorns. Bring to a boil, stirring occasionally, until the sugar and salt have dissolved.
2. Place the sliced fennel, garlic, and dill in a ball jar. Pour the hot vinegar mixture over the top, making sure to fully submerge the fennel.
3. Allow the jar to cool to room temperature, then seal the lid and refrigerate for at least 24 hours before serving. The pickled fennel will last for up to a month in the refrigerator. Enjoy!

PICKLED FENNEL AND CARROTS

This recipe for pickled fennel and carrots is a great way to preserve the flavors of summer and enjoy them all year round. The fennel and carrots are crisp and refreshing, and the pickling liquid gives them a tangy and slightly sweet flavor. They are perfect for serving as a side dish or adding to sandwiches and salads.

1 medium fennel bulb, thinly sliced

2 medium carrots, peeled and thinly sliced

1 cup apple cider vinegar

1 cup water

1 tablespoon sugar

1 tablespoon salt

1 teaspoon coriander seeds

1 teaspoon mustard seeds

1/2 teaspoon black peppercorns

2 cloves garlic, peeled and thinly sliced

1. In a small saucepan, combine the vinegar, water, sugar, salt, coriander seeds, mustard seeds, and peppercorns. Bring to a boil, then reduce the heat to a simmer.

2. Place the fennel and carrots in a sterilized ball jar. Add the garlic slices.

3. Pour the pickling liquid over the vegetables, making sure to cover them completely.

4. Close the jar tightly and store in the refrigerator for at least 24 hours before serving, to allow the flavors to develop. The pickled fennel and carrots will keep in the refrigerator for up to 3 weeks. Enjoy!

PICKLED FENNEL AND DILL

This pickled fennel and dill recipe is a refreshing and tasty way to enjoy the flavors of fennel and dill all year round. The combination of the crisp, slightly sweet fennel with the bold and aromatic dill is truly delightful, and the vinegar-based pickling liquid adds a bright and tangy kick. These pickled fennel and dill slices make a great addition to sandwiches, salads, and charcuterie boards, and they're also delicious on their own as a snack.

1 medium fennel bulb, thinly sliced
1 bunch fresh dill, roughly chopped
1 cup white vinegar
1 cup water
2 tablespoons granulated sugar
1 tablespoon pickling salt
1 teaspoon mustard seeds
1 teaspoon coriander seeds
1 teaspoon black peppercorns

1. In a medium saucepan, combine the vinegar, water, sugar, pickling salt, mustard seeds, coriander seeds, peppercorns, and garlic. Bring the mixture to a boil over medium-high heat, stirring occasionally to dissolve the sugar and salt.

2. Once the mixture has reached a boil, add the fennel and dill to a clean and sterilized ball jar.

3. Pour the hot pickling liquid over the fennel and dill, making sure to fully cover the vegetables.

4. Secure the lid on the ball jar and let the pickled fennel and dill cool to room temperature.

5. Once cooled, transfer the ball jar to the refrigerator and let it sit for at least 24 hours before serving. The pickled fennel and dill will keep in the refrigerator for up to 1 month. Enjoy!

GARLIC AND FENNEL PICKLE DELIGHT

This pickled fennel and garlic recipe is a tasty and unique addition to any meal. The combination of the sweet, licorice-like flavor of fennel with the sharp tang of garlic creates a pickle that is sure to delight your taste buds. Perfect for adding some extra flavor to sandwiches, salads, or as a topping for grilled meats, these pickles are a must-try.

1 large bulb of fennel, thinly sliced

6 cloves of garlic, thinly sliced

1 cup white vinegar

1 cup water

1 tbsp sugar

1 tsp salt

1 tsp mustard seeds

1 tsp coriander seeds

1 tsp fennel seeds

1. Sterilize a large ball jar by boiling it in a pot of water for 10 minutes.
2. In a medium saucepan, combine the vinegar, water, sugar, salt, mustard seeds, coriander seeds, and fennel seeds. Bring to a boil, then reduce heat and simmer for 5 minutes.
3. Add the sliced fennel and garlic to the ball jar.
4. Pour the hot vinegar mixture over the fennel and garlic, making sure to fully submerge the vegetables.
5. Tightly seal the ball jar and let it cool to room temperature.
6. Transfer the ball jar to the refrigerator and let it pickle for at least 24 hours before serving. The pickles will keep in the refrigerator for up to 1 month. Enjoy!

PICKLED FENNEL AND LEMON

This pickled fennel and lemon is a refreshing and zesty addition to any meal. Its bright, citrusy flavor pairs well with a variety of dishes, from sandwiches and salads to charcuterie boards and more. Plus, it's easy to make and can be stored in a ball jar for up to a few months in the refrigerator.

2 medium fennel bulbs, thinly sliced
1 lemon, thinly sliced
1 cup white vinegar
1/2 cup granulated sugar
1 tsp salt
1 tsp black peppercorns
1 tsp coriander seeds
1 tsp fennel seeds

1. In a large pot, bring the vinegar, sugar, salt, peppercorns, coriander seeds, and fennel seeds to a boil.

2. Add the fennel and lemon slices to the pot and reduce the heat to a simmer. Cook for about 10 minutes, or until the vegetables are tender.

3. Using a slotted spoon, transfer the fennel and lemon to a sterilized ball jar.

4. Pour the remaining liquid from the pot over the vegetables in the jar, making sure to fully cover them.

5. Close the jar and let it sit at room temperature for about an hour to allow the flavors to meld.

6. Once cooled, store the jar in the refrigerator for up to a few months. Enjoy!

PICKLED FIG AND ONION RELISH

This pickled fig and onion relish is the perfect combination of sweet and savory. It's a great addition to any charcuterie board or as a topping for sandwiches and burgers. It's also a great way to use up any extra figs you may have on hand.

1-pound figs, stems removed and quartered
1 large onion, thinly sliced
1 cup apple cider vinegar
1 cup sugar
1 tablespoon kosher salt
1 teaspoon mustard seeds
1 teaspoon coriander seeds
1 teaspoon black peppercorns
1 cinnamon stick

1. In a medium saucepan, combine the figs, onion, vinegar, sugar, salt, mustard seeds, coriander seeds, peppercorns, and cinnamon stick. Bring to a boil over medium heat, stirring occasionally.
2. Reduce the heat to low and simmer for 10 minutes, or until the figs are tender.
3. Remove the pan from the heat and let the mixture cool to room temperature.
4. Transfer the fig and onion relish to a clean ball jar and refrigerate until ready to use. The relish will keep in the refrigerator for up to 2 weeks.

SAVORY AND SWEET PICKLED FIG AND ONION RELISH

Introducing a unique blend of savory and sweet flavors, this pickled fig and onion relish is perfect for topping sandwiches, burgers, and even hot dogs. Plus, it's easy to make and can be stored in a ball jar for future use. Here's how to make it

1-pound fresh figs, quartered

1 large red onion, thinly sliced

1 cup white vinegar

1 cup sugar

1 tablespoon kosher salt

1 teaspoon mustard seeds

1 teaspoon black peppercorns

1. In a large saucepan, bring the vinegar, sugar, salt, mustard seeds, and peppercorns to a boil over medium heat, stirring occasionally to dissolve the sugar.

2. Add the figs and onion to the saucepan and bring the mixture back to a boil.

3. Reduce the heat to low and simmer for 5 minutes.

4. Remove the saucepan from the heat and let the mixture cool for 5 minutes.

5. Transfer the fig and onion mixture to a sterilized ball jar, making sure to pack the figs and onions tightly.

6. Pour the pickling liquid over the figs and onions, filling the jar to within 1/2 inch of the top.

7. Seal the jar and let it sit at room temperature for 24 hours before refrigerating.

8. The pickled fig and onion relish can be stored in the refrigerator for up to 1 month. Enjoy!

PICKLED FIG AND THYME

This pickled fig and thyme recipe is a delicious and unique way to preserve figs and add a pop of flavor to your meals. The figs are pickled in a mixture of vinegar, sugar, and thyme, giving them a tangy and slightly sweet taste. They can be eaten as a snack or used as a condiment for sandwiches and salads.

1-pound fresh figs

1 cup white vinegar

1/2 cup sugar

2 sprigs fresh thyme

1 teaspoon salt

1. Wash and slice the figs into 1/4-inch slices.
2. In a small saucepan, combine the vinegar, sugar, thyme, and salt. Bring to a boil, stirring until the sugar is dissolved.
3. Place the sliced figs in a sterilized ball jar. Pour the hot vinegar mixture over the figs, making sure they are fully covered.
4. Let the jar cool to room temperature, then seal and store in the refrigerator for at least a week before serving to allow the flavors to fully develop. The pickled figs will keep for up to 3 months in the refrigerator.
5. To serve, remove the figs from the jar and enjoy as a snack or use as a condiment for sandwiches and salads.

SPICY PICKLED GARLIC AND CHILI

Looking for a tasty and unique addition to your next charcuterie board or sandwich? These spicy pickled garlic and chili will surely do the trick! The combination of the pungent garlic and the heat from the chili creates a flavor explosion in every bite. Plus, the vinegar brine helps to preserve the garlic and chili, so you can enjoy them for weeks to come. Here's how to make them at home

1 cup vinegar (white vinegar or apple cider vinegar work well)
1 cup water
2 tablespoons sugar
1 tablespoon salt
1 teaspoon black peppercorns
1 bay leaf
1 cup garlic cloves, peeled
1 cup chili peppers, stemmed and sliced

1. In a small saucepan, bring the vinegar, water, sugar, salt, peppercorns, and bay leaf to a boil. Stir until the sugar and salt have dissolved.
2. Place the garlic and chili peppers in a clean, sterilized ball jar.
3. Pour the hot vinegar mixture over the garlic and chili peppers, making sure to cover them completely.
4. Let the jar cool to room temperature, then seal and store in the refrigerator for at least 24 hours before serving. The pickled garlic and chili will last for several weeks in the refrigerator.
5. To serve, remove the garlic and chili peppers from the jar and chop or slice as desired. Enjoy on sandwiches, charcuterie boards, or as a condiment for grilled meats.

ZESTY PICKLED GARLIC AND DILL CAULIFLOWER

If you're a fan of pickled vegetables, you'll love this recipe for pickled garlic and dill cauliflower. The crisp cauliflower is combined with spicy garlic and fresh dill for a flavor combination that is simply unbeatable. This recipe is easy to make and can be stored in the refrigerator for up to a month, making it perfect for quick and easy snacks or side dishes.

---

1 head of cauliflower, cut into florets

1 cup white vinegar

1 cup water

1 tbsp sugar

1 tsp salt

2 cloves garlic, minced

1 tbsp fresh dill, chopped

1. In a small saucepan, bring the vinegar, water, sugar, and salt to a boil.
2. Place the cauliflower florets in a ball jar and add the minced garlic and chopped dill.
3. Pour the hot vinegar mixture over the cauliflower, making sure to completely cover the vegetables.
4. Let the jar cool to room temperature, then seal with a lid and refrigerate for at least 24 hours before serving.
5. The pickled cauliflower can be stored in the refrigerator for up to a month. Enjoy as a snack or as a side dish for sandwiches and salads.

DELICIOUSLY PICKLED GARLIC AND DILL GREEN BEANS

These pickled garlic and dill green beans are the perfect addition to any sandwich or charcuterie board. The briny, garlicky flavor pairs perfectly with meats and cheeses, and the crunch of the green beans adds a nice texture. Plus, they're super easy to make and can be stored in the fridge for several weeks.

1-pound green beans, trimmed
1 cup white vinegar
1 cup water
2 tablespoons sugar
2 teaspoons salt
3 cloves garlic, peeled and thinly sliced
1 tablespoon dill weed
1 teaspoon black peppercorns
1 ball jar with a tight-fitting lid

1. Wash and trim the green beans, cutting them into desired length.
2. In a small saucepan, combine the vinegar, water, sugar, and salt. Bring to a boil and stir to dissolve the sugar and salt.
3. Place the green beans, garlic, dill, and peppercorns in the ball jar.
4. Pour the hot vinegar mixture over the green beans, making sure to cover them completely.
5. Tightly seal the jar and let it cool to room temperature.
6. Once cooled, place the jar in the refrigerator for at least 24 hours before serving. The green beans will keep in the fridge for up to 3 weeks. Enjoy!

ZESTY PICKLED GARLIC AND ONION RELISH

This pickled garlic and onion relish is the perfect addition to any sandwich or burger. The tangy and flavorful combination of pickled garlic and onion brings a burst of flavor to any dish.

1 cup garlic cloves, peeled

1 cup diced onions

1 cup white vinegar

1 cup water

1 tbsp sugar

1 tsp salt

2 tbsp pickling spice

1. In a small saucepan, combine the vinegar, water, sugar, and salt. Bring to a boil.
2. In a ball jar, add the garlic cloves and diced onions.
3. Pour the hot vinegar mixture over the garlic and onions, making sure to fully cover them.
4. Add the pickling spice to the jar.
5. Close the jar tightly and let it sit in the refrigerator for at least 24 hours before serving. The relish will last for up to 2 weeks in the refrigerator. Enjoy!

ROSEMARY AND GARLIC PICKLED DELIGHT

Pickling is a great way to preserve the flavors and textures of your favorite ingredients. In this recipe, we will be pickling garlic and rosemary to create a flavorful condiment that can be added to a variety of dishes. The combination of the two herbs creates a unique and delicious taste that will surely become a staple in your kitchen.

1 cup white vinegar

1 cup water

1 tablespoon sugar

2 teaspoons salt

1 teaspoon black peppercorns

1 sprig of rosemary

6 cloves of garlic, peeled

1 ball jar

1. In a small saucepan, combine the vinegar, water, sugar, salt, and peppercorns. Bring to a boil over medium heat, stirring occasionally to dissolve the sugar and salt.
2. Meanwhile, prepare the rosemary and garlic. Break the rosemary sprig into small pieces and place in the bottom of the ball jar. Add the garlic cloves on top of the rosemary.
3. Once the vinegar mixture has come to a boil, carefully pour it over the rosemary and garlic in the ball jar.
4. Seal the ball jar tightly and allow it to cool to room temperature. Once cooled, place the jar in the refrigerator for at least 24 hours before serving.
5. The pickled garlic and rosemary will keep in the refrigerator for up to 2 weeks. Enjoy as a condiment on sandwiches, salads, and more.

SPICY PICKLED GARLIC AND SOY

Introducing our spicy pickled garlic and soy recipe! This recipe is a delicious and flavorful twist on traditional pickled garlic. The soy sauce adds a savory depth of flavor to the pickling liquid, while the addition of red pepper flakes gives it a nice kick of heat. This pickled garlic is great on sandwiches, in stir fries, or as a topping for grilled meats.

---

1 cup water

1 cup white vinegar

1/2 cup soy sauce

1/4 cup sugar

1 tablespoon red pepper flakes

2 cloves garlic, minced

1 ball jar

1. In a small saucepan, combine the water, vinegar, soy sauce, sugar, and red pepper flakes. Bring to a boil over medium heat, stirring until the sugar has dissolved.

2. Add the minced garlic to the ball jar.

3. Pour the hot pickling liquid over the garlic in the jar, making sure to completely cover the garlic.

4. Let the jar cool to room temperature, then cover with a lid and refrigerate for at least 24 hours before serving. The pickled garlic will last for up to a month in the refrigerator.

5. To serve, simply spoon out the desired amount of pickled garlic and enjoy!

DILL-ICIOUS PICKLED GHERKINS

Pickled gherkins are a classic accompaniment to sandwiches and burgers, and they're super easy to make at home. This recipe is perfect for those who love the flavors of dill and vinegar, and it's a great way to preserve cucumbers for the winter months.

1-pound small cucumbers

1 cup vinegar (white vinegar or apple cider vinegar work well)

1 cup water

2 tablespoons sugar

1 tablespoon salt

1 tablespoon dill seeds

1 teaspoon black peppercorns

1 garlic clove, sliced

1 small, dried chili pepper (optional)

1. Wash the cucumbers and slice them into thin rounds.

2. In a small saucepan, combine the vinegar, water, sugar, salt, dill seeds, peppercorns, garlic, and chili pepper (if using). Bring the mixture to a boil over medium heat, stirring occasionally to dissolve the sugar and salt.

3. Place the cucumber slices in a clean ball jar and pour the hot vinegar mixture over them, making sure to completely cover the cucumbers.

4. Allow the jar to cool to room temperature, then seal the jar and store it in the refrigerator for at least 24 hours before serving. The pickled gherkins will keep for up to 1 month in the refrigerator.

GINGER PICKLES A CRUNCHY AND REFRESHING TREAT

1 pound ginger, peeled and thinly sliced
1 cup rice vinegar
1 cup water
1/2 cup sugar
1 tablespoon salt
1 teaspoon mustard seeds
1 teaspoon black peppercorns
1 bay leaf
1 cinnamon stick
5 whole cloves

1. In a small saucepan, combine the vinegar, water, sugar, salt, mustard seeds, peppercorns, bay leaf, cinnamon stick, and cloves. Bring to a boil over medium heat, stirring occasionally to dissolve the sugar and salt.

2. Place the sliced ginger in a large jar, such as a Ball jar.

3. Pour the hot pickling liquid over the ginger, making sure to cover the ginger completely.

4. Let the ginger pickles cool to room temperature, then seal the jar and refrigerate for at least 24 hours before serving. The pickles will keep in the refrigerator for up to 3 months.

5. To serve, simply scoop out a few slices of pickled ginger and enjoy as a refreshing snack or as a condiment with sushi or other dishes.

GINGER LEMON PICKLES

These pickled ginger and lemon slices are the perfect balance of sweet and tangy, with a spicy kick from the ginger. They are a great addition to any sushi plate or can be enjoyed as a snack on their own.

1 cup white vinegar

1 cup water

1/2 cup sugar

1 tablespoon salt

1 small lemon, thinly sliced

1/2 cup thinly sliced ginger

1. In a small saucepan, combine the vinegar, water, sugar, and salt. Bring to a boil, stirring until the sugar and salt are dissolved.
2. Place the lemon and ginger slices in a clean ball jar.
3. Pour the hot vinegar mixture over the lemon and ginger slices, making sure they are completely covered.
4. Let the jar cool to room temperature, then seal and refrigerate for at least 2 hours before serving.
5. The pickles will keep in the refrigerator for up to 2 weeks. Enjoy!

GINGER AND ONION RELISH WITH A KICK

This pickled ginger and onion relish is the perfect condiment to add a punch of flavor to any dish. It's easy to make and can be stored in the fridge for weeks, making it a great addition to have on hand for quick meals.

---

1 cup rice vinegar

1/2 cup sugar

1 tablespoon salt

1/4 cup water

1 large red onion, thinly sliced

1/2 cup peeled and thinly sliced ginger

1 tablespoon mustard seeds

1 teaspoon coriander seeds

1 teaspoon black peppercorns

1 bay leaf

1. In a small saucepan, combine the rice vinegar, sugar, salt, and water. Bring to a boil, stirring to dissolve the sugar and salt.

2. Place the onion, ginger, mustard seeds, coriander seeds, peppercorns, and bay leaf in a large ball jar.

3. Pour the hot vinegar mixture over the ingredients in the jar, making sure to fully cover them.

4. Close the jar tightly and let it sit at room temperature for at least 2 hours to allow the flavors to meld.

5. Transfer the jar to the fridge and let it sit for at least 1 week before serving. The relish will keep in the fridge for several weeks. Enjoy!

GINGER AND SCALLION PICKLED CARROTS

Growing up, my grandma always had a jar of pickled carrots in the refrigerator. They were sweet, tangy, and oh so delicious. When I moved out on my own, I started experimenting with different flavors and came up with this recipe for ginger and scallion pickled carrots. They're the perfect addition to a sandwich or a charcuterie board.

1-pound carrots, peeled and thinly sliced

1 cup white vinegar

1 cup water

1/2 cup sugar

2 tablespoons salt

2 tablespoons grated ginger

1/2 cup thinly sliced scallions

1. In a small saucepan, combine the vinegar, water, sugar, and salt. Bring to a boil, stirring until the sugar and salt have dissolved.

2. In a sterilized ball jar, layer the carrots, ginger, and scallions.

3. Pour the vinegar mixture over the carrots, making sure to completely cover them.

4. Seal the jar and store in the refrigerator for at least 24 hours before serving. The carrots will keep in the refrigerator for up to a month.

ZESTY PICKLED GINGER AND SESAME CAULIFLOWER

This recipe combines the tangy and spicy flavors of pickled ginger with the nutty taste of sesame seeds and the crunch of cauliflower. It's a unique twist on traditional pickled vegetables that is sure to become a favorite in your home.

---

1 head of cauliflower, broken into florets

1 cup rice vinegar

1 cup water

1/2 cup sugar

1 tablespoon pickled ginger, chopped

1 tablespoon sesame seeds

1 tablespoon salt

1 ball jar

1. In a small saucepan, combine the vinegar, water, sugar, and salt. Bring to a boil, stirring until the sugar and salt are dissolved.

2. Place the cauliflower florets in the ball jar.

3. Add the pickled ginger and sesame seeds to the jar.

4. Pour the vinegar mixture over the cauliflower, making sure to cover all the florets.

5. Seal the jar and let it sit at room temperature for at least 24 hours before serving.

6. Refrigerate any leftovers. Enjoy your zesty pickled ginger and sesame cauliflower as a tasty side dish or topping for salads and sandwiches.

SWEET AND TANGY PICKLED GRAPE AND ONION RELISH

Growing up, my grandma always made this delicious, pickled relish to go with our summer barbeques. It's the perfect balance of sweet and tangy, and the combination of grapes and onions is surprisingly tasty. This recipe is perfect for preserving the end-of-season grapes and using them throughout the year. It's a great addition to sandwiches, hot dogs, and more.

1-pound red grapes

1 medium red onion, thinly sliced

1 cup apple cider vinegar

1/2 cup white sugar

1 tablespoon salt

1 teaspoon mustard seeds

1 teaspoon coriander seeds

1. Wash and thinly slice the red grapes and red onion.
2. In a medium saucepan, combine the vinegar, sugar, salt, mustard seeds, and coriander seeds. Bring to a boil, stirring occasionally.
3. Place the grapes and onions in a clean ball jar.
4. Pour the hot vinegar mixture over the grapes and onions, making sure they are completely submerged.
5. Close the ball jar tightly and allow to cool.
6. Store in the refrigerator for at least 24 hours before serving. The relish will keep in the refrigerator for up to 3 weeks. Enjoy!

GRAPE THYME PICKLES - A PERFECT PAIRING

Looking for a unique twist on your traditional pickle recipe? Look no further than these grape and thyme pickles! The combination of sweet grapes and savory thyme creates a flavor explosion in every bite. Perfect for adding to sandwiches or serving as an appetizer.

1 lb red grapes
1 cup water
1 cup white vinegar
1/2 cup sugar
1 tbsp pickling salt
2 sprigs fresh thyme

1. Wash and dry the grapes, removing any stems.
2. In a small saucepan, combine the water, vinegar, sugar, and pickling salt. Bring to a boil, stirring until the sugar and salt have dissolved.
3. Place the grapes and thyme sprigs in a clean ball jar.
4. Pour the hot vinegar mixture over the grapes, making sure they are fully submerged.
5. Let the jar cool to room temperature before sealing and storing in the refrigerator for at least 1 week before serving. The pickles will last up to 3 months in the refrigerator. Enjoy!

SUN-KISSED PICKLED GRAPEFRUIT AND CHAMOMILE

Growing up, my grandma always had a jar of pickled grapefruits in her pantry. She claimed they were the perfect accompaniment to a hot summer day, and boy was she right! The combination of sweet and tangy grapefruit with the floral notes of chamomile creates a unique and refreshing pickle. Give this recipe a try and see for yourself!

2 medium grapefruits, peeled and sliced into wedges

2 cups white vinegar

2 cups water

1/2 cup sugar

1 tablespoon chamomile flowers

1 tablespoon kosher salt

2 ball jars with lids

1. In a small saucepan, bring the vinegar, water, sugar, chamomile flowers, and salt to a boil. Stir until the sugar and salt have dissolved.

2. Place the grapefruit wedges into the ball jars.

3. Pour the vinegar mixture over the grapefruits, making sure to completely cover them.

4. Close the ball jars tightly and let them sit at room temperature for at least 2 hours.

5. Transfer the ball jars to the fridge and let them sit for at least 24 hours before serving.

6. The pickled grapefruits will last for up to 2 weeks in the fridge. Enjoy as a tangy and refreshing snack or as a garnish for cocktails and salads.

ZESTY PICKLED GRAPEFRUIT AND JALAPENO

This recipe is perfect for adding some kick to your next taco night or for serving as a unique appetizer. The combination of sweet grapefruit and spicy jalapeno is a match made in heaven.

1 large grapefruit, sliced into thin wedges

1 jalapeno, thinly sliced

1 cup white vinegar

1 cup water

1 tablespoon sugar

1 tablespoon salt

1 bay leaf

1 ball jar

1. In a small saucepan, combine the vinegar, water, sugar, salt, and bay leaf. Bring to a boil, then reduce heat and simmer for 5 minutes.
2. Place the grapefruit and jalapeno slices in the ball jar.
3. Pour the hot vinegar mixture over the fruit and jalapeno in the jar.
4. Close the jar and let it cool to room temperature.
5. Once cooled, store the jar in the refrigerator for at least 24 hours before serving to allow the flavors to develop.
6. Enjoy your pickled grapefruit and jalapeno on tacos, sandwiches, or as a tangy appetizer.

TANGY AND REFRESHING PICKLED GRAPEFRUIT AND LEMON

This recipe is perfect for those who love a bit of tang in their food. The combination of pickled grapefruit and lemon adds a burst of flavor to any dish.

1 grapefruit

1 lemon

1 cup water

1 cup vinegar

1 cup sugar

1 tsp salt

2-3 cloves garlic, minced

1 tsp black peppercorns

1 tsp mustard seeds

1. Wash the grapefruit and lemon thoroughly and slice into thin wedges.

2. In a small saucepan, bring the water, vinegar, sugar, and salt to a boil.

3. Once the mixture has boiled, add the garlic, peppercorns, and mustard seeds.

4. Place the grapefruit and lemon wedges into a clean ball jar.

5. Pour the hot pickling liquid over the fruit in the jar, making sure to fully cover the fruit.

6. Seal the ball jar and let it sit at room temperature for at least 24 hours before refrigerating.

7. The pickled grapefruit and lemon can be enjoyed as is or used in salads, sandwiches, or as a garnish for cocktails. Enjoy!

TANGY PICKLED GRAPEFRUIT AND LIME

Growing up, my mom always had a jar of pickled grapefruit and lime in the pantry. It's a delicious, refreshing treat that's perfect for adding a little extra flavor to any dish. This recipe is easy to make and can be stored in the pantry for months. Here's how to make it

2 grapefruits, peeled and sliced into thin wedges
2 limes, sliced into thin wedges
1 cup water
1 cup white vinegar
1/2 cup sugar
1 tsp salt
2 cloves garlic, minced
1 tsp whole peppercorns
1 tsp dill seeds
1 tsp mustard seeds

1. In a small saucepan, combine the water, vinegar, sugar, and salt. Bring to a boil, then reduce heat and simmer for 5 minutes.

2. Meanwhile, place the grapefruit and lime wedges in a sterilized ball jar. Add the garlic, peppercorns, dill seeds, and mustard seeds.

3. Pour the hot vinegar mixture over the fruit, making sure to cover all the slices.

4. Secure the lid on the ball jar and let it cool to room temperature. Once cooled, store in the pantry for up to 3 months.

5. When ready to use, remove the fruit from the jar and slice as desired. Enjoy as a topping for salads, sandwiches, or as a garnish for cocktails.

SUNSHINE IN A JAR PICKLED GRAPEFRUIT AND MINT

This refreshing pickle combines the bright flavor of grapefruit with the cool, refreshing taste of mint. Perfect for adding a burst of flavor to any dish, this pickle is a great addition to any pantry.

---

3 grapefruits, peeled and sliced into wedges

1 cup white vinegar

1 cup water

1/2 cup sugar

1 tablespoon kosher salt

1/4 cup mint leaves

1. In a small saucepan, combine the vinegar, water, sugar, and salt. Bring to a boil and stir until the sugar and salt have dissolved.

2. Add the grapefruit wedges and mint leaves to a sterilized ball jar. Pour the hot vinegar mixture over the top, making sure to fully cover the grapefruit and mint.

3. Secure the lid on the ball jar and allow the pickle to cool to room temperature. Once cooled, store in the refrigerator for at least 24 hours before enjoying.

4. Serve the pickled grapefruit and mint as a topping for salads, grilled meats, or as a refreshing snack on its own. Enjoy!

TART AND SWEET PICKLED GRAPEFRUIT AND ONION RELISH

This pickled grapefruit and onion relish is the perfect addition to any savory dish. The combination of tart grapefruit and sweet onions creates a unique and flavorful condiment that will surely impress your friends and family.

1 grapefruit, peeled and cut into small pieces
1 medium red onion, sliced thin
1 cup white vinegar
1 cup sugar
1 tsp salt
1 tsp mustard seeds
1 tsp black peppercorns
1 ball jar with lid

1. In a small saucepan, combine the vinegar, sugar, salt, mustard seeds, and black peppercorns. Bring to a boil and stir until the sugar has dissolved.

2. Place the grapefruit and onion slices in the ball jar. Pour the hot vinegar mixture over the top of the fruit and onions, making sure to completely cover them.

3. Close the lid on the ball jar and let it cool to room temperature.

4. Once cool, place the ball jar in the fridge for at least 24 hours before serving to allow the flavors to meld together.

5. Serve as a condiment for sandwiches, burgers, or grilled meats. The pickled grapefruit and onion relish will keep in the fridge for up to 1 month.

PICKLED GRAPEFRUIT AND ROSEMARY A REFRESHING TWIST ON CLASSIC PICKLES

Intro This recipe combines the tartness of grapefruit with the woodsy flavors of rosemary to create a unique pickle that is perfect for adding a burst of flavor to any dish. Whether you're serving them as a side at a BBQ or using them to add a pop of color to a salad, these pickled grapefruit and rosemary are sure to be a hit.

2 large grapefruits, peeled and sliced into wedges

1 cup water

1 cup white vinegar

1/2 cup sugar

2 sprigs of rosemary

1 tsp salt

4 ball jars with lids

1. In a small saucepan, combine the water, vinegar, sugar, rosemary, and salt. Bring to a boil, stirring until the sugar and salt have dissolved.
2. Place the grapefruit wedges in the ball jars, packing them in tightly.
3. Pour the vinegar mixture over the grapefruit, making sure to cover all of the wedges.
4. Close the ball jars tightly and place them in the fridge to chill for at least 24 hours before serving.
5. The pickled grapefruit and rosemary will keep in the fridge for up to 2 weeks. Enjoy!

GARLICKY PICKLED GRAPEFRUIT WITH THYME

This recipe is a delicious and unique twist on traditional pickled grapefruit. The addition of garlic and thyme adds depth and flavor to the grapefruit, making it perfect for a refreshing snack or topping for a salad.

3 grapefruits, peeled and thinly sliced

1 cup white vinegar

1 cup water

1/2 cup sugar

3 garlic cloves, minced

1 tablespoon thyme leaves

1 teaspoon salt

2 ball jars

1. In a small saucepan, combine the vinegar, water, sugar, garlic, thyme, and salt. Bring to a boil over medium heat, stirring until the sugar has dissolved.
2. Place the sliced grapefruit in the ball jars.
3. Pour the vinegar mixture over the grapefruit, making sure to cover all of the slices.
4. Close the ball jars tightly and let cool to room temperature.
5. Once cool, store the pickled grapefruit in the refrigerator for at least 24 hours before serving. Enjoy as a snack or use as a topping for salads, sandwiches, or cocktails.

TANTALIZINGLY TART PICKLED GRAPES

As the weather starts to cool and grape season approaches, I love to preserve some of the bounty for snacking on throughout the year. These pickled grapes are the perfect balance of sweet and tangy and make for a unique addition to cheese boards or charcuterie spreads.

2 cups red grapes, halved

1 cup white wine vinegar

1 cup water

1/2 cup sugar

1 cinnamon stick

2 cloves

1 star anise

1 bay leaf

1. In a small saucepan, bring the vinegar, water, sugar, and spices to a boil, stirring to dissolve the sugar.
2. Pack the halved grapes into a clean ball jar.
3. Pour the hot vinegar mixture over the grapes, making sure to cover them completely.
4. Let the jar cool to room temperature, then seal and refrigerate for at least 24 hours before enjoying. The pickled grapes will keep in the refrigerator for up to 2 months.

GARLIC-INFUSED PICKLED GREEN BEANS

Growing up, my grandma always had a jar of pickled green beans in her pantry. She would serve them as a tangy side dish to many of our family dinners. These pickled green beans are a twist on her classic recipe, with the addition of garlic for extra flavor. They're the perfect addition to any sandwich or charcuterie board.

1-pound green beans, trimmed

4 cloves garlic, sliced

1 cup white vinegar

1 cup water

2 tablespoons sugar

1 tablespoon salt

1 teaspoon black peppercorns

1 dried red chili pepper (optional)

1. Fill a large pot with water and bring to a boil. Add the green beans and blanch for 2 minutes. Drain and rinse with cold water.

2. In a ball jar, combine the sliced garlic, vinegar, water, sugar, salt, peppercorns, and chili pepper (if using). Stir until the sugar and salt have dissolved.

3. Add the blanched green beans to the jar. Press down to ensure they are fully submerged in the liquid.

4. Seal the jar and let it sit at room temperature for at least 24 hours before refrigerating. The pickled green beans will keep in the refrigerator for up to 3 months.

ZESTY PICKLED GREEN BEAN AND ONION RELISH

Growing up, my grandma always had a jar of this pickled green bean and onion relish in her pantry. It was the perfect addition to any sandwich or as a topping for a savory hot dog. This recipe has been passed down in my family for generations and I'm excited to share it with you.

1 lb green beans, trimmed

1 small red onion, thinly sliced

1 cup white vinegar

1/2 cup sugar

1 tsp salt

1 tsp mustard seeds

1 tsp celery seeds

1. Bring a large pot of salted water to a boil. Add the green beans and blanch for 2-3 minutes until bright green and crisp-tender. Drain and rinse under cold water to stop the cooking process.
2. In a medium saucepan, combine the vinegar, sugar, salt, mustard seeds, and celery seeds. Bring to a boil and stir until the sugar is dissolved.
3. Place the green beans and onion slices in a clean ball jar. Pour the vinegar mixture over the top, making sure to completely cover the vegetables.
4. Tightly seal the ball jar and place in the fridge for at least 2 hours before serving. The pickled green beans and onions will keep in the fridge for up to 2 weeks. Enjoy!

ZESTY PICKLED GREEN BEANS

These pickled green beans are a classic addition to any barbecue or picnic spread. The brine is full of zesty flavors, including garlic, dill, and red pepper flakes, which give these beans a bit of a kick. Plus, the canning process preserves the beans for months, making them a perfect pantry staple.

1-pound fresh green beans, trimmed

2 cloves garlic, minced

1 teaspoon dill seeds

1/2 teaspoon red pepper flakes

1 cup white vinegar

1 cup water

1 tablespoon sugar

1 teaspoon salt

1. In a small saucepan, combine the vinegar, water, sugar, and salt. Bring to a boil, stirring occasionally, until the sugar and salt have dissolved. Remove from heat.

2. In a large ball jar, place the green beans, garlic, dill seeds, and red pepper flakes.

3. Pour the vinegar mixture over the green beans, making sure to fully cover them.

4. Close the ball jar and let it sit at room temperature for at least 2 hours, or until the brine has cooled.

5. Once the brine has cooled, place the ball jar in the refrigerator and let it sit for at least 24 hours before serving. The pickled green beans will keep in the refrigerator for up to 2 weeks.

THYME-INFUSED PICKLED GREEN BEANS

These pickled green beans are the perfect addition to any charcuterie board or sandwich. The thyme adds a subtle, herbal flavor that pairs well with the vinegar-y brine.

1-pound green beans, trimmed

2 sprigs of thyme

1 cup white vinegar

1 cup water

2 teaspoons sugar

1 teaspoon salt

1 ball jar with a tight-fitting lid

1. Wash and trim the green beans, cutting them into bite-sized pieces.
2. In a small saucepan, combine the vinegar, water, sugar, and salt. Bring to a boil, stirring until the sugar and salt have dissolved.
3. Place the green beans and thyme sprigs in the ball jar.
4. Pour the vinegar mixture over the green beans, making sure they are completely covered.
5. Tightly seal the ball jar and let it cool to room temperature.
6. Once cooled, store the ball jar in the refrigerator for at least 24 hours before serving. The pickled green beans will last up to a week in the refrigerator. Enjoy!

ZESTY PICKLED GREEN OLIVE AND FENNEL

This pickled green olive and fennel recipe is the perfect combination of tangy and aromatic flavors. The combination of briny olives and anise-flavored fennel is sure to satisfy your taste buds.

1 cup green olives, pitted

1 bulb fennel, thinly sliced

1 cup white vinegar

1 cup water

2 tablespoons sugar

2 teaspoons salt

1 teaspoon fennel seeds

4 garlic cloves, sliced

2 bay leaves

1. In a small saucepan, combine the vinegar, water, sugar, salt, fennel seeds, and garlic. Bring to a boil and let simmer for 5 minutes.
2. In a ball jar, layer the sliced fennel and pitted olives.
3. Pour the hot vinegar mixture over the olives and fennel, making sure to fully cover the vegetables.
4. Add the bay leaves to the jar.
5. Tightly seal the jar and let it cool to room temperature.
6. Once cooled, store the jar in the refrigerator for at least 2 days before serving to allow the flavors to fully develop. Enjoy as a topping for sandwiches, as a garnish for cocktails, or on their own as a snack.

TROPICAL PICKLED GUAVA WITH A HINT OF BASIL

This recipe combines the sweet and tart flavors of pickled guava with the fresh and aromatic taste of basil. It's a unique and flavorful addition to any charcuterie board or sandwich. Plus, the pretty pink color of the pickled guava is sure to impress your guests.

2 cups guava, peeled and sliced
1 cup white vinegar
1 cup water
1/2 cup sugar
2 tablespoons basil, finely chopped
1 teaspoon salt
1 ball jar with a lid

1. In a small saucepan, combine the vinegar, water, sugar, salt, and basil. Bring the mixture to a boil, stirring to dissolve the sugar and salt.
2. Add the sliced guava to the ball jar.
3. Pour the hot vinegar mixture over the guava, making sure to fully cover the fruit.
4. Close the lid tightly and let the jar cool to room temperature.
5. Once cooled, transfer the jar to the refrigerator and let it sit for at least 24 hours before serving. The pickled guava will keep for up to 2 weeks in the refrigerator.
6. Serve the pickled guava as a unique and flavorful topping for sandwiches, burgers, or as a side to any charcuterie board. Enjoy!

SPICY PICKLED GUAVA WITH A HINT OF CINNAMON

This pickled guava recipe is perfect for those who love a little sweet and spice in their preserved fruit. The combination of guava and cinnamon creates a unique and flavorful treat that can be enjoyed on its own or used as a topping for meats or salads. The recipe calls for a ball jar, so be sure to have one on hand before getting started.

---

2 cups guava, peeled and sliced

1 cinnamon stick

1 cup white vinegar

1 cup water

1/2 cup sugar

1 tablespoon pickling salt

2 cloves

2-star anise

1 teaspoon red pepper flakes (optional for added heat)

1. Begin by sterilizing your ball jar by running it through the dishwasher or washing it with hot soapy water and rinsing it well. Set it aside to dry.

2. In a small saucepan, combine the vinegar, water, sugar, pickling salt, cloves, and star anise. Bring the mixture to a boil, stirring to dissolve the sugar and salt.

3. Once the mixture has boiled, remove the saucepan from the heat and add in the red pepper flakes, if using.

4. Place the sliced guava and cinnamon stick in the ball jar.

5. Pour the hot vinegar mixture over the guava and cinnamon, making sure to cover the fruit completely.

6. Secure the lid on the ball jar and allow the pickled guava to cool to room temperature.

7. Once cool, transfer the ball jar to the refrigerator and allow the pickled guava to marinate for at least 24 hours before serving. The pickled guava will keep in the refrigerator for up to 2 weeks. Enjoy!

SPICY PICKLED GUAVA WITH CLOVES

This recipe for pickled guava with cloves is a unique twist on traditional pickling techniques. The combination of sweet guava and spicy cloves creates a flavorful and aromatic pickle that is perfect for adding to sandwiches, salads, or as a topping for cheese plates. The best part is, it's incredibly easy to make with just a few simple ingredients and a trusty ball jar.

---

1 pound guava, peeled and sliced into wedges
2 cups white vinegar
1 cup water
1 cup granulated sugar
1 tablespoon whole cloves
1 tablespoon mustard seeds
1 teaspoon salt

1. In a small saucepan, combine the vinegar, water, sugar, cloves, mustard seeds, and salt. Bring to a boil, stirring occasionally, until the sugar has dissolved.

2. Place the sliced guava in a clean ball jar. Pour the hot vinegar mixture over the top of the guava, making sure to cover all of the slices.

3. Secure the lid on the jar and allow the pickles to cool to room temperature. Once cooled, store in the refrigerator for at least 3 days before serving to allow the flavors to fully develop.

4. Serve the pickled guava as a condiment or topping for sandwiches, salads, or cheese plates. Enjoy!

TART AND TANGY PICKLED GUAVA AND LEMON

This pickled guava and lemon recipe is a unique and tasty twist on traditional pickled vegetables. The combination of sweet guava and tart lemon creates a balance of flavors that is sure to delight your taste buds. The pickling process adds an extra layer of flavor and preserves the fruit, making it perfect for enjoying all year round.

---

1 pound guava, peeled and cut into wedges
1 lemon, sliced thin
1 cup white vinegar
1 cup water
1/2 cup sugar
1 tablespoon salt
1 cinnamon stick
5 whole cloves
1 bay leaf

1. In a small saucepan, combine the vinegar, water, sugar, salt, cinnamon stick, cloves, and bay leaf. Bring to a boil, stirring to dissolve the sugar and salt.

2. Place the guava wedges and lemon slices into a clean ball jar.

3. Pour the hot vinegar mixture over the fruit, making sure to completely cover the fruit.

4. Tightly seal the jar and place in the refrigerator for at least 48 hours before enjoying. The pickled guava and lemon will keep in the refrigerator for up to 1 month.

5. Serve the pickled guava and lemon as a tangy side dish or use as a topping for sandwiches and salads. Enjoy!

TART AND TANGY PICKLED GUAVA AND LIME

This pickled guava and lime recipe is a perfect balance of sweet and sour flavors. The guava adds a tropical twist to the classic pickled lime, and the combination is perfect for serving as a side dish or topping for tacos and sandwiches.

4 cups water

2 cups white vinegar

1 cup sugar

1 tablespoon kosher salt

2 cups sliced guava

2 cups sliced limes

1. In a medium saucepan, combine the water, vinegar, sugar, and salt. Bring to a boil, stirring until the sugar and salt have dissolved.

2. Place the sliced guava and limes in a large heat-safe jar, such as a Ball jar.

3. Pour the hot pickling liquid over the fruit, making sure to fully cover the slices.

4. Let the jar cool to room temperature, then seal and store in the refrigerator for at least 24 hours before serving. The pickled fruit will keep in the refrigerator for up to 1 month.

5. Serve the pickled guava and lime slices as a side dish or topping for tacos and sandwiches. Enjoy!

TROPICAL TWIST PICKLED GUAVA AND ONION RELISH

This pickled relish combines the sweet and tangy flavors of guava with the sharpness of onions for a unique and tasty condiment. It's perfect for adding a tropical twist to sandwiches, burgers, or even using as a topping for tacos or nachos.

2 cups guava, peeled and finely diced
1 cup red onion, finely diced
1/2 cup apple cider vinegar
1/2 cup white sugar
1 teaspoon salt
1/2 teaspoon black pepper
1/2 teaspoon mustard seeds
1/2 teaspoon coriander seeds
1/2 teaspoon cumin seeds
1/2 teaspoon fennel seeds
2 cloves garlic, minced

1. In a small saucepan, combine the vinegar, sugar, salt, pepper, mustard seeds, coriander seeds, cumin seeds, fennel seeds, garlic, and chilies (if using). Bring the mixture to a boil over medium heat, stirring occasionally.

2. Add the diced guava and onion to a clean and sterilized ball jar. Pour the hot vinegar mixture over the top of the guava and onion, making sure to cover them completely.

3. Seal the ball jar and let it cool to room temperature. Once cooled, store the jar in the refrigerator for at least 24 hours to allow the flavors to meld and the pickling process to occur.

4. The pickled guava and onion relish is now ready to use. It will keep in the refrigerator for up to 3 weeks. Enjoy!

TANTALIZINGLY TART PICKLED GUAVA AND SAGE

This recipe is inspired by the unique flavors of the Caribbean, where guava is a popular fruit and sage is used in traditional medicinal remedies. The combination of sweet, tropical guava and earthy, aromatic sage creates a pickle that is both refreshing and complex. These pickles are perfect as a condiment for sandwiches or as a garnish for cocktails.

4 cups guava, peeled and cut into wedges

1 cup white vinegar

1 cup water

1/2 cup sugar

2 tablespoons salt

4 sage leaves

4 small ball jars with lids

1. In a small saucepan, combine the vinegar, water, sugar, and salt. Bring to a boil, stirring until the sugar and salt have dissolved.

2. Pack the guava wedges and sage leaves into the ball jars.

3. Pour the hot vinegar mixture over the guava and sage, making sure to completely cover the fruit.

4. Secure the lids on the ball jars and allow to cool to room temperature.

5. Once cooled, store the pickled guava and sage in the refrigerator for at least 24 hours before serving to allow the flavors to fully develop.

6. The pickles will keep for up to 1 month in the refrigerator. Enjoy!

BALL JAR BLISS PICKLED GUAVA AND THYME

If you're a fan of sweet and savory flavors, you're going to love this recipe for pickled guava and thyme. It's a unique and tasty way to preserve guavas and add some extra flavor to your meals. The thyme gives the pickled guavas a subtle herbaceous note, while the guavas themselves are slightly sweet and tart. This recipe is perfect for adding some zing to sandwiches, salads, and more.

---

2 cups guavas, peeled and sliced

1 cup white vinegar

1 cup water

1/2 cup sugar

2 tablespoons salt

1 tablespoon thyme leaves

1 teaspoon black peppercorns

2 cloves garlic, minced

1. In a small saucepan, combine the vinegar, water, sugar, salt, thyme, peppercorns, and garlic. Bring the mixture to a boil over medium heat, stirring until the sugar and salt are dissolved.

2. Place the sliced guavas in a clean, sterilized ball jar. Pour the hot pickling liquid over the guavas, making sure they are fully covered.

3. Tightly seal the ball jar and place it in the refrigerator for at least 24 hours before serving. The pickled guavas will keep in the refrigerator for up to 2 weeks.

4. Serve the pickled guavas as a condiment on sandwiches, salads, or enjoy them on their own as a snack. Enjoy!

VANILLA AND GUAVA PICKLES A TROPICAL TWIST ON A CLASSIC RECIPE

If you're a fan of sweet and sour flavors, these pickled guava and vanilla pickles are sure to become a new favorite. The combination of tangy guava and fragrant vanilla creates a unique and delicious pickle that is perfect for topping sandwiches or serving as a tangy condiment. Plus, the beautiful pink color of the pickles makes them a visually appealing addition to any dish.

---

1 pound guava, peeled and sliced into 1/4-inch rounds

1 cup white vinegar

1 cup water

1/2 cup sugar

2 vanilla beans, split lengthwise

1 tablespoon whole cloves

1 tablespoon mustard seeds

1 tablespoon pickling salt

1. In a medium saucepan, combine the vinegar, water, sugar, vanilla beans, cloves, mustard seeds, and pickling salt. Bring the mixture to a boil over medium heat, stirring until the sugar is dissolved.

2. Add the sliced guava to a clean and sterilized ball jar. Pour the hot vinegar mixture over the guava, making sure to fully cover the fruit.

3. Seal the jar tightly and place it in the refrigerator for at least 24 hours before serving. The pickles will keep in the refrigerator for up to 1 month. Enjoy!

ZESTY PICKLED GREEN TOMATOES

If you have a surplus of green tomatoes at the end of the growing season, or if you just love the unique flavor of pickled green tomatoes, this recipe is for you! These zesty pickled green tomatoes are the perfect addition to any sandwich or salad, and they make a great snack straight from the jar.

---

2 lbs green tomatoes, sliced into rounds
1 cup white vinegar
1 cup water
2 tbsp pickling salt
1 tbsp sugar
2 cloves garlic, minced
1 tsp mustard seeds
1 tsp dill seeds
1 tsp red pepper flakes (optional)

1. Wash and slice the green tomatoes into rounds.
2. In a small saucepan, combine the vinegar, water, pickling salt, sugar, garlic, mustard seeds, dill seeds, and red pepper flakes (if using). Bring to a boil over high heat, stirring until the salt and sugar have dissolved.
3. Place the tomato slices in a clean, sterile ball jar.
4. Pour the hot pickling liquid over the tomatoes, making sure to cover them completely.
5. Secure the lid on the ball jar and allow the tomatoes to cool to room temperature.
6. Once cooled, place the ball jar in the refrigerator for at least 24 hours to allow the flavors to meld.
7. Enjoy your pickled green tomatoes on sandwiches, salads, or as a snack! They will last for up to 3 months in the refrigerator.

LIVELY PICKLED GREEN OLIVES AND LEMONS

Introducing our lively pickled green olives and lemons! This recipe is perfect for those who love a tangy, briny flavor with a pop of citrus. The combination of the two might seem unconventional, but trust us, it is a match made in heaven. These pickled olives and lemons are perfect for snacking on their own or adding to a charcuterie board.

1 cup green olives, pitted
1 lemon, thinly sliced
1 cup white vinegar
1 cup water
1 tsp salt
1 tsp sugar
2 cloves garlic, minced
1 tsp whole black peppercorns

1. In a medium saucepan, combine the vinegar, water, salt, sugar, garlic, and peppercorns. Bring to a boil over medium heat, stirring occasionally.

2. Once the mixture has reached a boil, remove from heat and let it cool for a few minutes.

3. In a clean ball jar, place the olives and lemon slices. Pour the cooled vinegar mixture over the top, making sure to fully cover the olives and lemons.

4. Close the ball jar and let it sit at room temperature for at least 24 hours before storing in the refrigerator.

5. The pickled olives and lemons can be enjoyed after 24 hours, but they will taste even better after a few days of pickling. Enjoy!

SAVORY ROSEMARY AND OLIVE PICKLE

Have you ever tried adding rosemary to your olives? It's a game-changer! This pickle combines briny green olives with aromatic rosemary for a unique and flavorful twist on a classic snack. Perfect for snacking on its own or adding to a cheese plate.

---

1 cup green olives, pitted
2 sprigs fresh rosemary
1 cup white vinegar
1 cup water
2 tbsp sugar
1 tsp salt

1. In a small saucepan, combine the vinegar, water, sugar, and salt. Bring to a boil over medium heat, stirring until the sugar and salt dissolve.
2. Place the olives and rosemary sprigs in a clean and sterilized ball jar.
3. Pour the hot vinegar mixture over the olives and rosemary, making sure to cover them completely.
4. Let the jar cool to room temperature before sealing and storing in the refrigerator.
5. These pickled olives will be ready to eat in 3-5 days and will keep in the refrigerator for up to 2 months. Enjoy!

ZESTY PICKLED GREEN ONION AND CILANTRO

Growing up in a Mexican household, pickled vegetables were always a staple in our pantry. These pickled green onions and cilantro add the perfect amount of tang and flavor to any dish. They're also super easy to make and can last for months in the fridge. Here's my recipe for Zesty Pickled Green Onion and Cilantro.

1 bunch green onions
1 cup cilantro, roughly chopped
1 cup white vinegar
1 cup water
2 tbsp sugar
1 tsp salt
3 cloves garlic, thinly sliced
1 jalapeno, thinly sliced
2 ball jars

1. Wash and thinly slice the green onions. Roughly chop the cilantro.
2. In a small saucepan, bring the vinegar, water, sugar, and salt to a boil. Stir until the sugar and salt are dissolved.
3. Divide the green onions, cilantro, garlic, and jalapeno slices evenly between the two ball jars.
4. Pour the hot vinegar mixture over the vegetables, making sure to cover them completely.
5. Seal the ball jars and let them cool to room temperature.
6. Once cooled, place the jars in the fridge and let them sit for at least 24 hours before serving. These pickled green onions and cilantro will last for several weeks in the fridge. Enjoy!

SPICY PICKLED GREEN ONION AND GINGER

There's nothing quite like the tangy and spicy flavor of pickled green onions and ginger to add some zing to your dishes. Whether you're using them as a topping for burgers, sandwiches, or salads, these pickled goodies will surely bring life to your meals. Here's how to make them at home

1 cup green onions, sliced

1/2 cup ginger, sliced

1 cup white vinegar

1/2 cup water

1 tsp salt

1 tsp sugar

1 tsp red pepper flakes

1. Wash and slice the green onions and ginger.
2. In a small saucepan, combine the vinegar, water, salt, sugar, and red pepper flakes. Bring to a boil.
3. Once the mixture has boiled, pour it over the sliced green onions and ginger in a ball jar.
4. Close the ball jar and let it sit in the fridge for at least 1 hour before using. The pickled green onions and ginger will last in the fridge for up to 1 month.
5. Enjoy your spicy pickled green onions and ginger on top of your favorite dishes!

ZESTY PICKLED GREEN ONIONS WITH MUSTARD SEED

Growing up, my grandma always had a jar of these pickled green onions in her refrigerator. They were a staple at every family barbecue and added the perfect tangy and spicy kick to any sandwich or salad. Now, I love making my own batch to keep on hand for those summer cookouts.

1 cup white vinegar

1 cup water

1 tablespoon sugar

1 tablespoon mustard seeds

1 teaspoon salt

1 bunch green onions, thinly sliced

1. In a small saucepan, combine vinegar, water, sugar, mustard seeds, and salt. Bring to a boil, stirring occasionally.
2. Place the sliced green onions in a clean, sterilized ball jar.
3. Pour the vinegar mixture over the green onions, making sure to fully cover them.
4. Let the jar cool to room temperature before sealing and placing in the refrigerator.
5. Allow the pickled green onions to sit in the refrigerator for at least 24 hours before enjoying. These pickled green onions will last for up to a month in the refrigerator.

ZESTY PICKLED GREEN TOMATOES AND BASIL

When summer's bounty starts to wane and the first frost is on the horizon, it's time to start preserving the last of the green tomatoes. These zesty pickled green tomatoes are the perfect way to use up any remaining tomatoes and add a bit of flavor to your winter meals.

4 cups green tomatoes, quartered

1 cup white vinegar

1 cup water

1/4 cup sugar

2 tablespoons kosher salt

4 cloves garlic, minced

1 tablespoon black peppercorns

1 teaspoon mustard seeds

1/2 teaspoon dill seeds

1/2 cup fresh basil, chopped

1. In a medium saucepan, combine the vinegar, water, sugar, salt, garlic, peppercorns, mustard seeds, and dill seeds. Bring to a boil over medium-high heat, stirring to dissolve the sugar and salt.

2. Pack the green tomatoes and basil into a clean ball jar. Pour the hot vinegar mixture over the top, making sure to cover all of the ingredients.

3. Tightly seal the jar and allow it to cool to room temperature. Once cooled, store the jar in the refrigerator for at least 24 hours before serving to allow the flavors to develop.

4. These pickled green tomatoes will keep in the refrigerator for up to 2 weeks. Serve as a condiment on sandwiches or as a side dish. Enjoy!

SPICY PICKLED GREEN TOMATO AND CHILI DELIGHT

Growing up on a farm, I learned that there was always a way to preserve the bounty of the garden. One of my favorite ways to use up an abundance of green tomatoes was to pickle them with a kick of chili peppers. This recipe is easy and can be enjoyed year round as a topping for sandwiches, in salads, or as a tasty snack.

---

3 cups green tomatoes, sliced into rounds

2 cups white vinegar

1 cup water

1/2 cup sugar

2 tbsp salt

1 tbsp pickling spice

2-3 chili peppers, sliced

1. In a large saucepan, combine vinegar, water, sugar, salt, and pickling spice. Bring to a boil and stir until sugar and salt have dissolved.

2. Pack sliced green tomatoes and sliced chili peppers into a clean, sterilized ball jar.

3. Pour the hot vinegar mixture over the tomatoes and peppers, making sure to leave about 1 inch of headspace at the top of the jar.

4. Secure the lid on the jar and let cool to room temperature.

5. Once cooled, store in the refrigerator for at least 24 hours before serving. The pickled tomatoes will keep in the refrigerator for up to 1 month.

DELICIOUS PICKLED GREEN TOMATO AND DILL

There's nothing quite like the tangy, refreshing flavor of pickled green tomatoes. And when you add a generous helping of dill, the result is truly irresistible. This recipe is a great way to preserve your excess green tomatoes at the end of the growing season, and it's a tasty addition to any sandwich or salad.

---

3 lbs green tomatoes, sliced

2 cups white vinegar

2 cups water

2 tbsp pickling salt

2 tsp sugar

2 cloves garlic, minced

1 tbsp dill seeds

1 tsp mustard seeds

1 tsp peppercorns

1. In a large pot, combine the vinegar, water, pickling salt, and sugar. Bring to a boil.
2. Add the green tomato slices to the pot and cook for 5 minutes.
3. In a separate bowl, mix together the minced garlic, dill seeds, mustard seeds, and peppercorns.
4. Carefully pack the green tomato slices into a sterilized ball jar, making sure to leave enough space at the top for the brine.
5. Pour the brine over the green tomatoes, making sure to cover them completely.
6. Secure the lid on the ball jar and store in the refrigerator for at least 24 hours before serving. Enjoy!

TANGY PICKLED GREEN TOMATOES AND GARLIC

Growing up on a farm, I always had an abundance of green tomatoes at the end of the season. Instead of letting them go to waste, my mom taught me how to pickle them and create a delicious condiment to enjoy all year round. This recipe is a simple and tasty way to preserve green tomatoes and add some zesty flavor to your meals.

---

4 cups green tomatoes, quartered

1 cup garlic cloves, peeled

2 cups white vinegar

1 cup water

2 tablespoons sugar

2 tablespoons salt

2 teaspoons mustard seeds

1 teaspoon dill seeds

1. In a large saucepan, combine the vinegar, water, sugar, and salt. Bring to a boil over medium heat, stirring until the sugar and salt are dissolved.

2. Pack the green tomatoes and garlic into a clean ball jar.

3. Pour the hot vinegar mixture over the tomatoes and garlic, making sure to cover them completely.

4. Add the mustard seeds and dill seeds to the jar.

5. Close the jar tightly and let it cool to room temperature.

6. Once cooled, store the pickled green tomatoes and garlic in the refrigerator for at least 2 days before enjoying. These will keep in the refrigerator for up to 3 months.

7. Serve as a tangy condiment on sandwiches, burgers, or alongside grilled meats. Enjoy!

MINTY PICKLED GREEN TOMATOES

When I was growing up, my grandma used to make these pickled green tomatoes every year. She would always add a little bit of mint to give them a refreshing twist. These pickled green tomatoes are perfect for adding a tangy kick to sandwiches, salads, and more.

4 cups green tomatoes, sliced into wedges
1 cup white vinegar
1 cup water
1 tablespoon salt
1 teaspoon black peppercorns
1 teaspoon dill seeds
3 cloves garlic, thinly sliced
1/4 cup fresh mint leaves, roughly chopped

1. In a small saucepan, combine vinegar, water, salt, peppercorns, and dill seeds. Bring to a boil over medium heat, stirring occasionally.

2. Pack the green tomato wedges into a clean ball jar. Add the sliced garlic and chopped mint leaves on top.

3. Pour the hot vinegar mixture over the tomatoes, making sure to fully cover the tomatoes.

4. Let the jar cool to room temperature, then seal and store in the refrigerator. The pickled green tomatoes will be ready to eat in about 3 days and will keep in the refrigerator for up to a month. Enjoy!

TANGY GREEN TOMATO AND ONION RELISH

This pickled green tomato and onion relish is the perfect addition to any sandwich or burger. The tangy and slightly sweet flavor pairs well with a variety of meats and adds a pop of color to any dish. Plus, the green tomatoes and onions are preserved in a vinegar and sugar brine, making it a delicious and convenient condiment to have on hand all year round.

2 cups green tomatoes, diced
1 cup diced onion
1 cup vinegar
1 cup sugar
1 tbsp mustard seeds
1 tsp salt
1 tsp celery seeds

1. In a medium saucepan, combine vinegar, sugar, mustard seeds, salt, and celery seeds. Bring to a boil, stirring until the sugar is dissolved.
2. Add the diced green tomatoes and onions to a clean and sterilized ball jar. Pour the hot vinegar mixture over the top, making sure to cover the vegetables completely.
3. Seal the jar with the lid and let cool to room temperature. Once cooled, store in the refrigerator for at least 24 hours before serving to allow the flavors to develop.
4. Serve as a condiment on sandwiches or burgers, or as a topping for pulled pork or grilled chicken. Enjoy!

TANGY PICKLED GREEN TOMATOES WITH A HINT OF OREGANO

Green tomatoes are a staple of southern cuisine and pickling them adds a delicious tangy flavor. The addition of oregano gives these pickles a unique and aromatic twist.

---

4 green tomatoes, sliced

1 cup white vinegar

1 cup water

2 tbsp sugar

1 tsp salt

1 tsp oregano

2 cloves garlic, minced

1 small onion, thinly sliced

1. In a small saucepan, combine the vinegar, water, sugar, salt, and oregano. Bring to a boil, stirring occasionally.
2. Meanwhile, place the tomato slices, garlic, and onion slices in a sterilized ball jar.
3. Once the vinegar mixture has come to a boil, pour it over the tomato slices in the jar.
4. Seal the jar and let it sit at room temperature for at least one hour before refrigerating.
5. These pickled green tomatoes will keep in the refrigerator for up to 2 weeks. Enjoy on sandwiches, in salads, or as a flavorful snack.

SUMMER'S LAST HURRAH PICKLED GREEN TOMATO AND THYME

As summer ends and the tomato plants in the garden start to wither, it's time to preserve the last of the green tomatoes. This pickled green tomato and thyme recipe is a delicious way to extend the life of your summer bounty and add a tangy and herbaceous twist to your meals.

1-pound green tomatoes, sliced into 1/4 inch rounds
1/2 cup white vinegar
1/2 cup water
1/4 cup sugar
2 cloves garlic, sliced
1 tablespoon thyme leaves
1 teaspoon salt
1/2 teaspoon black peppercorns

1. In a small saucepan, combine the vinegar, water, sugar, garlic, thyme, salt, and peppercorns. Bring to a boil, then reduce heat to a simmer and cook for 5 minutes.

2. Place the green tomato slices in a clean ball jar. Pour the hot vinegar mixture over the tomatoes, making sure to cover all slices.

3. Close the jar tightly and let it cool to room temperature.

4. Store the pickled green tomatoes in the refrigerator for at least 24 hours before serving. They will keep for up to 2 weeks.

GARLIC AND HERB PICKLE PERFECTION

This pickled herb and garlic mix is the perfect addition to any sandwich or charcuterie board. The combination of fresh herbs and pungent garlic is sure to elevate any dish.

---

1 cup white vinegar

1 cup water

2 tbsp sugar

2 tbsp salt

1 ball jar

1 bunch fresh herbs (such as dill, parsley, and thyme)

1 head of garlic, peeled and thinly sliced

1. In a small saucepan, combine the vinegar, water, sugar, and salt. Bring to a boil and stir until the sugar and salt have dissolved.

2. Meanwhile, pack the herbs and sliced garlic into the ball jar.

3. Once the vinegar mixture has come to a boil, pour it over the herbs and garlic in the jar, making sure to cover them completely.

4. Let the jar sit at room temperature for at least 30 minutes to allow the flavors to meld.

5. Once cooled, seal the jar and store in the refrigerator for up to 2 weeks. Enjoy on sandwiches, charcuterie boards, or as a condiment on any dish.

HERBED HEAVEN PICKLED CARROTS AND ONIONS

This recipe is a delicious twist on the classic pickled carrot and onion combination. The addition of herbs adds an extra layer of flavor that will make these pickles a new favorite in your kitchen. Perfect for topping off sandwiches or serving as a tangy side dish.

1 lb carrots, peeled and thinly sliced
1 small onion, thinly sliced
1 cup white vinegar
1 cup water
1 tsp salt
1 tsp sugar
1 sprig rosemary
1 sprig thyme
1 sprig oregano
1 ball jar (1 pint size)

1. In a small saucepan, combine vinegar, water, salt, and sugar. Bring to a boil and stir until the salt and sugar have dissolved.
2. Place the sliced carrots and onions in the ball jar.
3. Add the sprigs of rosemary, thyme, and oregano to the jar.
4. Pour the hot vinegar mixture over the vegetables, making sure to cover them completely.
5. Close the jar and let it cool to room temperature. Once cooled, store in the refrigerator for at least 2 hours before serving.
6. These pickles will keep in the refrigerator for up to 3 weeks. Enjoy!

SLIGHTLY SWEET AND SAVORY PICKLED HONEY MUSTARD CUCUMBERS

These pickled honey mustard cucumbers are the perfect blend of sweet and savory flavors. They are great for adding to sandwiches or as a refreshing snack on their own.

1 pound of cucumbers, sliced

1/2 cup honey

1/2 cup white vinegar

1/4 cup dijon mustard

1 tablespoon sugar

2 cloves garlic, minced

1 teaspoon salt

1. In a small saucepan, combine the honey, vinegar, mustard, sugar, garlic, and salt. Heat over medium heat until the sugar is dissolved.

2. Place the cucumber slices in a large ball jar. Pour the honey mustard mixture over the cucumbers, making sure to cover them completely.

3. Secure the lid on the ball jar and place in the refrigerator for at least 1 hour before serving.

4. These pickled cucumbers will keep in the refrigerator for up to 1 week. Enjoy!

SPICY AND SWEET PICKLED HONEYDEW

This recipe is a unique twist on traditional pickled fruits, combining the sweetness of honeydew with the heat of chili peppers. Perfect as a condiment for grilled meats or a tangy addition to a cheese platter.

1 medium honeydew, cut into small cubes
1 red chili pepper, thinly sliced
1/2 cup white vinegar
1/2 cup water
1/4 cup sugar
1 tablespoon salt
1 garlic clove, minced
1 teaspoon mustard seeds
1/2 teaspoon black peppercorns

1. In a small saucepan, bring the vinegar, water, sugar, and salt to a boil. Stir until the sugar and salt are fully dissolved.
2. Place the honeydew, chili pepper, garlic, mustard seeds, and peppercorns in a clean ball jar.
3. Pour the hot vinegar mixture over the honeydew and spices, making sure to fully cover the honeydew.
4. Close the ball jar and let it cool to room temperature before placing it in the refrigerator.
5. Allow the pickled honeydew to marinate in the refrigerator for at least 24 hours before serving. The pickled honeydew will last up to 2 weeks in the refrigerator.

GINGER-INFUSED HONEYDEW PICKLES

When I was traveling through Southeast Asia, I tasted a honeydew pickle that was infused with ginger, and it was love at first bite. I knew I had to recreate it at home, so I experimented with different ratios of honeydew, ginger, and vinegar until I found the perfect balance. These pickles are sweet and spicy, with a refreshing crunch that pairs well with almost any dish. Plus, they make a beautiful addition to any charcuterie board or party spread. Here's my recipe for Ginger-Infused Honeydew Pickles.

1 small honeydew melon, peeled and sliced into 1/4-inch rounds

2 inches of fresh ginger, peeled and sliced into thin rounds

1 cup white vinegar

1 cup water

1/2 cup sugar

1 tablespoon kosher salt

1 teaspoon mustard seeds

1 teaspoon coriander seeds

4 ball jars with lids

1. Begin by sterilizing your ball jars and lids. You can do this by boiling them in a pot of water for 10 minutes, or by running them through a dishwasher cycle.
2. In a medium saucepan, combine the vinegar, water, sugar, salt, mustard seeds, and coriander seeds. Bring the mixture to a boil, stirring occasionally to dissolve the sugar and salt.
3. Meanwhile, place the sliced honeydew and ginger into the prepared ball jars.
4. Once the vinegar mixture has come to a boil, pour it over the honeydew and ginger in the jars, making sure to leave about 1/2 inch of headspace at the top of the jar.
5. Wipe the rims of the jars with a clean cloth, then place the lids on top and screw on the bands until they are finger tight.
6. Place the jars in a large pot or canning kettle, making sure they are covered by at least 1 inch of water. Bring the water to a boil, then reduce the heat to a simmer and process the jars for 15 minutes.
7. Carefully remove the jars from the pot using a jar lifter or tongs and place them on a clean kitchen towel. Allow the jars to cool completely before storing them in a cool, dark place for up to 6 months.
8. Once opened, these pickles will keep for about a week in the refrigerator. Enjoy!

HONEYDEW MINT PICKLES - A REFRESHING SUMMER TREAT

These pickles are the perfect blend of sweet and savory, making them a unique and refreshing addition to any summer BBQ or picnic. The combination of honeydew and mint gives these pickles a bright and refreshing flavor that pairs well with a variety of dishes. Plus, they're super easy to make and can be stored in a ball jar for up to 6 months in the fridge.

---

1 medium honeydew, peeled and cut into small cubes
1 cup apple cider vinegar
1 cup water
1/4 cup sugar
1/4 cup salt
1/4 cup honey
2 sprigs fresh mint
2 cloves garlic, minced

1. In a small saucepan, combine the vinegar, water, sugar, salt, and honey. Bring to a boil, stirring occasionally until the sugar and salt have dissolved.
2. In a sterilized ball jar, add the honeydew cubes, minced garlic, and mint sprigs.
3. Pour the hot vinegar mixture over the honeydew, making sure to completely cover the fruit.
4. Place the lid on the ball jar and let it cool to room temperature. Once cooled, store the jar in the fridge for at least 2 days before serving.
5. Serve the pickles as a side dish or add them to sandwiches, salads, or any other dish that needs a little boost of flavor. Enjoy!

GOLDEN PICKLED JACKFRUIT

This recipe is a delicious and unique twist on traditional pickled vegetables. The combination of jackfruit and turmeric creates a vibrant, golden color and adds a hint of spice to the pickling liquid. Perfect for serving as a side dish or topping on sandwiches and salads.

---

2 cups sliced jackfruit

1 cup white vinegar

1 cup water

2 tablespoons sugar

1 tablespoon turmeric

1 tablespoon salt

2 cloves garlic, minced

1 teaspoon mustard seeds

1. In a small saucepan, combine the vinegar, water, sugar, turmeric, salt, garlic, and mustard seeds. Bring to a boil, stirring to dissolve the sugar.

2. Place the sliced jackfruit in a clean ball jar. Pour the hot pickling liquid over the jackfruit, making sure to cover it completely.

3. Allow the jar to cool to room temperature, then cover and refrigerate for at least 24 hours before serving. The pickled jackfruit will last for up to 1 month in the refrigerator. Enjoy!

SPICY PICKLED JALAPENO AND GARLIC

These spicy pickled jalapeno and garlic are the perfect addition to any Mexican-inspired dish. The tangy, spicy flavors add a kick to tacos, burritos, or even just eaten straight out of the jar. Plus, the jar of pickled jalapenos and garlic makes for a beautiful gift for any foodie friend.

1 cup white vinegar

1 cup water

2 tablespoons sugar

1 tablespoon salt

2 cloves garlic, peeled

1 cup jalapeno slices, seeds removed

1. In a small saucepan, combine the vinegar, water, sugar, and salt. Bring to a boil, stirring until the sugar and salt have dissolved.

2. Place the garlic and jalapeno slices in a clean ball jar.

3. Pour the vinegar mixture over the garlic and jalapenos, making sure to cover them completely.

4. Let the jar cool to room temperature, then seal and store in the refrigerator for at least 24 hours before serving.

5. The pickled jalapenos and garlic will last up to 3 months in the refrigerator. Enjoy on tacos, burritos, or as a condiment on any dish.

SPICY AND TANGY PICKLED JALAPENO AND ONION RELISH

This pickled jalapeno and onion relish is the perfect condiment for adding a little kick to any dish. It's easy to make and can be stored in a ball jar for up to a month in the fridge.

2 cups diced onions
1 cup diced jalapeno peppers (seeds and ribs removed)
1 cup white vinegar
1 tsp salt
1 tsp sugar
1 tsp mustard seeds

1. In a small saucepan, combine the vinegar, salt, sugar, and mustard seeds. Bring to a boil, then reduce the heat to low and let simmer for 5 minutes.

2. Place the diced onions and jalapeno peppers in a ball jar.

3. Pour the vinegar mixture over the onions and jalapeno peppers in the ball jar, making sure to cover all the vegetables.

4. Close the ball jar and let it sit at room temperature for at least 1 hour before transferring to the fridge.

5. The pickled jalapeno and onion relish can be enjoyed after an hour of refrigeration, but it tastes even better after a few days. Enjoy!

FIERY HABANERO AND ONION RELISH

This recipe for pickled habanero and onion relish is perfect for adding a spicy kick to burgers, sandwiches, and more. The habaneros give it a bold flavor, while the onions add a touch of sweetness. And the best part? It's easy to make and can be stored in a ball jar for months on end.

---

1 cup habanero peppers, chopped
1 cup onions, chopped
1 cup white vinegar
1/2 cup sugar
1 tsp salt
1 tsp mustard seeds
1 tsp celery seeds

1. In a small saucepan, bring the vinegar, sugar, salt, mustard seeds, and celery seeds to a boil.
2. Add the habanero peppers and onions to a sterilized ball jar.
3. Pour the hot vinegar mixture over the peppers and onions, making sure to cover them completely.
4. Seal the jar and let it cool to room temperature.
5. Once cool, store the jar in the refrigerator for at least a week before using. The longer it sits, the more flavorful it will become.
6. Use the relish as a topping for sandwiches, burgers, hot dogs, or any other dish that needs a little extra kick. Enjoy!

SPICY AND SWEET PICKLED JALAPENO AND PINEAPPLE

If you're looking for a unique twist on your typical pickled dish, this recipe is for you. The combination of spicy jalapeno and sweet pineapple creates a flavor explosion in your mouth with every bite. Plus, these pickles are perfect for topping burgers, sandwiches, or even just snacking on straight from the ball jar.

---

1 cup pineapple, diced

1 cup jalapeno peppers, sliced

1 cup white vinegar

1 cup water

1/2 cup sugar

1 tbsp salt

1 tbsp whole peppercorns

1 tsp mustard seeds

1 tsp coriander seeds

1. In a medium saucepan, bring the vinegar, water, sugar, salt, peppercorns, mustard seeds, and coriander seeds to a boil.

2. Once boiling, add in the diced pineapple and sliced jalapenos.

3. Reduce heat to a simmer and let cook for 5 minutes.

4. Using a slotted spoon, transfer the pineapple and jalapenos to a clean ball jar.

5. Pour the hot brine over the top, making sure to cover the fruit completely.

6. Let the jar cool to room temperature before sealing and storing in the refrigerator.

7. These pickles will be ready to eat after 24 hours but will taste even better after a few days in the fridge. Enjoy!

SPICY PICKLED JALAPENO PEPPERS

These spicy pickled jalapeno peppers are the perfect addition to any Mexican dish or for a spicy kick to any sandwich. They are easy to make and will last for months in the fridge.

---

1 pound jalapeno peppers
1 cup white vinegar
1 cup water
2 tablespoons sugar
2 teaspoons salt
1 garlic clove, minced
1 ball jar

1. Wash the jalapeno peppers and slice them into thin rounds.
2. In a small saucepan, combine the vinegar, water, sugar, salt, and garlic. Bring to a boil, stirring until the sugar and salt are dissolved.
3. Place the sliced jalapeno peppers into the ball jar.
4. Pour the vinegar mixture over the jalapeno peppers, making sure to fully cover them.
5. Close the ball jar and let it sit at room temperature for at least 24 hours before transferring to the refrigerator.
6. The pickled jalapeno peppers will last for up to 3 months in the refrigerator. Enjoy!

FIESTA-INSPIRED PICKLED JICAMA AND CHILI

If you're looking to add a little zest to your next taco night, look no further than these fiesta-inspired pickled jicama and chili. The crunchy jicama is perfectly balanced by the heat of the chili peppers, creating a unique and flavorful addition to any dish.

1 medium jicama, peeled and sliced into thin rounds

1 small red chili pepper, thinly sliced

1 small green chili pepper, thinly sliced

1/2 cup white vinegar

1/2 cup water

2 tbsp sugar

1 tsp salt

1 garlic clove, minced

1 small onion, thinly sliced

1. In a small saucepan, combine the vinegar, water, sugar, salt, and garlic. Bring to a boil over medium heat.

2. Place the jicama and chili pepper slices in a clean, sterilized ball jar.

3. Top with the onion slices.

4. Pour the hot vinegar mixture over the vegetables, making sure to completely cover them.

5. Secure the lid on the ball jar and allow to cool to room temperature.

6. Once cooled, refrigerate the pickled jicama and chili for at least 24 hours before serving.

7. These pickles will keep in the refrigerator for up to 2 weeks. Enjoy as a topping for tacos, burritos, or as a snack on their own.

ZESTY JICAMA PICKLES WITH A CILANTRO TWIST

These pickled jicama and cilantro pickles are the perfect addition to any Mexican-inspired meal or as a tangy topping for a sandwich or burger. The combination of the crisp jicama and the fresh cilantro gives these pickles a refreshing flavor that will leave you wanting more.

---

1 medium jicama, peeled and sliced into thin strips

1 cup white vinegar

1 cup water

1 tablespoon sugar

1 tablespoon kosher salt

1 teaspoon black peppercorns

1 teaspoon mustard seeds

1 teaspoon coriander seeds

1 bay leaf

1/4 cup cilantro leaves, finely chopped

1. In a small saucepan, combine the vinegar, water, sugar, salt, peppercorns, mustard seeds, and coriander seeds. Bring to a boil over medium-high heat.
2. Place the jicama slices in a clean and sterilized ball jar.
3. Add the bay leaf, cilantro, and minced garlic to the jar with the jicama.
4. Pour the hot vinegar mixture over the jicama and spices in the jar. Make sure all of the jicama is covered by the vinegar mixture.
5. Seal the ball jar and let it cool to room temperature.
6. Once cooled, refrigerate the pickled jicama for at least 24 hours before serving. The pickles will last up to 2 weeks in the refrigerator. Enjoy!

GINGER-INFUSED JICAMA PICKLES

There's nothing quite like a crunchy, refreshing pickle on a hot summer day. These pickled jicama and ginger slices are the perfect addition to any barbecue or picnic spread. The combination of sweet jicama and spicy ginger is a match made in heaven, and the pickling process helps to preserve the flavors for weeks to come. So, grab a ball jar and get pickling!

1 jicama, peeled and thinly sliced
1 cup white vinegar
1 cup water
1/2 cup sugar
2 tablespoons kosher salt
1 tablespoon grated ginger
1 teaspoon mustard seeds
1/2 teaspoon black peppercorns
2 cloves garlic, minced
1/4 teaspoon red pepper flakes (optional)

1. In a small saucepan, combine the vinegar, water, sugar, salt, ginger, mustard seeds, peppercorns, garlic, and red pepper flakes (if using). Bring to a boil over medium heat, stirring occasionally, until the sugar and salt have dissolved.

2. Place the jicama slices in a clean, sterilized ball jar. Pour the hot pickling liquid over the jicama, making sure to fully cover the slices.

3. Let the jar cool to room temperature, then seal the jar and refrigerate for at least 24 hours before serving. The pickles will keep in the refrigerator for up to 2 weeks. Enjoy!

SPICY PICKLED JICAMA AND ONION RELISH

This pickled jicama and onion relish is a perfect addition to any BBQ spread or sandwich. The combination of the sweet jicama and the tangy onions is enhanced by the spicy kick from the chili flakes. Plus, it's super easy to make and can be stored in a ball jar for future use.

1 jicama, peeled and diced
1 onion, diced
1 cup apple cider vinegar
1 cup water
1/4 cup sugar
1 tbsp chili flakes
1 tsp salt

1. In a medium saucepan, combine the vinegar, water, sugar, chili flakes, and salt. Bring to a boil, stirring until the sugar is dissolved.
2. Add the jicama and onion to the saucepan and simmer for 5 minutes.
3. Remove from heat and let the mixture cool for a few minutes.
4. Transfer the mixture to a ball jar and seal the lid tightly.
5. Place the jar in the fridge for at least an hour to allow the flavors to develop. The relish can be stored in the fridge for up to a week.
6. Serve as a condiment or topping on sandwiches, burgers, or tacos. Enjoy!

BRINY BLISS PICKLED KALAMATA OLIVE AND GARLIC

Looking for a unique and flavorful addition to your charcuterie board? These pickled kalamata olives and garlic will surely impress. The tangy and slightly salty flavor pairs perfectly with cheese and meats. Plus, the garlicky kick adds a nice touch of heat.

1 cup kalamata olives, pitted

5 cloves garlic, peeled

1 cup white vinegar

1 cup water

1 tsp sugar

1 tsp dried oregano

1 tsp dried basil

1 tsp red pepper flakes (optional for added heat)

1 ball jar with a tight-fitting lid

1. In a small saucepan, combine the vinegar, water, sugar, oregano, basil, and red pepper flakes (if using). Bring to a boil and stir to dissolve the sugar.
2. Place the olives and garlic in the ball jar.
3. Once the vinegar mixture has come to a boil, pour it over the olives and garlic in the ball jar.
4. Tightly seal the ball jar and let it cool to room temperature.
5. Once cooled, store the ball jar in the fridge for at least 24 hours before serving. These pickled olives and garlic will last for up to 2 weeks in the fridge.
6. Serve on a charcuterie board or as a topping for sandwiches and salads. Enjoy!

PICKLED KALAMATA OLIVE AND LEMON DELIGHT

Introducing a twist on the classic pickled olive recipe! The combination of kalamata olives and lemon adds a tangy and slightly sour flavor that will have you reaching for another ball jar. Perfect for snacking or as a topping for salads and sandwiches.

---

1 cup kalamata olives

1 lemon, thinly sliced

1/2 cup white vinegar

1/2 cup water

1 tablespoon sugar

1/2 teaspoon salt

1. Rinse the olives and remove any stems.
2. Place the olives and lemon slices in a sterilized ball jar.
3. In a small saucepan, combine the vinegar, water, sugar, and salt. Bring to a boil, stirring until the sugar and salt are dissolved.
4. Pour the hot liquid over the olives and lemon slices, making sure they are fully covered.
5. Seal the ball jar and let it cool to room temperature.
6. Once cooled, place the ball jar in the refrigerator for at least 24 hours before serving. The olives will last up to 2 weeks in the refrigerator. Enjoy!

ZESTY PICKLED KALAMATA OLIVES WITH A MINTY TWIST

These pickled kalamata olives are the perfect addition to any charcuterie board or antipasto platter. The combination of the salty olives with the refreshing mint creates a unique and flavorful experience. Plus, they're easy to make and can be stored in a ball jar for up to a few months.

1 cup kalamata olives, pitted

1 cup white vinegar

1 cup water

1 tbsp sugar

2 tsp salt

1 sprig fresh mint

2 garlic cloves, sliced

1 tsp peppercorns

1 bay leaf

1. In a small saucepan, combine the vinegar, water, sugar, and salt. Bring to a boil, stirring occasionally, until the sugar and salt have dissolved.

2. Place the olives in a large ball jar. Add the mint, garlic, peppercorns, and bay leaf.

3. Pour the hot vinegar mixture over the olives and close the jar tightly. Let the olives sit at room temperature for at least 1 hour before transferring to the refrigerator.

4. The olives will be ready to eat after a few hours, but for best flavor, let them sit for at least a day before consuming. The olives will keep in the refrigerator for up to 3 months. Enjoy as a tasty snack or add to sandwiches, salads, or other dishes for an extra burst of flavor.

PICKLED KIMCHI A KOREAN DELIGHT

This pickled kimchi recipe combines spicy and tangy flavors to create a unique and delicious condiment. Perfect for adding some heat to sandwiches, burgers, or even as a topping for scrambled eggs.

---

1 head Napa cabbage, thinly sliced
1 cup Korean chili flakes
1 cup water
1/2 cup rice vinegar
1/4 cup sugar
1/4 cup fish sauce
2 cloves garlic, minced
1 inch ginger, grated
1/4 cup scallions, chopped

1. In a large bowl, mix together the chili flakes, water, rice vinegar, sugar, and fish sauce.
2. Add in the minced garlic, grated ginger, and chopped scallions.
3. Add in the sliced Napa cabbage and toss everything together until the cabbage is evenly coated.
4. Pack the mixture into a clean ball jar, pressing down firmly to remove any air pockets.
5. Let the jar sit at room temperature for at least 1 day before transferring to the refrigerator. The kimchi will continue to ferment in the fridge and will be ready to enjoy in about a week.

SPICY PICKLED KIMCHI AND THYME

If you're a fan of traditional Korean kimchi, you'll love this spicy pickled version with the added flavor of thyme. It's a perfect addition to any sandwich or bowl of rice.

---

1 large Napa cabbage, thinly sliced

1 cup radishes, thinly sliced

1 cup carrots, julienned

2 cloves garlic, minced

1 inch ginger, grated

1 tablespoon gochutgaru (Korean chili flakes)

1 teaspoon salt

1 teaspoon sugar

2 tablespoons white vinegar

1 tablespoon thyme leaves

2 Ball jars with lids

1. In a large bowl, mix together the cabbage, radishes, carrots, garlic, ginger, gochutgaru, salt, and sugar.
2. Pack the mixture into the two Ball jars, pressing down firmly to remove any air pockets.
3. In a small saucepan, heat the vinegar until it comes to a boil. Remove from heat and stir in the thyme leaves.
4. Pour the vinegar mixture over the vegetables in the Ball jars, making sure to cover all the vegetables.
5. Close the lids tightly and let the jars sit at room temperature for at least 24 hours before refrigerating.
6. The pickled kimchi will be ready to eat after 24 hours, but it will continue to ferment and become more flavorful as it sits in the refrigerator. Enjoy!

ZESTY PICKLED KIWI AND BLACK PEPPER DELIGHT

This recipe is a unique twist on traditional pickled vegetables. The combination of sweet kiwi and spicy black pepper creates a flavor explosion in every bite. Perfect for adding to sandwiches or serving as a tasty appetizer.

---

3 medium kiwis, peeled and sliced into 1/4-inch rounds
1 cup white vinegar
1 cup water
1/2 cup sugar
1 tablespoon black peppercorns
1 teaspoon salt
1 ball jar with lid

1. In a small saucepan, combine the vinegar, water, sugar, black peppercorns, and salt. Bring to a boil, stirring until the sugar has dissolved.
2. Place the sliced kiwis in the ball jar.
3. Pour the hot vinegar mixture over the kiwis, making sure to fully cover them.
4. Secure the lid on the ball jar and let cool to room temperature.
5. Once cooled, place the ball jar in the refrigerator and let pickle for at least 2 hours before serving. The pickled kiwi will keep in the refrigerator for up to 2 weeks. Enjoy!

TROPICAL PICKLED KIWI AND CORIANDER DELIGHT

If you're looking for a unique and flavorful twist on traditional pickled items, try out this recipe for pickled kiwi and coriander. The combination of sweet kiwi and fragrant coriander creates a truly unique and tasty pickled treat.

2 cups white vinegar

1 cup water

1 cup sugar

2 tbsp salt

2 tbsp coriander seeds

2 tbsp mustard seeds

4-6 kiwis, peeled and sliced

1 bunch coriander, roughly chopped

1. In a medium saucepan, combine the vinegar, water, sugar, salt, coriander seeds, and mustard seeds. Bring to a boil, stirring to dissolve the sugar and salt.
2. Place the sliced kiwis and chopped coriander in a clean ball jar.
3. Pour the hot vinegar mixture over the kiwis and coriander, making sure to cover all the ingredients.
4. Secure the lid on the ball jar and allow to cool to room temperature.
5. Once cooled, transfer the ball jar to the refrigerator and allow to pickle for at least 3 days before enjoying. These pickled kiwis and coriander can be stored in the refrigerator for up to 2 months.

KIWI FENNEL PICKLES A REFRESHING TWIST ON A CLASSIC RECIPE

If you're a fan of pickles but looking for something a little more unique and refreshing, these pickled kiwi and fennel pickles are sure to hit the spot. The combination of sweet and tart kiwi with the crunchy and slightly anise-flavored fennel creates a flavor explosion in every bite. These pickles are perfect for adding a pop of flavor to sandwiches, salads, or as a snack on their own.

---

3 kiwis, peeled and sliced into thin rounds
1 bulb fennel, thinly sliced
1 cup white vinegar
1 cup water
2 tbsp sugar
2 tsp salt
1 tsp black peppercorns
1 tsp fennel seeds

1. In a small saucepan, combine the vinegar, water, sugar, salt, peppercorns, and fennel seeds. Bring to a boil and stir until the sugar and salt have dissolved. Remove from heat and let cool slightly.
2. Place the kiwi slices and fennel slices in a clean, dry ball jar.
3. Pour the pickling liquid over the kiwi and fennel, making sure to cover all the slices completely.
4. Place the lid on the ball jar and let the pickles sit at room temperature for at least 1 hour to allow the flavors to meld.
5. Store in the refrigerator for up to 2 weeks. Enjoy!

DELICIOUSLY TANGY PICKLED KIWI AND LEMON

Introducing a new twist on traditional pickled foods! This recipe combines the unique flavor of kiwi with the bright and acidic taste of lemon for a tangy and refreshing pickle. It's the perfect addition to any charcuterie board or as a topping for sandwiches and burgers.

---

4 kiwis, peeled and sliced into thin rounds

2 lemons, thinly sliced

2 cups white vinegar

1 cup water

1/2 cup sugar

1 tablespoon kosher salt

2 cloves garlic, minced

1 tablespoon whole black peppercorns

2 cinnamon sticks

4 whole cloves

4 ball jars with lids

1. In a small saucepan, combine the vinegar, water, sugar, salt, garlic, peppercorns, cinnamon sticks, and cloves. Bring the mixture to a boil, stirring occasionally to dissolve the sugar and salt.

2. Pack the kiwi and lemon slices into the ball jars, leaving about 1/2 inch of headspace at the top.

3. Pour the hot vinegar mixture over the fruit, making sure to cover all of the slices.

4. Close the lids tightly and allow the jars to cool to room temperature.

5. Once cooled, store the jars in the refrigerator for at least 24 hours before serving. The pickles will keep for up to 2 weeks in the fridge. Enjoy!

TART AND TANGY PICKLED KIWI AND LIME

If you're looking for a unique twist on your typical pickled vegetables, these pickled kiwis and limes are the perfect addition to your pantry. The combination of the sweet kiwi and sour lime creates a balance of flavors that will have you coming back for more.

---

1 cup water

1 cup white vinegar

1/4 cup sugar

1 tsp salt

4 kiwis, peeled and sliced into rounds

2 limes, sliced into rounds

2 cloves garlic, peeled and thinly sliced

2 sprigs fresh dill

1 tsp black peppercorns

1. In a small saucepan, combine the water, vinegar, sugar, and salt. Bring to a boil, stirring until the sugar and salt have dissolved.
2. Place the kiwi slices, lime slices, garlic, dill, and peppercorns in a clean and sterilized ball jar.
3. Pour the hot vinegar mixture over the ingredients in the ball jar, making sure to cover all the fruit and vegetables.
4. Seal the ball jar and allow it to cool to room temperature.
5. Once cooled, place the ball jar in the refrigerator for at least 24 hours before serving.
6. These pickled kiwis and limes can be stored in the refrigerator for up to 2 weeks. Enjoy as a condiment or topping for sandwiches and salads.

TANGY PICKLED KIWI AND MUSTARD DELIGHT

This pickled kiwi and mustard recipe is a unique twist on traditional pickling recipes. The tangy kiwi pairs perfectly with the spicy mustard, creating a flavor combination that will leave your taste buds wanting more. Perfect for adding some zing to sandwiches or as a tasty snack on its own.

1 pound kiwi, peeled and sliced into rounds
1 cup white vinegar
1 cup water
1/2 cup sugar
1 tablespoon mustard seeds
1 tablespoon yellow mustard
1 tablespoon honey
1 teaspoon salt

1. In a medium saucepan, combine the vinegar, water, sugar, mustard seeds, yellow mustard, honey, and salt. Bring to a boil over medium heat, stirring until the sugar has dissolved.
2. Place the kiwi slices in a clean, sterilized ball jar. Pour the hot vinegar mixture over the kiwi, making sure to cover all the slices.
3. Tightly seal the ball jar and let it cool to room temperature. Once cool, place the jar in the refrigerator for at least 24 hours before serving.
4. The pickled kiwi and mustard will last for up to two weeks in the refrigerator. Enjoy on sandwiches, as a snack, or as a topping for salads.

ZESTY KIWI AND ONION RELISH

This pickled kiwi and onion relish is the perfect addition to any BBQ or picnic spread. The sweet and tangy flavors of the kiwi are balanced out by the savory onion, making it a unique and tasty condiment.

4 kiwis, peeled and diced
1 medium onion, diced
1 cup white vinegar
1/2 cup sugar
1 tbsp salt
1 tsp mustard seeds
1/2 tsp black peppercorns
1/2 tsp red chili flakes (optional)

1. In a medium saucepan, combine the vinegar, sugar, salt, mustard seeds, peppercorns, and chili flakes (if using). Bring to a boil, stirring occasionally, until the sugar has dissolved.
2. Add the diced kiwis and onion to a clean and sterilized ball jar.
3. Pour the hot vinegar mixture over the kiwis and onions, making sure to cover them completely.
4. Place the lid on the ball jar and allow to cool to room temperature.
5. Once cooled, refrigerate for at least 24 hours before serving. The relish will keep for up to 2 weeks in the refrigerator.
6. Serve with grilled meats, sandwiches, or as a topping for burgers and hot dogs. Enjoy!

ZESTY ROSEMARY PICKLED KIWI

If you're a fan of tart and savory flavors, then this recipe is for you! The combination of pickled kiwi and rosemary creates a unique and tasty treat that is perfect for snacking or as a condiment for sandwiches and salads.

---

4 kiwis, peeled and sliced into rounds
1 cup white vinegar
1 cup water
1/2 cup sugar
2 sprigs of fresh rosemary
2 cloves garlic, minced
1 teaspoon salt
1/2 teaspoon black peppercorns

1. In a small saucepan, combine the vinegar, water, sugar, rosemary, garlic, salt, and peppercorns. Bring to a boil, then reduce the heat and simmer for 5 minutes.

2. Place the kiwi slices in a clean ball jar. Pour the hot vinegar mixture over the kiwis, making sure they are fully submerged.

3. Let the kiwis cool to room temperature, then seal the ball jar and refrigerate for at least 24 hours before serving.

4. The pickled kiwis will keep in the refrigerator for up to 2 weeks. Enjoy as a snack or use as a condiment for sandwiches and salads.

DELICIOUSLY PICKLED KUMQUAT AND GINGER

When I first tasted pickled kumquat and ginger, I was immediately struck by the tangy and slightly sweet flavor. It's a perfect combination of flavors that's both refreshing and invigorating. If you've never tried pickling your own kumquats, now is the time to start! All you need is a few simple ingredients and a few hours of patience. Trust me, it's worth the wait!

---

1 cup white vinegar

1 cup water

1/2 cup sugar

1 tablespoon salt

1/2 teaspoon black peppercorns

1/2 teaspoon mustard seeds

1/2 teaspoon coriander seeds

1/2 teaspoon fennel seeds

1/2 teaspoon dill seeds

1/4 teaspoon red pepper flakes (optional)

1-pound kumquats,

1. In a small saucepan, combine the vinegar, water, sugar, and salt. Bring to a boil over medium heat, stirring until the sugar and salt have dissolved.

2. Place the black peppercorns, mustard seeds, coriander seeds, fennel seeds, dill seeds, and red pepper flakes (if using) in the bottom of a large ball jar.

3. Add the sliced kumquats and ginger on top of the spices.

4. Pour the hot vinegar mixture over the kumquats and ginger, making sure to cover all the fruit and spices.

5. Seal the ball jar tightly and let it cool to room temperature.

6. Once cooled, place the jar in the refrigerator and let it pickle for at least 24 hours before serving. The pickled kumquats and ginger will keep in the refrigerator for up to 2 weeks. Enjoy!

TANGY PICKLED KUMQUAT AND LEMON

If you're a fan of tart and tangy flavors, then this pickled kumquat and lemon recipe is for you! Kumquats are small, orange-like fruits that are often used in pickling and preserving. Combined with lemons, these pickles make for a delicious and unique addition to any meal.

1-pound kumquats, thinly sliced
1 lemon, thinly sliced
1 cup white vinegar
1 cup water
1 tablespoon kosher salt
2 tablespoons sugar
1 teaspoon whole coriander seeds
1 teaspoon black peppercorns
1 dried chili pepper (optional)

1. In a small saucepan, combine the vinegar, water, salt, sugar, coriander seeds, peppercorns, and chili pepper (if using). Bring to a boil over medium-high heat, stirring occasionally until the sugar and salt have dissolved.

2. Place the sliced kumquats and lemon in a clean ball jar.

3. Pour the hot pickling liquid over the sliced fruit, making sure to fully cover them.

4. Allow the jar to cool to room temperature, then seal the jar and store in the refrigerator for at least 24 hours before serving. The pickles will keep in the refrigerator for up to 1 month.

5. Serve the pickled kumquats and lemon as a condiment with grilled meats or as a topping for sandwiches and salads. Enjoy!

TART AND TANGY PICKLED LEEKS WITH A HINT OF DILL

Pickling is a great way to preserve vegetables and add a unique flavor to your dishes. These pickled leeks are a delicious and tangy addition to sandwiches, salads, and charcuterie boards. The dill adds a refreshing, herbaceous note to the pickling liquid, making these pickled leeks a flavorful and versatile condiment.

1-pound leeks, white and light green parts only
1 cup white vinegar
1 cup water
2 tablespoons sugar
2 teaspoons salt
2 cloves garlic, minced
1 tablespoon dill seeds
1 teaspoon mustard seeds
1 teaspoon peppercorns
4 ball jars with lids

1. Wash and trim the leeks, slicing them into thin rounds.
2. In a small saucepan, bring the vinegar, water, sugar, salt, garlic, dill seeds, mustard seeds, and peppercorns to a boil.
3. Divide the leeks among the ball jars, packing them tightly into the jars.
4. Pour the hot pickling liquid over the leeks, leaving about 1/2 inch of headspace at the top of the jar.
5. Wipe the rim of the jar with a clean cloth to remove any spills, then place the lid on top and screw on the ring until it is fingertip tight.
6. Place the jars in a pot of boiling water, making sure the water covers the jars by at least 1 inch. Boil the jars for 10 minutes, then remove them from the pot and let them cool to room temperature.
7. Once the jars are cool, check the seal by pressing down on the center of the lid. If it doesn't flex, the seal is good.

ZESTY PICKLED LEEK AND GARLIC

This pickled leek and garlic recipe is the perfect condiment to add some tangy flavor to your meals. The combination of leeks and garlic gives these pickles a unique and delicious taste that will complement a variety of dishes. Whether you serve them as a topping for sandwiches or as a garnish for cocktails, these pickled leeks and garlic are sure to be a hit.

---

2 leeks, white and light green parts only, sliced into thin rounds

4 cloves garlic, thinly sliced

1 cup white vinegar

1 cup water

2 tablespoons sugar

1 tablespoon salt

1 teaspoon black peppercorns

2 bay leaves

1 ball jar with a tight-fitting lid

1. Wash and slice the leeks and garlic.
2. In a small saucepan, combine the vinegar, water, sugar, salt, peppercorns, and bay leaves. Bring to a boil and stir until the sugar and salt are dissolved.
3. Place the sliced leeks and garlic in the ball jar.
4. Pour the hot vinegar mixture over the leeks and garlic, making sure they are fully covered.
5. Close the ball jar tightly and let it cool to room temperature.
6. Once cool, store the jar in the refrigerator for at least 24 hours before serving to allow the flavors to meld together.

These pickled leeks and garlic will last for several weeks in the refrigerator. Enjoy them on sandwiches, in salads, or as a garnish for cocktails.

LIVELY PICKLED LEEKS AND LEMONS

Pickling is a great way to preserve the taste and texture of fresh vegetables for later use. These pickled leeks and lemons are a refreshing and tangy addition to any dish. The combination of leeks and lemon adds a bright and lively flavor to the jar. Serve these pickled leeks and lemons as a condiment or topping for sandwiches, salads, or grain bowls.

1 large leek, white and light green parts only

1 lemon, thinly sliced

1 cup white vinegar

1 cup water

1 tablespoon sugar

1 teaspoon salt

1 bay leaf

4 black peppercorns

1. Wash and slice the leek into thin rounds.
2. Thinly slice the lemon.
3. In a small saucepan, combine the vinegar, water, sugar, salt, bay leaf, and peppercorns. Bring to a boil, then remove from heat.
4. Pack the sliced leeks and lemon slices into a clean, sterilized ball jar.
5. Pour the hot vinegar mixture over the leeks and lemon slices, making sure to cover them completely.
6. Close the jar tightly and let it cool to room temperature.
7. Once cooled, store the jar in the refrigerator for at least a week before serving to allow the flavors to meld. The pickled leeks and lemons will keep in the refrigerator for up to 3 months. Enjoy!

TANGY PICKLED LEEK AND ONION RELISH

This pickled leek and onion relish is the perfect addition to any sandwich or charcuterie board. The combination of sweet and sour flavors creates a delicious balance that pairs well with a variety of dishes. Plus, it's easy to make and can be stored in the refrigerator for up to a month.

2 medium leeks, sliced into thin rounds
1 medium onion, sliced into thin rounds
1 cup apple cider vinegar
1 cup water
1/2 cup sugar
1 tablespoon pickling spice
1 teaspoon salt

1. In a medium saucepan, combine the vinegar, water, sugar, pickling spice, and salt. Bring to a boil over medium heat, stirring occasionally to dissolve the sugar.
2. Once the mixture comes to a boil, add the leeks and onions to the pan. Reduce the heat to a simmer and cook for 5 minutes.
3. Remove the pan from the heat and allow the mixture to cool for 10 minutes.
4. Transfer the pickled leeks and onions to a clean ball jar and seal the jar with a lid.
5. Place the jar in the refrigerator to cool completely. The pickled leeks and onions will be ready to eat after 24 hours and will last in the refrigerator for up to a month.

DELICIOUS PICKLED LEEK AND THYME RECIPE

This recipe for pickled leek and thyme is a great way to add some tangy, flavorful goodness to your meals. The combination of leeks and thyme creates a unique and delicious taste that pairs well with a variety of dishes. Whether you're using the pickled leeks as a topping for sandwiches, a garnish for salads, or as an ingredient in your cooking, this recipe is sure to be a hit.

1-pound leeks

1 cup white vinegar

1 cup water

2 tablespoons sugar

2 teaspoons salt

1 teaspoon thyme leaves

2 cloves garlic, minced

2 ball jars

1. Wash and trim the leeks, making sure to remove any dirt or debris. Cut the leeks into 1/4-inch slices.

2. In a medium saucepan, combine the vinegar, water, sugar, salt, thyme, and garlic. Bring the mixture to a boil, stirring occasionally to dissolve the sugar and salt.

3. Once the mixture has come to a boil, add the sliced leeks to the pan. Reduce the heat to low and simmer for 5 minutes.

4. Remove the pan from the heat and allow the leeks to cool in the pickling liquid for 10 minutes.

5. Using a slotted spoon, transfer the pickled leeks to the ball jars, making sure to divide the leeks evenly between the two jars.

6. Pour the pickling liquid over the leeks, making sure to cover the leeks completely.

7. Close the jars tightly and store in the refrigerator for at least 24 hours before serving. The pickled leeks will keep in the refrigerator for up to 2 weeks. Enjoy!

ZESTY PICKLED LEMONS WITH A KICK OF CHILI

Pickled lemons are a staple in many Middle Eastern and North African cuisines and adding a bit of chili brings a nice balance of sweetness and heat to the finished product. These pickled lemons are great as a condiment for grilled meats, sandwiches, and even on their own as a snack. Plus, the bright yellow color is sure to add a pop of color to any dish.

---

2 lemons, thinly sliced

2 tablespoons chili flakes

2 tablespoons sugar

2 tablespoons salt

1 cup white vinegar

1 cup water

1. In a small saucepan, combine the vinegar, water, sugar, and salt. Bring to a boil, stirring until the sugar and salt have dissolved.

2. Place the sliced lemons and chili flakes in a clean, sterilized ball jar.

3. Pour the vinegar mixture over the lemons, making sure to fully submerge them.

4. Let the jar cool to room temperature, then seal and store in the refrigerator for at least 3 days before using. The pickled lemons will keep in the refrigerator for up to 3 months.

TANGY LEMON AND DILL PICKLED CUCUMBERS

If you're a fan of pickles, but looking for something a little different, these pickled cucumbers are the perfect option. The combination of lemon and dill gives them a bright and refreshing flavor that's perfect for summertime snacking.

---

4 medium cucumbers, thinly sliced

1 cup water

1 cup white vinegar

1/2 cup granulated sugar

1 tablespoon salt

4 cloves garlic, minced

1 tablespoon dill seeds

1 lemon, thinly sliced

4 ball jars, sterilized

1. In a small saucepan, combine the water, vinegar, sugar, and salt. Bring to a boil over medium heat, stirring until the sugar and salt have dissolved.

2. Place a few slices of garlic and lemon, as well as some dill seeds, in the bottom of each ball jar.

3. Pack the cucumber slices into the jars, leaving about 1 inch of space at the top.

4. Pour the hot pickling liquid over the cucumbers, making sure to fully cover them.

5. Seal the jars and allow to cool to room temperature. Once cooled, store in the refrigerator for at least 24 hours before serving to allow the flavors to meld. The pickled cucumbers will keep in the refrigerator for up to 2 weeks. Enjoy!

DELICIOUSLY PICKLED LEMON AND DILL GREEN BEANS

There's nothing quite like the refreshing crunch of a pickled green bean, and this recipe takes it to the next level with the addition of lemon and dill. Perfect for snacking on their own or adding to a salad or sandwich, these pickled green beans are sure to become a new favorite.

1-pound green beans, trimmed
1 cup white vinegar
1 cup water
1 tablespoon sugar
1 tablespoon kosher salt
2 cloves garlic, minced
1 teaspoon dill seeds
1/2 lemon, thinly sliced

1. Bring a large pot of water to a boil. Add the green beans and blanch for 2-3 minutes, until they are bright green and slightly tender.
2. Drain the green beans and place them in a large bowl filled with ice water. This will help stop the cooking process and preserve their bright green color.
3. In a small saucepan, combine the vinegar, water, sugar, and salt. Bring to a boil, stirring occasionally, until the sugar and salt have dissolved.
4. Divide the garlic, dill seeds, and lemon slices evenly among the jars.
5. Add the green beans to the jars, packing them in as tightly as possible.
6. Pour the hot vinegar mixture over the green beans, making sure to cover them completely.
7. Wipe the rims of the jars with a clean, damp cloth to remove any residue.
8. Cover the jars with the lids and rings and place them in a boiling water bath for 10 minutes.
9. Carefully remove the jars from the boiling water bath and allow them to cool to room temperature. Store the pickled green beans in the refrigerator for at least 24 hours before serving, to allow the flavors to fully develop. Enjoy!

FANCY FENNEL PICKLED LEMONS

Pickling is a great way to preserve the fresh flavors of produce, and these pickled lemons are the perfect balance of tangy and sweet. The fennel adds a unique, licorice-like flavor that pairs beautifully with the bright, citrusy lemons. These pickled lemons are a delicious addition to salads, sandwiches, and charcuterie boards.

---

2 lemons, thinly sliced
1 bulb of fennel, thinly sliced
1 cup white vinegar
1 cup water
1/2 cup sugar
1 tablespoon salt
1 teaspoon mustard seeds
1 teaspoon fennel seeds
4 garlic cloves, thinly sliced
2 sprigs of fresh thyme

1. In a small saucepan, combine the vinegar, water, sugar, salt, mustard seeds, and fennel seeds. Bring to a boil, stirring until the sugar and salt have dissolved.
2. Place the lemon and fennel slices in a clean, sterilized ball jar. Add the garlic and thyme sprigs.
3. Pour the hot vinegar mixture over the lemon and fennel slices, making sure to cover them completely.
4. Secure the lid on the ball jar and let it cool to room temperature.
5. Once cooled, store the jar in the refrigerator for at least 24 hours before serving. The pickled lemons will keep for up to 2 weeks in the refrigerator. Enjoy!

ZESTY PICKLED LEMON AND GARLIC OLIVES"

If you're a fan of tangy and bold flavors, then these pickled lemon and garlic olives are sure to become a new favorite. The combination of tart lemons and pungent garlic adds depth and complexity to the briny olives, creating a snack that's perfect for topping salads, adding to sandwiches, or simply enjoying on their own.

1 cup green olives

1 lemon, thinly sliced

3 cloves garlic, thinly sliced

1 cup white vinegar

1 cup water

1 tablespoon sugar

1 tablespoon salt

1 bay leaf

1. In a small saucepan, bring the vinegar, water, sugar, salt, and bay leaf to a boil.
2. Meanwhile, pack the olives, lemon slices, and garlic slices into a clean ball jar.
3. Once the brine has come to a boil, carefully pour it over the olives in the jar, making sure to cover them completely.
4. Close the jar and let it cool to room temperature.
5. Once cooled, store the jar in the refrigerator for at least 24 hours before serving. This will give the flavors time to meld and intensify.
6. The pickled olives will keep for up to a month in the refrigerator. Enjoy!

"ZESTY PICKLED LEMON AND ONION RELISH"

This pickled lemon and onion relish is a tangy and refreshing condiment that pairs perfectly with grilled meats or sandwiches. It's easy to make and can be stored in a ball jar in the refrigerator for several weeks.

2 lemons, sliced into thin rounds

1 medium onion, thinly sliced

1 cup apple cider vinegar

1/2 cup water

2 tbsp sugar

1 tsp salt

1 tsp mustard seeds

1/2 tsp coriander seeds

1. In a medium saucepan, combine the vinegar, water, sugar, salt, mustard seeds, and coriander seeds. Bring to a boil over medium heat, stirring until the sugar and salt have dissolved.
2. Add the lemon and onion slices to a clean and sterilized ball jar.
3. Pour the hot vinegar mixture over the lemon and onion slices, making sure to completely cover them.
4. Allow the mixture to cool to room temperature, then seal the jar and store in the refrigerator for at least 24 hours before serving.
5. The relish will keep in the refrigerator for up to 4 weeks. Enjoy!

LIVELY PICKLED LEMONS WITH FRESH PARSLEY"

This recipe is a twist on traditional pickled lemons, adding the brightness of parsley to the mix. It's a perfect addition to any charcuterie board or as a tangy condiment on grilled meats.

4 lemons, thinly sliced
1/2 cup white vinegar
1/2 cup water
2 tablespoons sugar
2 tablespoons kosher salt
1/4 cup fresh parsley, chopped

1. In a small saucepan, combine the vinegar, water, sugar, and salt. Bring to a boil over medium heat, stirring until the sugar and salt are dissolved.

2. Place the lemon slices and parsley in a clean, sterilized ball jar. Pour the vinegar mixture over the top, making sure the lemons are fully submerged.

3. Allow the jar to cool to room temperature, then seal the jar and store in the refrigerator.

4. The pickled lemons will be ready to eat after 24 hours, but they will continue to improve in flavor as they sit in the refrigerator for up to 2 weeks.

"LUSCIOUS LEMON AND ROSE PICKLES"

These pickled lemons are a unique and flavorful addition to any meal. The combination of tart lemons and floral rose is surprisingly delightful, and the pickling process helps to soften the rind and infuse the fruit with a delicious, pickled taste. These pickles are perfect for adding a pop of flavor to sandwiches, salads, or as a garnish for cocktails.

---

4 lemons, thinly sliced

2 cups water

1 cup white vinegar

1/2 cup sugar

1 tablespoon salt

2 tablespoons rose water

4 whole cloves

2 cinnamon sticks

1. In a medium saucepan, combine the water, vinegar, sugar, and salt. Bring to a boil and stir until the sugar and salt have dissolved.
2. Add the lemon slices, rose water, cloves, and cinnamon sticks to a clean, sterilized ball jar.
3. Pour the hot vinegar mixture over the lemon slices, making sure to cover the slices completely.
4. Close the jar tightly and allow to cool to room temperature.
5. Once cooled, store the jar in the refrigerator for at least 24 hours before serving. The pickles will last for several weeks in the refrigerator. Enjoy!

"ZESTY PICKLED LEMONS WITH ROSEMARY"

Pickling is a great way to preserve the taste and texture of fresh lemons and adding rosemary to the mix adds a lovely depth of flavor. These pickled lemons are perfect for adding a burst of citrus to salads, sandwiches, and more.

---

4 lemons, sliced into thin rounds
1 cup white vinegar
1 cup water
2 tablespoons sugar
1 tablespoon salt
2 sprigs of fresh rosemary
2 cloves garlic, minced
1 small red chili pepper, sliced (optional)

1. In a small saucepan, combine the vinegar, water, sugar, and salt. Bring to a boil, stirring until the sugar and salt are dissolved.
2. In a clean, sterile ball jar, place the lemon slices, rosemary, garlic, and chili pepper (if using).
3. Pour the hot vinegar mixture over the lemon slices, making sure to fully submerge them.
4. Close the jar tightly and let it cool to room temperature.
5. Once cooled, place the jar in the refrigerator for at least 24 hours to allow the flavors to meld. The pickled lemons will keep in the refrigerator for up to 1 month. Enjoy!

"LIVELY LEMON AND THYME PICKLES"

These pickled lemons are a tangy and aromatic addition to any dish. The combination of lemon and thyme adds a bright and herbaceous flavor that is perfect for summertime. They are easy to make and can be stored in the refrigerator for up to a month.

---

4 lemons, thinly sliced
1 cup white vinegar
1 cup water
1/2 cup sugar
2 tablespoons salt
4 sprigs fresh thyme

1. In a medium saucepan, bring the vinegar, water, sugar, and salt to a boil.
2. Place the lemon slices and thyme sprigs in a clean and sterilized ball jar.
3. Pour the hot vinegar mixture over the lemons, making sure to cover them completely.
4. Close the jar tightly and let it cool to room temperature.
5. Once cool, transfer the jar to the refrigerator and let it pickle for at least 24 hours before serving.
6. These pickles will keep in the refrigerator for up to a month. Enjoy them as a condiment or use them to add flavor to salads, sandwiches, and more.

"ZESTY PICKLED LEMON AND THYME BEETS"

This recipe for pickled beets is a refreshing twist on the classic pickled beet recipe. The combination of lemon and thyme adds a bright and fragrant flavor to the beets, making them a perfect addition to any salad or charcuterie board.

---

2 lbs fresh beets, trimmed and scrubbed

1 cup white vinegar

1 cup water

1/2 cup sugar

2 cloves garlic, minced

1 lemon, thinly sliced

1 tbsp fresh thyme leaves

2 tsp kosher salt

2 Ball jars with lids

1. Preheat your oven to 400 degrees F. Place the beets on a sheet of foil and wrap them tightly. Roast the beets for 45-60 minutes, or until they are tender when pierced with a fork.
2. Allow the beets to cool, then peel and slice them into 1/4-inch-thick rounds.
3. In a medium saucepan, combine the vinegar, water, sugar, garlic, lemon slices, thyme, and salt. Bring the mixture to a boil, then reduce the heat to a simmer and cook for 5 minutes.
4. Pack the beet slices into the Ball jars, making sure to leave about 1/2 inch of headspace at the top of each jar.
5. Pour the hot vinegar mixture over the beets, making sure to cover them completely. Tap the jars gently on the counter to remove any air bubbles, then seal the lids.
6. Allow the jars to cool to room temperature, then store them in the refrigerator for at least 24 hours before serving. The beets will keep in the refrigerator for up to 1 month. Enjoy!

"LUSCIOUS LEMON AND VANILLA PICKLES"

These pickles are a unique and delightful twist on the traditional pickled lemon. The addition of vanilla brings a subtle sweetness and depth of flavor that pairs perfectly with the tangy lemon. These pickles make a great addition to any charcuterie board or can be enjoyed as a snack on their own.

4 lemons, thinly sliced

2 cups water

1 cup white vinegar

1 cup sugar

2 teaspoons kosher salt

2 vanilla beans, split lengthwise

1. Place the lemon slices in a medium saucepan and cover with water. Bring to a boil and cook for 2 minutes. Drain and rinse the lemon slices under cold water.

2. In a separate saucepan, combine the water, vinegar, sugar, and salt. Scrape the seeds from the vanilla beans and add them to the saucepan, along with the beans. Bring the mixture to a boil, stirring until the sugar and salt have dissolved.

3. Place the lemon slices in a clean ball jar and pour the hot liquid over the top. Seal the jar and let it cool to room temperature.

4. Transfer the jar to the refrigerator and let it sit for at least 24 hours before serving. The pickles will keep in the refrigerator for up to 1 month. Enjoy!

"ZESTY PICKLED LEMON ZEST AND ONION RELISH"

This pickled lemon zest and onion relish is a tangy and flavorful condiment that adds a burst of acidity to any dish. It's perfect for topping burgers, sandwiches, or even grilled chicken. The combination of pickled lemon zest and onions gives this relish a unique and refreshing taste that will surely become a new favorite in your household.

---

1 lemon, zested and thinly sliced

1 small red onion, thinly sliced

1 cup white vinegar

1/2 cup water

2 tablespoons sugar

1 tablespoon salt

1 teaspoon mustard seeds

1/2 teaspoon black peppercorns

1 bay leaf

1 ball jar with a lid

1. In a small saucepan, combine the vinegar, water, sugar, salt, mustard seeds, black peppercorns, and bay leaf. Bring to a boil, stirring occasionally, until the sugar and salt have dissolved.

2. Place the lemon zest and onion slices in the ball jar.

3. Pour the hot vinegar mixture over the lemon zest and onions in the jar, making sure to cover them completely.

4. Let the jar cool to room temperature, then seal the lid tightly and refrigerate for at least 3 days before using. The relish will keep in the refrigerator for up to 3 weeks.

5. Enjoy your pickled lemon zest and onion relish on sandwiches, burgers, or as a condiment for grilled meats.

ZESTY PICKLED LIME AND JALAPENO PEPPERS"

These pickled lime and jalapeno peppers are the perfect addition to any Mexican-inspired dish, adding a burst of flavor and a little bit of heat. They're also great as a topping for sandwiches or as a snack on their own. Plus, they're super easy to make and can be stored in a ball jar in the fridge for up to a few months.

---

2 cups water

1 cup white vinegar

2 tablespoons sugar

2 tablespoons salt

4-6 limes, thinly sliced

2 jalapeno peppers, thinly sliced (seeds and ribs removed if you want less heat)

1 garlic clove, minced

1. In a small saucepan, combine the water, vinegar, sugar, and salt. Bring to a boil, stirring until the sugar and salt have dissolved.
2. Place the sliced limes, jalapeno peppers, and minced garlic in a ball jar.
3. Pour the hot vinegar mixture over the top of the lime and jalapeno slices, making sure they are fully covered.
4. Let the jar cool to room temperature, then seal with a lid and store in the fridge.
5. Allow the peppers to pickle for at least 24 hours before serving. They will keep in the fridge for up to a few months. Enjoy!

DELICIOUS PICKLED LIME AND ONION RELISH

This pickled lime and onion relish is a tangy and flavorful condiment that adds a burst of freshness to any dish. It's easy to make and can be stored in a ball jar for several months in the refrigerator.

2 limes, thinly sliced

1 onion, thinly sliced

1/2 cup white vinegar

1/2 cup water

1/4 cup sugar

1 tsp salt

1/2 tsp black peppercorns

1. In a small saucepan, combine the vinegar, water, sugar, salt, and peppercorns. Bring to a boil, stirring until the sugar and salt have dissolved.

2. Place the lime and onion slices in a sterilized ball jar. Pour the hot vinegar mixture over the top, making sure to cover the limes and onions completely.

3. Close the jar tightly and let it cool to room temperature. Then store it in the refrigerator for at least 24 hours before serving. The relish will keep for several months in the refrigerator.

4. Serve the pickled lime and onion relish as a condiment with grilled meats, sandwiches, or tacos. Enjoy!

PICKLED LIME AND PARSLEY: A REFRESHING TWIST ON PICKLES

If you're a fan of pickles, you're going to love this twist on the classic recipe. Pickled limes add a tangy and refreshing flavor to your pickle jar, while parsley adds a nice touch of freshness. This recipe is easy to make and is perfect for adding a unique touch to sandwiches, salads, and more.

---

1 cup water

1 cup white vinegar

1 tablespoon salt

1 tablespoon sugar

4 limes, thinly sliced

1/4 cup parsley leaves

1 clove garlic, minced

1/2 teaspoon peppercorns

1/2 teaspoon mustard seeds

1. In a small saucepan, bring the water, vinegar, salt, and sugar to a boil.
2. Place the lime slices, parsley, garlic, peppercorns, and mustard seeds in a clean 1-quart Ball jar.
3. Pour the hot vinegar mixture over the lime and parsley mixture, making sure to completely cover the ingredients.
4. Let the pickles cool to room temperature, then seal the jar and refrigerate for at least 24 hours before serving.
5. These pickles will last for up to 1 month in the refrigerator. Enjoy!

"TANGY PICKLED LIMES WITH ROSEMARY"

Pickling limes may seem like an unusual recipe, but the tangy and slightly sweet flavor of pickled limes is a delicious addition to many dishes. Whether you're adding them to a salad, using them as a garnish for cocktails, or adding them to your favorite Mexican dish, these pickled limes are sure to be a hit. And the addition of rosemary adds a woodsy, herbal flavor that pairs perfectly with the tanginess of the limes.

1-pound limes, cut into wedges
1 cup white vinegar
1 cup water
1/2 cup sugar
2 tablespoons kosher salt
2 sprigs fresh rosemary

1. In a small saucepan, combine the vinegar, water, sugar, and salt. Bring to a boil over medium heat, stirring until the sugar and salt have dissolved. Remove from heat and let cool to room temperature.
2. Place the lime wedges and rosemary sprigs in a large glass jar (such as a ball jar).
3. Pour the vinegar mixture over the limes, making sure to cover all the limes.
4. Tightly seal the jar and store in the refrigerator for at least 24 hours before using. The limes will keep in the refrigerator for up to 2 weeks.
5. To use, remove the limes and rosemary from the jar and chop or slice as desired. The pickling liquid can also be used as a tangy dressing or marinade. Enjoy!

"LIVELY LIME AND THYME PICKLES"

These pickled limes are a tangy and flavorful addition to any dish. The combination of lime and thyme gives them a unique and aromatic taste that will surely impress your friends and family. They are perfect for serving with grilled meats or as a topping for salads and sandwiches.

---

4 medium limes, thinly sliced
1 cup white vinegar
1 cup water
2 tablespoons sugar
1 tablespoon salt
1 tablespoon thyme leaves

1. In a small saucepan, bring the vinegar, water, sugar, and salt to a boil. Stir to dissolve the sugar and salt.
2. Place the lime slices in a clean and sterilized ball jar.
3. Add the thyme leaves to the jar with the lime slices.
4. Pour the vinegar mixture over the lime slices, making sure to completely cover them.
5. Close the jar tightly and allow it to cool to room temperature.
6. Once cooled, store the jar in the refrigerator for at least a week before serving to allow the flavors to fully develop. These pickles will keep in the refrigerator for up to 2 months. Enjoy!

TANTALIZING THAI PICKLED LONGAN AND BASIL"

Pickled longan and basil may not be a combination you're familiar with, but trust us, it's a match made in heaven. The sweet, tropical flavor of longan pairs perfectly with the aromatic basil, and the pickling process helps to enhance and intensify the flavors. This recipe is inspired by the flavors of Thailand and is sure to be a hit at any gathering.

---

1 cup longan fruit, peeled and pitted

1 cup white vinegar

1 cup water

1/2 cup sugar

1 tablespoon salt

2 sprigs fresh basil

2 cloves garlic, minced

1 small chili pepper, sliced (optional)

1. In a small saucepan, combine the vinegar, water, sugar, and salt. Bring to a boil and stir until the sugar and salt have dissolved.
2. Place the longan fruit, basil, garlic, and chili pepper (if using) in a clean, sterilized ball jar.
3. Pour the hot vinegar mixture over the fruit and herbs, making sure to cover everything completely.
4. Let the jar cool to room temperature, then seal it and store it in the refrigerator.
5. The pickled longan and basil will be ready to eat in about a week, but they'll continue to improve in flavor the longer they sit. Enjoy them as a snack, or use them as a flavorful addition to salads or sandwiches.

LIVELY PICKLED LOTUS ROOT AND LEMON"

This recipe for pickled lotus root and lemon is a refreshing and tangy twist on traditional pickled vegetables. The combination of the slightly sweet and crunchy lotus root with the tart and citrusy lemon creates a unique and flavorful experience. Plus, the pretty pink color of the pickled lotus root is sure to impress!

---

1 cup water

1 cup white vinegar

1/2 cup sugar

1 tablespoon salt

4 medium lemons, thinly sliced

4 medium lotus roots, thinly sliced

4 ball jars with lids

1. In a small saucepan, combine the water, vinegar, sugar, and salt. Bring to a boil over medium heat, stirring until the sugar and salt have dissolved. Remove from heat and set aside to cool.

2. Divide the lemon slices evenly among the ball jars.

3. Add the lotus root slices on top of the lemon slices in the ball jars.

4. Pour the cooled vinegar mixture over the lotus root and lemon slices, making sure to cover the slices completely.

5. Close the ball jars and refrigerate for at least 24 hours before serving. The pickled lotus root and lemon will last in the refrigerator for up to 1 month.

Note: You can also add other vegetables or herbs to the ball jars for added flavor, such as sliced red onions, sliced ginger, or fresh dill. Experiment with different combinations to find your favorite!

"TANGY SESAME PICKLED LOTUS ROOT"

Pickled lotus root is a popular condiment in many Asian cuisines and adding sesame seeds gives it a nutty and fragrant twist. It's easy to make at home and adds a burst of flavor to any dish. This recipe uses a ball jar to preserve the pickled lotus root for longer storage.

1 cup rice vinegar

1 cup water

1/4 cup sugar

1 tablespoon salt

2 cloves garlic, thinly sliced

1 teaspoon sesame seeds

1 pound lotus root, sliced into thin rounds

1. In a small saucepan, combine the vinegar, water, sugar, and salt. Bring to a boil and stir until the sugar and salt have dissolved.

2. Place the sliced garlic and sesame seeds in the bottom of a clean ball jar.

3. Add the sliced lotus root to the jar, packing it in tightly.

4. Pour the hot vinegar mixture over the lotus root, making sure to completely cover the slices.

5. Allow the jar to cool to room temperature, then seal the jar and store in the refrigerator. The pickled lotus root will be ready to eat after at least 24 hours of pickling and will last for up to a month in the refrigerator.

6. Serve the pickled lotus root as a condiment or topping for dishes like rice bowls, sandwiches, or salads. Enjoy!

DELICIOUS PICKLED LOTUS ROOT AND SOY

Pickled lotus root and soy is a tasty and unique way to preserve and enjoy lotus root. This recipe combines the crunchy texture of lotus root with the savory flavor of soy sauce to create a delicious, pickled snack or side dish.

1 pound lotus root, peeled and thinly sliced

1 cup water

1 cup soy sauce

1/2 cup rice vinegar

2 cloves garlic, minced

2 tablespoons sugar

1 tablespoon black peppercorns

1 ball jar with a tight-fitting lid

1. In a small saucepan, combine the water, soy sauce, rice vinegar, garlic, sugar, and peppercorns. Bring the mixture to a boil over medium heat, stirring occasionally to dissolve the sugar.

2. Once the mixture has come to a boil, add the sliced lotus root to the pan and reduce the heat to low. Simmer the lotus root in the soy sauce mixture for about 5 minutes, or until it is tender but still crisp.

3. Use a slotted spoon to transfer the lotus root slices to the ball jar, packing them in tightly. Pour the remaining soy sauce mixture over the lotus root slices in the jar.

4. Seal the jar tightly and allow it to cool to room temperature. Once cooled, store the jar in the refrigerator for at least 24 hours before serving to allow the flavors to develop.

To serve, simply open the jar and enjoy the pickled lotus root and soy as a snack or side dish. The pickled lotus root will last for several weeks in the refrigerator.

"REFRESHING PICKLED LYCHEE AND MINT"

This pickled lychee and mint recipe is a unique and refreshing twist on traditional pickled vegetables. The sweet and tart flavor of the lychees pairs perfectly with the refreshing and aromatic mint. It's the perfect addition to any charcuterie board or as a topping for grilled meat or fish.

1-pound fresh lychees, peeled and halved

1 cup white vinegar

1 cup water

1/2 cup granulated sugar

1 tablespoon salt

2 sprigs fresh mint

2 garlic cloves, thinly sliced

2 small chili peppers, thinly sliced (optional)

1. In a small saucepan, combine the vinegar, water, sugar, and salt. Bring to a boil and stir until the sugar and salt have dissolved.

2. Place the lychees, mint, garlic, and chili peppers (if using) in a clean 1 quart ball jar.

3. Pour the vinegar mixture over the lychees, making sure to cover them completely.

4. Let the jar cool to room temperature, then seal and refrigerate for at least 24 hours before serving. The pickled lychees will keep in the refrigerator for up to 1 month.

"TROPICAL BLISS: PICKLED MANGO AND CARDAMOM"

Welcome to the tropical paradise of pickled mango and cardamom. This sweet and tangy recipe is perfect for adding a burst of flavor to any dish. Whether you're using it as a topping for your favorite tacos or just snacking on a jar of pickled mango, this recipe is sure to become a new favorite.

2 cups diced mango
1 cup white vinegar
1 cup water
1/4 cup sugar
2 tablespoons salt
1 tablespoon cardamom seeds
1 ball jar

1. Combine the vinegar, water, sugar, and salt in a small saucepan and bring to a boil.
2. Once the mixture comes to a boil, remove from heat and stir in the cardamom seeds.
3. Place the diced mango in the ball jar and pour the vinegar mixture over the top.
4. Close the jar tightly and let it sit in the fridge for at least 24 hours before serving.
5. Enjoy your pickled mango and cardamom on top of your favorite dishes or as a tasty snack!

"SPICY PICKLED MANGO WITH A KICK"

If you're a fan of sweet and spicy flavors, this pickled mango recipe is for you. The combination of sweet mango and spicy chili creates a unique and delicious taste that will surely impress your friends and family. Plus, the mango can be preserved in a ball jar, making it a convenient snack to keep on hand for anytime cravings.

---

1 large mango, peeled and sliced into small pieces
1 cup white vinegar
1 cup water
1/2 cup sugar
2 tablespoons chili flakes
1 teaspoon salt

1. In a medium saucepan, combine the vinegar, water, sugar, chili flakes, and salt. Bring the mixture to a boil, stirring occasionally until the sugar has dissolved.

2. Place the mango slices into a clean, sterilized ball jar.

3. Pour the vinegar mixture over the mango slices, making sure to cover them completely.

4. Seal the ball jar and let it cool to room temperature before placing it in the refrigerator.

5. Let the pickled mango sit in the fridge for at least 24 hours before serving. The longer it sits, the more flavorful it will become.

6. Serve the pickled mango as a snack or use it as a condiment for sandwiches, tacos, or salads. Enjoy!

"TROPICAL PARADISE PICKLED MANGO AND CUMIN"

When I visited Thailand, I was blown away by the sweet and tangy flavors in their pickled mango. I knew I had to bring a bit of that tropical paradise back home with me, so I experimented with adding a hint of cumin for a unique twist on the traditional recipe. This pickled mango and cumin recipe is perfect for adding a pop of flavor to any dish, or for snacking on straight from the ball jar.

---

2 cups mango, peeled and sliced into thin wedges

1 cup white vinegar

1 cup water

1/2 cup sugar

1 tsp salt

1 tsp cumin seeds

1 small red chili pepper, thinly sliced (optional)

1. Place the mango wedges in a sterilized ball jar.
2. In a small saucepan, combine the vinegar, water, sugar, salt, and cumin seeds. Bring to a boil, stirring until the sugar and salt have dissolved.
3. Pour the hot liquid over the mango wedges in the jar, making sure to completely cover the mango.
4. Optional: add a few slices of red chili pepper for a spicy kick.
5. Tightly seal the jar and let it cool to room temperature.
6. Place the jar in the refrigerator for at least 24 hours before serving to allow the flavors to fully develop.
7. The pickled mango and cumin will last for up to 2 weeks in the refrigerator. Enjoy on sandwiches, in salads, or as a delicious snack straight from the jar.

SPICY PICKLED MANGO CURRY

This recipe is inspired by the flavors of South Asia, where mangoes and curry are common ingredients in many dishes. The pickling process adds a tangy and slightly sour element to the sweet mangoes, which is perfectly balanced out by the aromatic and flavorful curry spices. The result is a unique and tasty condiment that can be used to add some zing to sandwiches, salads, or even as a topping for grilled meats or tofu.

2 cups mangoes, peeled and sliced into thin wedges
1 cup white vinegar
1 cup water
1 tablespoon sugar
1 tablespoon salt
2 teaspoons mustard seeds
1 teaspoon cumin seeds
1 teaspoon coriander seeds
1 teaspoon fennel seeds
1 teaspoon black peppercorns
1 teaspoon red chili flakes (optional)
1 tablespoon curry powder

1. In a small saucepan, combine the vinegar, water, sugar, and salt. Bring to a boil and stir until the sugar and salt are dissolved. Remove from heat and set aside.
2. In a ball jar, combine the mango wedges, mustard seeds, cumin seeds, coriander seeds, fennel seeds, black peppercorns, and red chili flakes (if using).
3. Pour the curry powder over the top of the mango mixture.
4. Pour the vinegar mixture over the mangoes, making sure to cover them completely.
5. Close the ball jar tightly and let it sit at room temperature for at least 24 hours, or up to 3 days, before serving.
6. Once opened, store the pickled mango curry in the refrigerator for up to 3 weeks. Enjoy as a condiment or topping for sandwiches, salads, or grilled meats.

"EXPLOSIVELY DELICIOUS PICKLED MANGO AND HABANERO"

Looking for a spicy twist on your usual pickled fruit? This recipe combines the sweet and tangy flavors of mango with the heat of habanero peppers for a truly unique and flavorful pickle. Perfect for adding to sandwiches, charcuterie boards, or just snacking on straight from the ball jar.

---

4 mangoes, peeled and sliced

4 habanero peppers, seeded and thinly sliced

1 cup white vinegar

1 cup water

1/2 cup sugar

1 tbsp salt

4 cloves garlic, minced

4 sprigs fresh cilantro

1. In a small saucepan, combine the vinegar, water, sugar, and salt. Bring to a boil, stirring occasionally, until the sugar and salt have dissolved.

2. Pack the sliced mangoes and habanero peppers into a clean and sterilized ball jar.

3. Add the minced garlic and cilantro sprigs to the jar.

4. Pour the hot vinegar mixture over the fruit and peppers, making sure to completely cover them.

5. Place the lid on the jar and let cool to room temperature.

6. Once cooled, store in the refrigerator for at least 24 hours before serving to allow the flavors to develop. The pickled mango and habanero will keep in the refrigerator for up to 2 weeks. Enjoy!

"TROPICAL BLISS PICKLED MANGO AND LIME"

This recipe combines the sweet and tangy flavors of mango and lime to create a unique and refreshing pickled fruit. Perfect as a topping for tacos, a garnish for cocktails, or as a snack on its own.

---

2 mangoes, peeled and sliced
1 cup water
1 cup white vinegar
1/2 cup sugar
1/2 cup lime juice
1 tablespoon salt
2 cloves garlic, minced
2 small chili peppers, sliced
4 sprigs fresh cilantro
1 ball jar

1. In a small saucepan, bring the water, vinegar, sugar, lime juice, and salt to a boil. Stir until the sugar and salt are dissolved.
2. Place the mango slices, garlic, chili peppers, and cilantro sprigs in the ball jar.
3. Pour the hot liquid over the mango mixture, making sure to fully cover the fruit.
4. Secure the lid on the jar and let it cool to room temperature.
5. Place the jar in the refrigerator for at least 24 hours before serving to allow the flavors to meld.
6. Enjoy the pickled mango and lime as a topping for tacos, a garnish for cocktails, or as a snack on its own.

"TROPICAL BLISS PICKLED MANGO AND LIME"

This recipe combines the sweet and tangy flavors of mango and lime to create a unique and refreshing pickled fruit. Perfect as a topping for tacos, a garnish for cocktails, or as a snack on its own.

---

2 mangoes, peeled and sliced
1 cup water
1 cup white vinegar
1/2 cup sugar
1/2 cup lime juice
1 tablespoon salt
2 cloves garlic, minced
2 small chili peppers, sliced
4 sprigs fresh cilantro
1 ball jar

1. In a small saucepan, bring the water, vinegar, sugar, lime juice, and salt to a boil. Stir until the sugar and salt are dissolved.
2. Place the mango slices, garlic, chili peppers, and cilantro sprigs in the ball jar.
3. Pour the hot liquid over the mango mixture, making sure to fully cover the fruit.
4. Secure the lid on the jar and let it cool to room temperature.
5. Place the jar in the refrigerator for at least 24 hours before serving to allow the flavors to meld.
6. Enjoy the pickled mango and lime as a topping for tacos, a garnish for cocktails, or as a snack on its own.

"TROPICAL BLISS PICKLED MANGO AND MINT"

This recipe is a unique twist on traditional pickles, featuring the sweetness of mango and the freshness of mint. The combination creates a burst of flavor that is perfect for any summer barbecue or backyard gathering.

---

2 mangoes, peeled and sliced
1 cup water
1 cup white vinegar
1/2 cup sugar
1/2 cup lime juice
1 tablespoon salt
2 cloves garlic, minced
2 small chili peppers, sliced
4 sprigs fresh cilantro
1 ball jar

1. In a medium saucepan, combine water, vinegar, sugar, and salt. Bring to a boil over medium heat, stirring until the sugar and salt have dissolved.
2. Divide the mango slices and mint leaves evenly among the four ball jars.
3. Pour the hot pickling liquid over the mango and mint in the jars, making sure to fully cover the ingredients.
4. Close the jars tightly and let them cool to room temperature.
5. Once cooled, store the jars in the refrigerator for at least 24 hours before serving. The pickled mango and mint will keep in the refrigerator for up to two weeks.
6. Serve as a unique and refreshing condiment on sandwiches, tacos, or as a topping for grilled meats. Enjoy!

ZESTY PICKLED MANGO WITH MUSTARD SEED"

Pickled mango is a sweet and tangy addition to any meal, and the added mustard seeds give it a nice kick of flavor. This recipe is perfect for using up ripe mangoes and adding some unique flavor to your meals.

---

3 mangoes, peeled and thinly sliced
1 cup vinegar (white or apple cider)
1 cup water
1/2 cup sugar
2 tablespoons mustard seeds
1 tablespoon salt
1/2 teaspoon red pepper flakes (optional)

1. Combine the vinegar, water, sugar, mustard seeds, salt, and red pepper flakes (if using) in a small saucepan. Bring to a boil, stirring to dissolve the sugar.
2. Place the mango slices in a large ball jar. Pour the hot pickling liquid over the mangoes, making sure to cover them completely.
3. Seal the jar and let it sit at room temperature for at least 24 hours before transferring to the refrigerator. The pickled mango will be ready to enjoy after 48 hours, and will keep in the refrigerator for up to 1 month.
4. Serve as a condiment with sandwiches, in salads, or as a topping for grilled meat or tofu. Enjoy!

"TROPICAL TWIST PICKLED MANGO AND ONION RELISH"

This pickled mango and onion relish is the perfect blend of sweet and tangy flavors. The mango adds a tropical twist to the traditional pickled onion, making it a unique and delicious addition to any dish.

2 mangoes, peeled and diced

1 large onion, thinly sliced

1 cup apple cider vinegar

1/2 cup sugar

1 teaspoon salt

1/2 teaspoon black peppercorns

1/2 teaspoon mustard seeds

1/2 teaspoon coriander seeds

1/4 teaspoon cumin seeds

1/4 teaspoon red pepper flakes (optional for added heat)

1. Combine the mango and onion in a large bowl.
2. In a small saucepan, bring the apple cider vinegar, sugar, salt, peppercorns, mustard seeds, coriander seeds, cumin seeds, and red pepper flakes (if using) to a boil. Stir to dissolve the sugar.
3. Pour the hot vinegar mixture over the mango and onion mixture and stir to combine.
4. Transfer the pickled mango and onion relish to a clean ball jar, making sure to pack it down well.
5. Close the jar tightly and let it cool to room temperature.
6. Once cooled, store the jar in the refrigerator for at least 24 hours before serving to allow the flavors to fully develop. The pickled mango and onion relish will keep in the refrigerator for up to 2 weeks.
7. Serve the pickled mango and onion relish as a condiment for sandwiches, burgers, or grilled meats. It can also be used as a topping for salads, tacos, or bowls. Enjoy!

"TROPICAL THYME PICKLED MANGO"

This recipe combines the sweet and tangy flavors of mango with the floral and herbaceous notes of thyme for a unique and refreshing pickle. Perfect for topping salads, sandwiches, or even adding to a cheese board.

2 cups mango, peeled and thinly sliced

1 cup white vinegar

1 cup water

1/2 cup sugar

1 tablespoon salt

1 tablespoon thyme leaves

1 ball jar (16 ounces)

1. In a small saucepan, combine the vinegar, water, sugar, and salt. Bring to a boil, stirring to dissolve the sugar and salt.
2. Place the mango slices in the ball jar, packing them in tightly.
3. Pour the vinegar mixture over the mango slices, making sure they are fully submerged.
4. Add the thyme leaves to the jar.
5. Tightly seal the jar and let cool to room temperature.
6. Refrigerate the pickled mango for at least 2 hours before serving. The mango will keep in the refrigerator for up to 1 month. Enjoy!

"SWEET AND TANGY PICKLED CUCUMBERS"

Growing up, my grandma always had a jar of pickled cucumbers in her pantry. She called them "sour pickles" and they were always a hit at family gatherings. These pickled cucumbers have a twist with the addition of maple syrup and mustard, adding a sweet and tangy flavor. Perfect for topping sandwiches or eating on their own as a snack.

1 large cucumber, thinly sliced
1/4 cup white vinegar
2 tablespoons maple syrup
1 tablespoon yellow mustard
1 teaspoon salt
1/2 teaspoon black pepper

1. Start by sterilizing a ball jar and lid. Place them in a large pot of boiling water for 10 minutes. Remove from the water and set aside to cool.
2. In a small saucepan, combine the vinegar, maple syrup, mustard, salt, and pepper. Bring to a simmer over medium heat.
3. Place the thinly sliced cucumbers in the sterilized ball jar.
4. Pour the vinegar mixture over the cucumbers, making sure they are fully covered.
5. Close the ball jar tightly and place in the refrigerator for at least 24 hours before serving. These pickled cucumbers will last for up to 2 weeks in the refrigerator. Enjoy!

"GARLIC MUSHROOM PICKLE"

Introducing our "Garlic Mushroom Pickle," the perfect addition to any charcuterie board or as a topping for your favorite sandwich. This recipe features fresh mushrooms and cloves of garlic, pickled in a mixture of vinegar and spices. The result is a tangy, savory treat that is sure to impress your guests.

1-pound fresh mushrooms, sliced
6 cloves garlic, peeled and thinly sliced
1 cup white vinegar
1 cup water
1 tablespoon sugar
1 tablespoon pickling salt
1 teaspoon black peppercorns
1 teaspoon mustard seeds
1 ball jar with lid

1. In a small saucepan, combine the vinegar, water, sugar, pickling salt, peppercorns, and mustard seeds. Bring to a boil over medium heat, stirring occasionally.

2. Place the sliced mushrooms and garlic in the ball jar. Pour the hot vinegar mixture over the top, making sure to completely cover the mushrooms and garlic.

3. Secure the lid on the jar and let it cool to room temperature. Once cooled, place the jar in the refrigerator for at least 24 hours before serving.

4. The pickled mushrooms and garlic will keep in the refrigerator for up to one month. Enjoy on sandwiches, charcuterie boards, or as a flavorful addition to any dish.

DELICIOUS PICKLED MUSHROOM AND LEMON RECIPE

This recipe is perfect for those who love the combination of tangy and savory flavors. The pickled mushrooms are a great addition to any salad or sandwich, and the lemon adds a refreshing twist to the dish. Plus, it's easy to make and can be stored in a ball jar for later use.

1-pound mushrooms, sliced

1 lemon, thinly sliced

1 cup white vinegar

1 cup water

2 tablespoons sugar

1 tablespoon salt

1 teaspoon black peppercorns

1 bay leaf

2 cloves garlic, minced

1. In a small saucepan, combine the vinegar, water, sugar, salt, peppercorns, bay leaf, and garlic. Bring to a boil and then reduce the heat to a simmer.

2. Place the sliced mushrooms and lemon slices in a clean, sterilized ball jar.

3. Pour the hot pickling liquid over the mushrooms and lemon slices, making sure they are completely covered.

4. Let the jar sit at room temperature for 30 minutes to allow the flavors to meld.

5. Place the jar in the refrigerator to chill for at least 2 hours before serving. The pickled mushrooms and lemon will keep for up to 2 weeks in the refrigerator. Enjoy!

"HEARTY AND FLAVORFUL PICKLED MUSHROOM AND ONION RELISH"

This pickled mushroom and onion relish is a perfect addition to any sandwich or charcuterie board. The combination of earthy mushrooms and sweet onions is enhanced by the tangy vinegar and spices. It's a delicious and unique condiment that's sure to impress.

1-pound mushrooms, sliced

1 medium onion, thinly sliced

1 cup vinegar

1/2 cup sugar

1 teaspoon salt

1/2 teaspoon mustard seeds

1/2 teaspoon celery seeds

1/2 teaspoon black peppercorns

1. In a medium saucepan, combine the vinegar, sugar, salt, mustard seeds, celery seeds, and black peppercorns. Bring to a boil and stir until the sugar has dissolved.

2. Place the sliced mushrooms and onions in a ball jar or other glass jar.

3. Pour the hot vinegar mixture over the mushrooms and onions, making sure they are fully covered.

4. Let the jar cool to room temperature, then seal and refrigerate for at least 2 hours before serving. The relish will keep for up to 2 weeks in the refrigerator.

5. Serve the pickled mushroom and onion relish on sandwiches, as a topping for burgers or hot dogs, or as a condiment for grilled meats. Enjoy!

"ROSEMARY-INFUSED PICKLED MUSHROOMS"

Growing up, my grandfather was always tinkering in the kitchen and experimenting with different flavors. One of his signature dishes was these pickled mushrooms infused with the woodsy, aromatic flavor of rosemary. They're perfect as a snack on their own or added to sandwiches and salads for a burst of tangy flavor.

1-pound small mushrooms
1 cup apple cider vinegar
1 cup water
2 tablespoons sugar
1 tablespoon salt
4 sprigs fresh rosemary
2 cloves garlic, minced
1 bay leaf
1 teaspoon peppercorns
1 small ball jar

1. Clean and trim the mushrooms.
2. In a small saucepan, combine the vinegar, water, sugar, salt, rosemary, garlic, bay leaf, and peppercorns. Bring to a boil, stirring until the sugar and salt have dissolved.
3. Pack the mushrooms tightly into the ball jar.
4. Pour the hot vinegar mixture over the mushrooms, making sure they are completely covered.
5. Let the jar sit at room temperature for at least 2 hours, or until the mushrooms have cooled completely.
6. Place the jar in the refrigerator and let the mushrooms pickle for at least 3 days before serving. The pickled mushrooms will keep in the refrigerator for up to 3 weeks. Enjoy!

SAVORY AND SUCCULENT PICKLED MUSHROOMS WITH THYME"

This recipe is inspired by my love for pickled vegetables and the desire to add a unique twist to the classic pickled mushroom. The combination of thyme and mushrooms creates a delicious and aromatic flavor that is perfect for a snack or topping on a salad.

1-pound mushrooms, sliced

1 cup white vinegar

1 cup water

2 tablespoons sugar

1 tablespoon salt

1 teaspoon thyme

2 cloves garlic, minced

1 bay leaf

1 ball jar with a lid

1. In a small saucepan, combine the vinegar, water, sugar, salt, thyme, garlic, and bay leaf. Bring to a boil, stirring occasionally.

2. In the meantime, prepare the mushrooms by slicing them into desired thickness.

3. Once the vinegar mixture has come to a boil, add the mushrooms to the ball jar.

4. Pour the vinegar mixture over the mushrooms, making sure to completely cover them.

5. Close the ball jar with the lid and let it sit at room temperature for at least 24 hours before placing it in the refrigerator.

6. The pickled mushrooms can be eaten immediately or stored in the refrigerator for up to 2 weeks. Enjoy as a snack or topping on a salad.

"SAVORY AND SASSY PICKLED MUSHROOMS"

Growing up, my grandma would always keep a jar of pickled mushrooms in the fridge. They were the perfect addition to a summertime sandwich or a cheese platter at a party. This recipe is my spin on her classic pickled mushrooms, with a little added kick from red pepper flakes and garlic.

1 lb. fresh mushrooms, sliced
1 cup white vinegar
1 cup water
2 tbsp. sugar
1 tsp. salt
1 tsp. red pepper flakes
2 cloves garlic, minced
2 sprigs fresh dill

1. In a small saucepan, combine vinegar, water, sugar, salt, red pepper flakes, and garlic. Bring to a boil, stirring until sugar and salt are dissolved.
2. Place mushrooms in a clean, sterilized ball jar. Pour the hot vinegar mixture over the mushrooms, making sure they are fully submerged.
3. Add in the fresh dill sprigs.
4. Place the lid on the jar and allow the mushrooms to cool completely before refrigerating.
5. Let the mushrooms marinate in the fridge for at least 24 hours before enjoying. These pickled mushrooms will last for up to 2 weeks in the fridge.

"ZESTY MUSTARD AND ONION RELISH FOR ALL YOUR BARBECUE NEEDS"

This pickled mustard and onion relish is the perfect condiment for any barbecue or cookout. The tangy mustard pairs perfectly with the sweet and slightly spicy onions, creating a flavor that is sure to be a hit with your guests. This recipe is easy to follow and only requires a few simple ingredients that you likely already have in your pantry.

---

1 cup yellow mustard seeds
1 cup white vinegar
1/2 cup sugar
1/4 cup diced onions
1 teaspoon salt
1/2 teaspoon red pepper flakes (optional)

1. In a small saucepan, combine the mustard seeds, vinegar, sugar, onions, salt, and red pepper flakes (if using). Bring to a boil over medium heat, stirring frequently.
2. Reduce heat to low and simmer for 5 minutes, or until the onions are soft and the mustard seeds have absorbed some of the vinegar.
3. Remove from heat and let cool for a few minutes.
4. Pour the mixture into a clean ball jar and seal with a lid.
5. Let the pickled mustard and onion relish sit in the refrigerator for at least 24 hours before serving to allow the flavors to meld together.
6. Serve as a condiment for your favorite barbecue dishes or use as a topping for sandwiches and burgers. Enjoy!

"SUMMER IN A JAR: PICKLED NECTARINE AND ROSEMARY"

As the summer sun beats down, there's nothing like a refreshing pickle to cool you off. These pickled nectarines are a delicious twist on traditional pickles, with the added herbaceous kick of rosemary. Perfect for snacking on or adding to a charcuterie board, these pickled nectarines are sure to be a hit.

4 nectarines, sliced

1 cup white vinegar

1 cup water

1/2 cup sugar

2 sprigs fresh rosemary

1 teaspoon salt

1. In a small saucepan, bring the vinegar, water, sugar, and salt to a boil. Stir until the sugar and salt are dissolved.
2. Place the sliced nectarines and rosemary sprigs in a clean ball jar.
3. Pour the hot vinegar mixture over the nectarines, making sure they are fully covered.
4. Seal the jar and let it cool to room temperature.
5. Place the jar in the refrigerator for at least 24 hours before serving. The pickled nectarines will keep in the refrigerator for up to 2 weeks.

"SWEET AND SAVORY PICKLED NECTARINE AND THYME"

Looking for a unique and tasty addition to your charcuterie board? These pickled nectarines with a hint of thyme will impress your guests. The combination of the sweet fruit and the savory herb creates a balance of flavors that is sure to be a hit. Plus, the pretty pink color of the nectarines makes for a beautiful presentation in a ball jar.

---

3 nectarines, sliced into wedges
1 cup white vinegar
1 cup water
1/2 cup sugar
2 sprigs of thyme
1 tablespoon salt
1 teaspoon peppercorns
1 cinnamon stick (optional)

1. In a small saucepan, combine the vinegar, water, sugar, salt, peppercorns, and cinnamon stick (if using). Bring to a boil, stirring occasionally, until the sugar has dissolved.
2. Place the nectarine wedges and thyme sprigs in a clean ball jar.
3. Pour the hot vinegar mixture over the nectarines, making sure to fully cover them.
4. Let the jar cool to room temperature, then seal and refrigerate for at least 2 hours before serving. The pickled nectarines will keep in the refrigerator for up to 2 weeks.
5. Serve the pickled nectarines as a snack or use them to add a pop of flavor to sandwiches and salads. Enjoy!

"VANILLA-INFUSED PICKLED NECTARINES"

This recipe combines the sweetness of nectarines with the subtle flavor of vanilla to create a unique and delicious pickled fruit. Perfect for adding a little something special to your charcuterie board or as a topping for ice cream or cheesecake.

---

4 nectarines, quartered and pits removed
1 cup white vinegar
1 cup water
1/2 cup sugar
1 vanilla bean, split and seeds scraped
2 cinnamon sticks
4 cloves
4 allspice berries
4 ball jars with lids

1. In a small saucepan, combine the vinegar, water, sugar, vanilla bean and seeds, cinnamon sticks, cloves, and allspice berries. Bring to a boil over medium heat, stirring occasionally, until the sugar has dissolved.

2. Place the nectarine quarters in the ball jars, packing them in tightly.

3. Pour the hot pickling liquid over the nectarines, filling the jars to the top.

4. Secure the lids on the ball jars and allow the nectarines to cool to room temperature.

5. Once cooled, transfer the jars to the refrigerator and allow the nectarines to pickle for at least 24 hours before serving.

6. The pickled nectarines will last for up to 2 weeks in the refrigerator. Enjoy as a unique addition to your charcuterie board or as a topping for ice cream or cheesecake.

"ZESTY PICKLED OKRA"

Pickled okra is a southern classic that adds a tangy and crunchy element to any dish. It's the perfect addition to a charcuterie board or as a topping for burgers and sandwiches. This recipe uses a mixture of vinegar, sugar, and spices to create a zesty brine that perfectly preserves the crisp texture of the okra.

1-pound fresh okra

1 cup white vinegar

1 cup water

2 tablespoons sugar

1 teaspoon salt

1 teaspoon mustard seeds

1 teaspoon coriander seeds

1/2 teaspoon red pepper flakes (optional for added heat)

2 cloves garlic, thinly sliced

2 sprigs fresh dill

1. Wash and dry the okra, removing the stem end.
2. In a small saucepan, combine the vinegar, water, sugar, salt, mustard seeds, coriander seeds, and red pepper flakes (if using). Bring to a boil over medium heat, stirring until the sugar and salt have dissolved.
3. Pack the okra, garlic slices, and dill sprigs into a sterilized ball jar.
4. Carefully pour the hot brine over the okra, making sure to cover the vegetables completely.
5. Close the jar tightly and let it cool to room temperature.
6. Once cooled, place the jar in the refrigerator and let it sit for at least 24 hours before serving. The okra will keep in the refrigerator for up to 2 weeks. Enjoy!

"SUN-KISSED TOMATO SAUCE"

"Sun-Kissed Tomato Sauce" This recipe for homemade tomato sauce is a great way to use up a bounty of fresh tomatoes from the garden. By preserving them in a ball jar, you can enjoy the taste of summer all year round.

---

2 lbs ripe tomatoes
1 small onion, diced
2 cloves garlic, minced
1 tbsp olive oil
1 tsp salt
1 tsp sugar
1 tsp dried basil
1 tsp dried oregano

1. Wash and slice the tomatoes into quarters.
2. Heat the olive oil in a large pot over medium heat. Add the diced onion and minced garlic and cook until the onion is translucent.
3. Add the sliced tomatoes to the pot and bring to a simmer. Cook for about 10 minutes, or until the tomatoes are soft and beginning to break down.
4. Using a blender or immersion blender, puree the tomato mixture until smooth.
5. Add the salt, sugar, basil, and oregano to the pot and stir to combine.
6. Bring the tomato sauce back to a simmer and cook for an additional 5 minutes.
7. Ladle the tomato sauce into clean, sterilized ball jars, leaving about 1/2 inch of headspace.
8. Process the jars in a boiling water bath for 35 minutes. Remove the jars from the water bath and let them cool completely before storing in a cool, dark place.

"SPICY PICKLED OKRA"

Pickled okra is a southern classic that adds a tangy and spicy kick to any dish. This recipe uses a mixture of vinegar, water, and spices to create a flavorful brine for the okra to soak in. The result is a delicious and addictive snack that is perfect for serving at BBQs or enjoying as a tasty addition to a sandwich or salad.

1-pound fresh okra, washed and trimmed

1 cup white vinegar

1 cup water

2 tablespoons sugar

1 tablespoon salt

1 teaspoon red pepper flakes

1 teaspoon mustard seeds

1 teaspoon coriander seeds

4 garlic cloves, thinly sliced

4 small, dried chili peppers (optional)

1. Sterilize a large ball jar by boiling it in a pot of water for 10 minutes.

2. In a small saucepan, combine the vinegar, water, sugar, salt, red pepper flakes, mustard seeds, coriander seeds, garlic, and chili peppers (if using). Bring to a boil over high heat, stirring to dissolve the sugar and salt.

3. Place the okra in the sterilized ball jar, making sure to pack them in tightly. Pour the hot brine over the okra, filling the jar to the top.

4. Let the jar cool to room temperature, then seal with a lid and refrigerate for at least 24 hours before serving. The okra will keep in the refrigerator for up to 1 month. Enjoy!

"ZESTY PICKLED OKRA WITH CORIANDER"

Pickling is a great way to preserve vegetables and add flavor to them at the same time. These pickled okra with coriander is the perfect combination of tangy and spicy, and they're sure to be a hit at any party or as a snack on their own.

1 pound okra

1 tablespoon coriander seeds

2 cloves garlic, minced

1 teaspoon red pepper flakes

1 cup white vinegar

1 cup water

2 tablespoons sugar

1 tablespoon kosher salt

1 ball jar with a lid

1. Wash the okra and trim the stem ends.
2. In a small pan, toast the coriander seeds over medium heat for 1-2 minutes until fragrant.
3. In a small saucepan, combine the vinegar, water, sugar, salt, toasted coriander seeds, garlic, and red pepper flakes. Bring to a boil, stirring until the sugar and salt are dissolved.
4. Pack the okra into the ball jar, leaving about 1 inch of headspace at the top.
5. Pour the hot pickling liquid over the okra, making sure to cover the okra completely.
6. Place the lid on the ball jar and let it cool to room temperature. Once cooled, store the jar in the refrigerator for at least 24 hours before serving to allow the flavors to develop. The pickled okra will keep in the refrigerator for up to 2 weeks. Enjoy!

"SPICY PICKLED OKRA AND GARLIC"

Pickling okra is a great way to preserve the summer vegetable and add a tangy, spicy flavor to your dishes. These pickled okra and garlic are the perfect addition to a charcuterie board or can be used as a condiment for sandwiches and burgers. The combination of okra and garlic adds depth and complexity to the pickling liquid, making for a truly delicious pickle.

1-pound fresh okra, stemmed and cut into 1-inch pieces

6 cloves garlic, thinly sliced

1 cup white vinegar

1 cup water

2 tablespoons sugar

1 tablespoon salt

1 teaspoon red pepper flakes (optional for added heat)

1 teaspoon mustard seeds

1/2 teaspoon coriander seeds

1. Wash and sterilize a 1-quart Ball jar and its lid.
2. In a medium saucepan, combine the vinegar, water, sugar, salt, and red pepper flakes (if using). Bring to a boil, stirring to dissolve the sugar and salt.
3. Add the okra, garlic, mustard seeds, coriander seeds, fennel seeds, and peppercorns to the Ball jar. Pour the hot vinegar mixture over the top, making sure to fully cover the okra and garlic.
4. Place the lid on the Ball jar and let it cool to room temperature.
5. Once cooled, store the jar in the refrigerator for at least 24 hours before serving to allow the flavors to fully develop. The pickled okra and garlic will last for several weeks in the refrigerator. Enjoy!

ZESTY PICKLED OKRA AND ONION RELISH"

This pickled okra and onion relish is the perfect accompaniment to any barbecue or southern-style meal. The combination of pickled okra, onions, and spices creates a zesty and flavorful condiment that is sure to impress. It's also incredibly easy to make and can be stored in a ball jar in the refrigerator for up to a month.

1-pound fresh okra, trimmed and sliced into 1/4 inch rounds

1 large onion, thinly sliced

1 cup apple cider vinegar

1 cup water

1 tablespoon sugar

1 teaspoon salt

1/2 teaspoon red pepper flakes

1/2 teaspoon mustard seeds

1/2 teaspoon celery seeds

4 garlic cloves, minced

4 sprigs fresh dill

1. In a medium saucepan, combine the vinegar, water, sugar, salt, red pepper flakes, mustard seeds, and celery seeds. Bring the mixture to a boil, stirring occasionally.

2. Add the okra, onions, and garlic to the saucepan. Reduce the heat to a simmer and cook for 5 minutes.

3. Remove the saucepan from the heat and add the dill sprigs. Let the mixture cool to room temperature.

4. Transfer the pickled okra and onion relish to a ball jar and seal the jar. Store in the refrigerator for at least 24 hours before serving to allow the flavors to fully develop.

5. Serve the pickled okra and onion relish with your favorite barbecue dishes or as a topping for burgers, sandwiches, or hot dogs. Enjoy!

"THYME-INFUSED PICKLED OKRA"

If you're a fan of southern cooking, you're probably familiar with pickled okra. It's a tasty snack that adds a tangy, crunchy bite to sandwiches, salads, and more. In this recipe, we'll take pickled okra to the next level by adding a hint of thyme for a unique and flavorful twist.

1-pound fresh okra

1 cup white vinegar

1 cup water

2 tablespoons sugar

1 tablespoon kosher salt

2 cloves garlic, minced

2 sprigs thyme

2-3 fresh chili peppers, optional (for a spicy kick)

1. Wash and dry the okra. Trim the stems and slice the okra into 1/4-inch rounds.

2. In a small saucepan, combine the vinegar, water, sugar, salt, garlic, thyme, and chili peppers (if using). Bring the mixture to a boil over medium heat, stirring occasionally to dissolve the sugar and salt.

3. Pack the sliced okra into a clean, sterilized ball jar. Pour the hot vinegar mixture over the okra, making sure to cover all the slices.

4. Seal the jar and let it sit at room temperature for at least 24 hours before refrigerating. The pickled okra will keep in the refrigerator for up to 3 months.

5. Serve the pickled okra as a snack or use it to add flavor and crunch to sandwiches, salads, and other dishes. Enjoy!

SPICY PICKLED OLIVES WITH CHILIES

There's nothing like a good ol' pickled olive to add some tang and bite to a dish. And when you add some heat with chilies, it takes things to the next level. These spicy pickled olives are perfect for adding to sandwiches, charcuterie boards, or as a snack on their own. Plus, they're super easy to make and can be stored in the pantry for months. Here's how to make them:

1-pound green olives, pitted

1 cup white vinegar

2 tablespoons sugar

2 cloves garlic, peeled and minced

1 teaspoon dried oregano

1 teaspoon dried thyme

2 dried chilies, such as chili de arbol or guajillo

1 teaspoon salt

1. In a small saucepan, combine the vinegar, sugar, garlic, oregano, thyme, chilies, and salt. Bring to a boil, then reduce the heat to low and simmer for 5 minutes.

2. Place the olives in a large jar, such as a Ball jar. Pour the hot vinegar mixture over the olives, making sure they are fully covered.

3. Let the jar cool to room temperature, then seal and store in the pantry for at least 1 week before serving. The olives will keep for several months in the pantry.

"ZESTY PICKLED OLIVES WITH CUMIN"

These pickled olives are the perfect addition to any charcuterie board or as a tangy topping for salads and sandwiches. The cumin adds a warm, earthy flavor that pairs well with the briny olives.

1 cup green olives, pitted

1 cup black olives, pitted

2 cloves garlic, thinly sliced

1 teaspoon cumin seeds

1 teaspoon coriander seeds

1/2 teaspoon red pepper flakes (optional)

1 cup white vinegar

1 cup water

2 tablespoons sugar

1 tablespoon salt

1. In a medium-sized pot, combine the vinegar, water, sugar, and salt. Bring to a boil, stirring until the sugar and salt have dissolved.

2. Place the olives, garlic, cumin seeds, coriander seeds, and red pepper flakes (if using) in a clean 1-quart Ball jar.

3. Pour the hot vinegar mixture over the olives, making sure to completely cover the olives.

4. Secure the lid on the Ball jar and let cool to room temperature.

5. Once cooled, refrigerate the jar for at least 24 hours before serving to allow the flavors to meld. The olives will keep in the refrigerator for up to 2 months. Enjoy!

"ZESTY PICKLED OLIVES WITH FRESH MINT"

These pickled olives are the perfect combination of salty, tangy, and refreshing. The addition of fresh mint adds a unique and bright flavor that will have you coming back for more. They are the perfect accompaniment to any charcuterie board or as a snack on their own.

1 cup green olives

1 cup black olives

1 cup white vinegar

1 cup water

2 tablespoons sugar

2 tablespoons salt

2 cloves garlic, minced

1 teaspoon peppercorns

1 sprig fresh mint

1. Wash and dry the olives.
2. In a small saucepan, combine the vinegar, water, sugar, salt, garlic, and peppercorns. Bring to a boil and stir until the sugar and salt are dissolved.
3. Place the olives in a clean and sterilized ball jar.
4. Pour the hot vinegar mixture over the olives, making sure to cover them completely.
5. Add the sprig of fresh mint to the jar.
6. Close the jar tightly and let it cool to room temperature.
7. Once cooled, place the jar in the refrigerator for at least 24 hours before serving. The olives will keep in the refrigerator for up to 2 months. Enjoy!

"ZESTY MUSTARD PICKLED OLIVES"

These pickled olives are the perfect addition to any charcuterie board or antipasto platter. The mustard seeds add a pop of flavor that pairs well with the briny olives. Plus, they're super easy to make and can be stored in a ball jar for up to 3 months in the refrigerator.

---

1 cup green olives, pitted

1 cup black olives, pitted

1 cup white vinegar

1 cup water

2 tablespoons mustard seeds

2 cloves garlic, minced

1 teaspoon dried oregano

1 teaspoon dried thyme

1 teaspoon sea salt

1. In a small saucepan, combine the vinegar, water, mustard seeds, garlic, oregano, thyme, and salt. Bring to a boil, then reduce heat to a simmer.

2. Add the olives to a large ball jar.

3. Pour the vinegar mixture over the olives in the jar, making sure to cover the olives completely.

4. Allow the jar to cool to room temperature, then cover and refrigerate for at least 24 hours before serving.

5. The olives will keep in the refrigerator for up to 3 months. Enjoy as a snack or use as a garnish for cocktails and other dishes.

"ZESTY PICKLED OLIVES WITH A KICK OF OREGANO"

These pickled olives are the perfect addition to any Mediterranean inspired meal. The brine is infused with oregano and other aromatic spices, giving the olives a bold and flavorful taste. Plus, the added bonus of being able to store them in a ball jar means you can enjoy them for weeks to come.

1-pound green olives, pitted
1 cup white vinegar
1 cup water
2 tablespoons oregano
2 cloves garlic, minced
1 teaspoon red pepper flakes (optional for added heat)
1 tablespoon sugar
1 tablespoon salt

1. In a small saucepan, combine the vinegar, water, oregano, garlic, red pepper flakes, sugar, and salt. Bring to a boil, then reduce the heat and simmer for 5 minutes.
2. In a sterilized ball jar, add the pitted olives.
3. Pour the hot brine over the olives, making sure they are fully submerged.
4. Allow the jar to cool to room temperature, then seal and store in the refrigerator for at least 24 hours before serving. The olives will continue to develop flavor as they sit in the brine.
5. Serve the olives as a snack or add them to a salad or sandwich for a burst of flavor. Enjoy!

SPICY PICKLED OLIVES WITH PAPRIKA"

These spicy pickled olives are the perfect addition to any charcuterie board or as a tangy topping for salads and sandwiches. The combination of brine, paprika, and red pepper flakes give them a bold flavor that will definitely turn heads at your next gathering.

---

1 cup pitted green olives

1 cup pitted black olives

2 cups water

1 cup white vinegar

2 tablespoons paprika

1 teaspoon red pepper flakes

2 cloves garlic, minced

1 tablespoon sugar

1 teaspoon salt

1. In a medium saucepan, bring the water, vinegar, paprika, red pepper flakes, garlic, sugar, and salt to a boil over medium-high heat.
2. Place the olives in a large, sterilized ball jar.
3. Pour the hot brine mixture over the olives, making sure to cover them completely.
4. Let the jar cool to room temperature, then seal the jar and store it in the refrigerator for at least 24 hours before serving.
5. The olives will keep for up to 1 month in the refrigerator. Enjoy!

"CRISP AND FRESH PICKLED OLIVES WITH PARSLEY"

This recipe for pickled olives with parsley is a simple and delicious way to preserve olives and add a burst of flavor to your meals. The brine is flavored with garlic, red pepper flakes, and parsley, giving the olives a tangy and slightly spicy taste. These pickled olives are great as a snack on their own or added to salads, sandwiches, and more.

---

1 cup green olives, pitted

1 cup parsley leaves

3 cloves garlic, peeled and thinly sliced

1/2 teaspoon red pepper flakes

2 cups water

1 cup white vinegar

2 tablespoons kosher salt

1. Rinse the olives and parsley leaves under cold water and set aside.
2. In a small saucepan, bring the water, vinegar, and salt to a boil.
3. In a clean and sterilized ball jar, layer the olives, parsley, garlic, and red pepper flakes.
4. Once the brine has come to a boil, carefully pour it over the ingredients in the jar, making sure to cover the olives and parsley completely.
5. Secure the lid on the jar and let it cool to room temperature.
6. Once the jar has cooled, transfer it to the refrigerator and let the olives pickle for at least 3 days before enjoying. The olives will keep for up to 1 month in the refrigerator.

"ZESTY ROSEMARY OLIVE PICKLE"

Looking for a unique twist on classic pickled olives? This recipe combines the briny flavor of olives with the fresh, woodsy taste of rosemary for a delicious and sophisticated snack.

1 cup olives, pitted
1/4 cup white vinegar
1/4 cup water
1 tablespoon sugar
1 tablespoon salt
2 sprigs fresh rosemary

1. In a small saucepan, combine the vinegar, water, sugar, and salt. Bring to a boil, stirring until the sugar and salt have dissolved.

2. Place the olives and rosemary sprigs in a clean ball jar.

3. Pour the hot vinegar mixture over the olives, making sure they are fully submerged.

4. Allow the jar to cool to room temperature, then seal and refrigerate for at least 24 hours before serving. The pickled olives will keep for up to 2 weeks in the refrigerator.

"SAGE-INFUSED PICKLED OLIVES"

These pickled olives are a tasty and unique addition to any charcuterie board or antipasto platter. The addition of sage adds a subtle, earthy flavor to the olives, making them stand out from traditional pickled olives. These can be made in a large batch and stored in a ball jar in the refrigerator for up to several months.

1 cup green olives, pitted

1 cup black olives, pitted

1 cup white vinegar

1 cup water

1 tablespoon salt

2 cloves garlic, minced

1 tablespoon fresh sage, chopped

1 teaspoon peppercorns

1 teaspoon mustard seeds

1. In a small saucepan, combine the vinegar, water, salt, garlic, sage, peppercorns, and mustard seeds. Bring to a boil over medium heat, stirring occasionally.

2. Add the olives to a large bowl. Pour the hot vinegar mixture over the olives and stir to combine.

3. Let the olives sit in the vinegar mixture for at least 2 hours, or overnight for the best flavor.

4. Using a slotted spoon, transfer the olives to a clean ball jar. Pour the vinegar mixture over the olives, making sure they are completely covered.

5. Close the jar tightly and refrigerate for at least 24 hours before serving. The olives will keep in the refrigerator for up to several months. Enjoy!

THYME-INFUSED PICKLED OLIVES"

Olives are a staple in many Mediterranean cuisines and adding a touch of thyme gives these pickled olives a unique and sophisticated flavor. They make a great addition to a cheese platter or as a tasty snack on their own.

1 cup green olives, pitted

1 cup black olives, pitted

1 sprig fresh thyme

1 cup white vinegar

1 cup water

1 tablespoon sugar

1 teaspoon salt

1. In a small saucepan, combine the vinegar, water, sugar, and salt. Bring to a boil and stir until the sugar and salt have dissolved.
2. Place the olives in a sterilized ball jar. Add the thyme sprig to the jar.
3. Pour the vinegar mixture over the olives, making sure they are fully covered.
4. Seal the jar and let it sit at room temperature for at least 24 hours before serving. The olives will keep for up to a month in the refrigerator. Enjoy!

"SPICY PICKLED ONIONS AND CHILIES"

If you love the tangy and spicy flavor of pickled onions and chilies, then this recipe is for you! It's the perfect addition to any Mexican dish, sandwich, or charcuterie board. And the best part is, it's so easy to make at home using a ball jar.

---

1 red onion, thinly sliced

1 jalapeno pepper, thinly sliced

1 red chili pepper, thinly sliced (optional)

1 garlic clove, thinly sliced

1/2 cup white vinegar

1/2 cup water

1 tablespoon sugar

1 teaspoon salt

1. In a small saucepan, combine the vinegar, water, sugar, and salt. Bring to a boil and stir until the sugar and salt are dissolved.

2. In a ball jar, layer the onions, jalapeno pepper, chili pepper, and garlic.

3. Pour the hot vinegar mixture over the onions and peppers, making sure to cover them completely.

4. Let the jar cool to room temperature, then seal and store in the refrigerator.

5. Allow the onions and peppers to pickle for at least 24 hours before serving. They will last for up to a month in the refrigerator.

Enjoy your spicy pickled onions and chilies on tacos, burritos, sandwiches, or as a tasty snack on their own!

"TROPICAL PICKLED PAPAYA WITH FRESH PARSLEY"

This pickled papaya recipe is the perfect balance of sweet and tangy, with a refreshing burst of parsley. It's a unique twist on traditional pickled vegetables and is great as a topping for tacos or sandwiches, or as a snack on its own.

1 small papaya, peeled and sliced into thin strips

1/2 cup white vinegar

1/2 cup water

1/4 cup sugar

1 tablespoon salt

1 bunch parsley, finely chopped

1 garlic clove, minced

1 teaspoon mustard seeds

1 teaspoon coriander seeds

In a small saucepan, combine the vinegar, water, sugar, and salt. Bring to a boil, stirring to dissolve the sugar and salt.

Place the papaya slices in a clean ball jar, and add the minced garlic, mustard seeds, and coriander seeds.

Pour the hot vinegar mixture over the papaya, making sure to cover the slices completely.

Let the jar cool to room temperature, then seal and refrigerate for at least 24 hours before serving. The pickled papaya will keep in the refrigerator for up to 1 week.

Just before serving, stir in the finely chopped parsley. Enjoy!

"TROPICAL TWIST PICKLED PAPAYA AND ONION RELISH"

This pickled papaya and onion relish is the perfect balance of sweet and tangy flavors. The papaya adds a unique tropical twist to this traditional pickled onion recipe, making it a standout condiment for any barbecue or picnic. Plus, it's easy to make and can be stored in a ball jar for future use.

1 large papaya, peeled and diced into small pieces

1 large red onion, thinly sliced

1 cup white vinegar

1 cup sugar

1 teaspoon salt

1 teaspoon mustard seeds

1 teaspoon coriander seeds

1/2 teaspoon black peppercorns

1. In a medium saucepan, combine the vinegar, sugar, salt, mustard seeds, coriander seeds, and black peppercorns. Bring to a boil over medium heat, stirring until the sugar is dissolved.

2. Add the diced papaya and sliced onion to the saucepan and stir to combine. Reduce the heat to low and simmer for 5 minutes.

3. Using a slotted spoon, transfer the papaya and onion to a ball jar. Pour the pickling liquid over the top, making sure to cover the vegetables completely.

4. Close the ball jar tightly and let it cool to room temperature. Once cooled, store the jar in the refrigerator for at least a few hours to allow the flavors to meld.

5. The pickled papaya and onion relish will keep in the refrigerator for up to 1 month. Enjoy as a condiment on sandwiches, burgers, or hot dogs, or as a topping for grilled meats or vegetables.

"SPICY PICKLED PAPAYA WITH CUMIN"

Pickling is a great way to preserve the flavor and crunch of fresh fruit, and this pickled papaya recipe is a unique and delicious twist on the traditional pickled cucumber. The combination of sweet, tangy papaya with warm, aromatic cumin is sure to be a hit with your taste buds. Plus, the beautiful pink color of the pickled papaya makes it a visually stunning addition to any plate.

---

1 medium papaya, peeled and sliced into thin wedges
1 cup white vinegar
1 cup water
1/2 cup sugar
2 teaspoons cumin seeds
2 teaspoons mustard seeds
1 tablespoon salt
4 cloves garlic, peeled and sliced
2 dried red chilies (optional)

1. In a small saucepan, combine the vinegar, water, sugar, cumin seeds, mustard seeds, salt, garlic, and chilies (if using). Bring to a boil, stirring occasionally to dissolve the sugar.
2. Place the papaya wedges in a clean, sterilized ball jar. Pour the hot pickling liquid over the papaya, making sure to cover the fruit completely.
3. Tightly seal the jar and let it sit at room temperature for at least 24 hours before serving. The pickled papaya will keep in the refrigerator for up to 2 weeks.
4. To serve, simply drain the pickled papaya and enjoy as a side dish or topping for sandwiches and salads.

TANGY PICKLED PAPAYA AND FENUGREEK"

This recipe combines the unique flavor of pickled papaya with the earthy, slightly bitter taste of fenugreek seeds. The result is a tangy and addictive condiment that is perfect for adding a burst of flavor to sandwiches, salads, and more. The best part? It's easy to make and can be stored in a ball jar for up to a month in the refrigerator.

---

1 small papaya, peeled and cut into thin slices
1/4 cup white vinegar
2 tablespoons sugar
1 teaspoon fenugreek seeds
1/2 teaspoon salt

1. In a small saucepan, bring the vinegar, sugar, and salt to a boil.
2. Add the fenugreek seeds and let the mixture simmer for a minute.
3. Remove the saucepan from the heat and let the mixture cool for a few minutes.
4. Place the papaya slices in a ball jar and pour the vinegar mixture over them.
5. Close the jar and refrigerate for at least 1 hour before serving. The pickled papaya will keep in the refrigerator for up to 1 month. Enjoy!

"SUN-KISSED ORANGE AND ONION RELISH"

This pickled orange zest and onion relish is the perfect combination of sweet and tangy flavors. It's a great addition to any sandwich or charcuterie board, and it's also delicious when paired with grilled meats or seafood. Plus, it's super easy to make and can be stored in the fridge for up to a month. So, let's get pickling!

---

1 orange, zested and juiced
1 small red onion, thinly sliced
1 cup white vinegar
1 cup water
1/2 cup sugar
1 tablespoon pickling spices
1 teaspoon salt

1. In a small saucepan, combine the orange juice, vinegar, water, sugar, pickling spices, and salt. Bring to a boil over medium heat, stirring until the sugar is dissolved.
2. Place the orange zest and onion slices in a clean, quart-sized ball jar. Pour the hot pickling liquid over the top, making sure to fully cover the orange zest and onion slices.
3. Let the jar cool to room temperature, then cover and refrigerate for at least 24 hours before serving. The relish will keep in the fridge for up to a month. Enjoy!

"CINNAMON-INFUSED PICKLED PAPAYA"

Looking for a unique twist on your traditional pickled vegetables? Try this recipe for pickled papaya with a hint of cinnamon. The combination of sweet and savory flavors will add a burst of flavor to any dish.

2 cups papaya, cut into bite-sized pieces

1 cup white vinegar

1 cup water

1/2 cup sugar

2 cinnamon sticks

1 teaspoon whole cloves

1 teaspoon whole allspice

1 teaspoon mustard seeds

1. In a small saucepan, combine the vinegar, water, and sugar. Bring to a boil, stirring until the sugar is dissolved.

2. Add the cinnamon sticks, cloves, allspice, and mustard seeds to the vinegar mixture.

3. Place the papaya pieces in a clean ball jar. Pour the vinegar mixture over the papaya, making sure to cover the pieces completely.

4. Close the ball jar tightly and place it in the refrigerator for at least 24 hours before serving. The pickled papaya will last for up to 2 weeks in the refrigerator.

5. Serve the pickled papaya as a topping for sandwiches, mixed into salads, or as a side dish. Enjoy!

"SUN-KISSED PICKLED ORANGES WITH THYME"

This recipe combines the bright, tangy flavor of pickled oranges with the earthy, aromatic notes of thyme. The result is a unique and flavorful condiment that is perfect for adding a burst of flavor to sandwiches, salads, or charcuterie boards. Plus, the beautiful golden color of the pickled oranges makes them a stunning addition to any dish.

---

4 medium oranges, thinly sliced

1 cup white vinegar

1 cup water

1/2 cup sugar

2 sprigs of fresh thyme

1 teaspoon salt

1 tablespoon whole black peppercorns

1 small, dried chili pepper (optional)

1. Begin by preparing your oranges. Using a sharp knife, slice the oranges as thinly as possible.
2. Next, combine the vinegar, water, sugar, salt, peppercorns, and chili pepper (if using) in a small saucepan. Bring the mixture to a boil, stirring occasionally to dissolve the sugar.
3. Once the mixture has come to a boil, add the thyme sprigs and orange slices to the pot.
4. Reduce the heat to a simmer and cook the oranges for 5-7 minutes, or until they have softened slightly.
5. Remove the pot from the heat and allow the oranges to cool in the pickling liquid for at least 30 minutes.
6. Once the oranges have cooled, transfer them to a clean ball jar along with the pickling liquid.
7. Seal the jar and store it in the refrigerator for at least 24 hours before serving to allow the flavors to fully develop.
8. The pickled oranges will keep in the refrigerator for up to 2 weeks. Enjoy!

"ZESTY PICKLED ORANGE AND ONION RELISH"

This colorful and vibrant relish is a unique twist on traditional pickle recipes. The combination of sweet oranges and tangy onions is sure to wake up your taste buds and add some zest to any dish. Plus, it's easy to make and can be stored in a ball jar for future use.

3 medium oranges, peeled and thinly sliced

1 medium onion, thinly sliced

1 cup white vinegar

1/2 cup granulated sugar

1 tsp salt

1 tsp mustard seeds

1/2 tsp coriander seeds

1/4 tsp red pepper flakes (optional for a little extra kick)

1. In a medium saucepan, combine the vinegar, sugar, salt, mustard seeds, coriander seeds, and red pepper flakes (if using). Bring to a boil over medium heat, stirring occasionally, until the sugar has dissolved.

2. Add the sliced oranges and onions to the saucepan and stir to combine. Reduce the heat to low and simmer for 5 minutes.

3. Remove the saucepan from the heat and let the mixture cool to room temperature.

4. Transfer the pickled orange and onion relish to a ball jar and seal it tightly. Store in the refrigerator for at least 24 hours before serving to allow the flavors to meld together.

5. Serve the pickled orange and onion relish as a condiment or use it to add flavor to sandwiches, salads, or any other dish that could use a little zing. Enjoy!

"SPICED ORANGE PICKLES WITH A HINT OF CINNAMON"

These pickled oranges are a unique and flavorful addition to any charcuterie board or as a condiment for grilled meats. The combination of orange and cinnamon gives these pickles a warm and cozy flavor, perfect for the colder months.

---

4 oranges, thinly sliced

2 cups white vinegar

1 cup water

1/2 cup sugar

2 cinnamon sticks

1 tablespoon whole cloves

1 tablespoon whole allspice

4 ball jars with lids

1. In a medium saucepan, combine the vinegar, water, sugar, cinnamon sticks, cloves, and allspice. Bring to a boil over medium-high heat, stirring until the sugar has dissolved.

2. Arrange the orange slices in the ball jars, packing them in tightly.

3. Carefully pour the hot vinegar mixture over the oranges in the jars, making sure to cover them completely.

4. Place the lids on the jars and let them cool to room temperature.

5. Once cooled, store the jars in the refrigerator for at least 3 days before serving to allow the flavors to fully develop. The pickles will keep in the refrigerator for up to 2 weeks. Enjoy!

PICKLED ORANGE AND CHILI: A SPICY AND SWEET TREAT

This pickled orange and chili recipe is a unique twist on traditional pickles. The combination of sweet oranges and spicy chili peppers creates a balance of flavors that is both refreshing and addictive. These pickles are perfect for adding a pop of flavor to sandwiches, salads, and more.

---

4 medium oranges, thinly sliced

2 jalapeno peppers, thinly sliced

1 red bell pepper, thinly sliced

1 cup white vinegar

1 cup water

1/2 cup sugar

1 tablespoon salt

1 tablespoon coriander seeds

1 tablespoon mustard seeds

1 tablespoon fennel seeds

1 bay leaf

1. Place the orange, jalapeno, and bell pepper slices in a large glass ball jar.
2. In a small saucepan, combine the vinegar, water, sugar, salt, coriander seeds, mustard seeds, fennel seeds, and bay leaf. Bring the mixture to a boil, stirring until the sugar and salt are dissolved.
3. Pour the hot liquid over the orange and pepper slices in the jar. Make sure the slices are completely covered with the liquid.
4. Close the jar tightly and let it sit at room temperature for at least 2 hours, or until the pickles are cooled to room temperature.
5. Transfer the jar to the refrigerator and let the pickles marinate for at least 24 hours before serving. The pickles will last for up to 2 weeks in the refrigerator. Enjoy!

"LUSCIOUS LEMON PRESERVES"

If you have an abundance of lemons, this recipe for lemon preserves is the perfect way to use them up and enjoy their bright, tangy flavor all year round. Spread it on toast, add a dollop to yogurt, or use it to flavor cakes and cookies. With just a few simple ingredients and a ball jar, you can easily make a batch of these luscious lemon preserves at home.

4 cups lemon slices, seeds removed
4 cups granulated sugar
4 tbsp lemon juice
1 tbsp butter

1. In a large saucepan, combine the lemon slices, sugar, and lemon juice. Cook over medium heat, stirring frequently, until the sugar has dissolved.

2. Bring the mixture to a boil, then reduce the heat to low and simmer for about 45 minutes, or until the lemon slices are translucent and the mixture has thickened. Stir in the butter.

3. Carefully ladle the lemon preserve into a sterilized ball jar, leaving about 1/2 inch of headspace. Wipe the rim of the jar with a clean cloth, then seal and let cool to room temperature.

4. Store the jar of lemon preserves in the refrigerator for up to 3 months. Enjoy!

"GARLICKY WHITE WINE PICKLED ONIONS"

These pickled onions are the perfect addition to any charcuterie board or sandwich. The white wine and garlic give them a unique and flavorful twist. Plus, they're super easy to make and can be stored in the fridge for weeks in a airtight ball jar.

1 large red onion, thinly sliced
1 cup white wine
1/2 cup white vinegar
2 cloves garlic, minced
1 tablespoon sugar
1 teaspoon salt
1 bay leaf

1. In a medium saucepan, combine the white wine, vinegar, sugar, salt, and bay leaf. Bring to a boil over medium heat, stirring until the sugar and salt have dissolved.
2. Add the sliced onions to the boiling liquid and stir to coat. Reduce the heat to low and simmer for 2-3 minutes, or until the onions have softened slightly.
3. Remove the saucepan from the heat and stir in the minced garlic.
4. Transfer the onions and pickling liquid to a clean ball jar. Make sure to press down on the onions to remove any air bubbles and ensure they are fully submerged in the liquid.
5. Seal the jar and place it in the fridge to cool completely. The onions will be ready to eat in about 24 hours, but they'll taste even better after a few days in the fridge.
6. Serve the pickled onions on a charcuterie board, in a sandwich, or as a topping for burgers or salads. Enjoy!

"GRANDMA'S TANGY PICKLED ONION RELISH"

This pickled onion relish recipe has been passed down in our family for generations. My grandma always used to make a big batch every summer, and we would enjoy it on burgers, sandwiches, and hot dogs all year round. The combination of sweet and tangy flavors is truly addictive!

---

2 cups thinly sliced onions
1 cup white vinegar
1 cup sugar
1 tsp salt
1 tsp mustard seeds
1 tsp celery seeds
1 tsp turmeric

1. In a small saucepan, combine the vinegar, sugar, salt, mustard seeds, celery seeds, and turmeric. Bring to a boil over medium heat, stirring to dissolve the sugar.

2. Place the sliced onions in a heat-resistant bowl. Pour the hot vinegar mixture over the onions and let sit for 10 minutes.

3. Transfer the onions and vinegar mixture to a sterilized ball jar. Make sure the onions are fully submerged in the vinegar mixture.

4. Seal the jar and let it cool to room temperature. Then store in the refrigerator for at least 24 hours before serving. The pickled onions will keep in the refrigerator for up to 3 months.

"ZESTY PICKLED ONIONS"

Pickled onions are a tangy and flavorful addition to any sandwich, salad, or charcuterie board. They are also incredibly easy to make at home with just a few simple ingredients and a trusty ball jar. This recipe combines red onions with white vinegar, sugar, and a blend of spices for a zesty and savory pickle.

---

1 red onion, thinly sliced

1 cup white vinegar

2 tbsp sugar

1 tsp salt

1 tsp mustard seeds

1 tsp coriander seeds

1 tsp peppercorns

1 bay leaf

1. Slice the red onion thinly and set aside.

2. In a small saucepan, combine the vinegar, sugar, salt, mustard seeds, coriander seeds, peppercorns, and bay leaf. Bring the mixture to a boil, stirring to dissolve the sugar.

3. Once the mixture is boiling, add the sliced onions to a clean and sterilized ball jar. Pour the hot vinegar mixture over the onions, making sure to fully cover the onions with liquid.

4. Secure the lid on the ball jar and allow the pickled onions to cool to room temperature. Once cooled, store the jar in the refrigerator for at least 24 hours before serving to allow the flavors to meld. The pickled onions will keep for up to 1 month in the refrigerator. Enjoy!

"ZESTY PICKLED ONIONS WITH THYME"

Pickled onions are a classic condiment that add a burst of flavor to any dish. These zesty pickled onions with thyme are the perfect addition to sandwiches, salads, and even as a topping for tacos. They are easy to make and can be stored in the refrigerator for up to a month. Plus, the combination of onion and thyme adds a unique and delicious twist to the traditional pickled onion.

1 large red onion, thinly sliced
1 cup white vinegar
1 cup water
2 tablespoons sugar
1 tablespoon salt
2 sprigs fresh thyme
1 ball jar with a tight-fitting lid

1. In a small saucepan, combine the vinegar, water, sugar, and salt. Bring to a boil over medium heat, stirring occasionally to dissolve the sugar and salt.
2. Once the mixture has come to a boil, add in the thyme sprigs.
3. Place the sliced onion in the ball jar.
4. Pour the hot vinegar mixture over the onions, making sure to completely cover the onions.
5. Secure the lid on the ball jar and let the onions cool to room temperature.
6. Once the onions have cooled, place the jar in the refrigerator. The onions will be ready to eat after 24 hours but will taste even better after a few days of marinating.
7. Enjoy the pickled onions as a condiment on sandwiches, salads, or as a topping for tacos. They will last in the refrigerator for up to a month.

"SPICY PICKLED ONIONS WITH SESAME SEEDS"

These pickled onions are the perfect addition to any sandwich or salad. The sesame seeds add a nutty flavor and the pickling process gives the onions a tangy, spicy kick. They're easy to make and can be stored in a ball jar for up to a month in the refrigerator.

---

1 large red onion, thinly sliced
1/4 cup white vinegar
1/4 cup water
1 tablespoon sugar
1 teaspoon salt
1/2 teaspoon red pepper flakes
1/2 teaspoon sesame seeds

1. In a small saucepan, combine the vinegar, water, sugar, salt, and red pepper flakes. Bring to a boil and stir until the sugar and salt have dissolved.
2. Place the sliced onions in a clean ball jar. Pour the hot vinegar mixture over the onions and add the sesame seeds.
3. Close the jar and let it cool to room temperature. Once cooled, store the jar in the refrigerator for at least 24 hours before serving. The onions will keep in the refrigerator for up to a month.
4. To serve, simply remove the onions from the jar and enjoy them as a topping on sandwiches, salads, or as a snack on their own.

"ZESTY PICKLED ONION AND PARSLEY"

Pickled onions are a staple in many cultures and add a tangy, flavorful twist to sand-wiches, salads, and more. This recipe combines pickled onions with fresh parsley for a bright and refreshing twist.

1 large red onion, thinly sliced
1 cup white vinegar
1 cup water
2 tablespoons sugar
1 teaspoon salt
1/2 teaspoon black peppercorns
2 sprigs fresh parsley
1 garlic clove, sliced

1. In a small saucepan, combine the vinegar, water, sugar, salt, and peppercorns. Bring to a boil over high heat, stirring to dissolve the sugar and salt.
2. Place the sliced onion and parsley in a clean, sterilized ball jar. Add the sliced garlic.
3. Pour the hot vinegar mixture over the onions and parsley, making sure to cover them completely.
4. Let the jar cool to room temperature, then seal and refrigerate for at least 24 hours before serving. The pickled onions will keep for up to 2 weeks in the refrigerator.
5. Serve the pickled onions on sandwiches, salads, or as a tangy condiment on their own. Enjoy!

PICKLED ONION AND MISO

Deliciously tangy and savory, these pickled onions are a perfect match for the rich and complex flavor of miso. They're easy to make and can be stored in the fridge for a quick snack or added to your favorite dishes for a burst of flavor.

---

1 large onion, sliced thinly
1 cup white vinegar
1 cup water
2 tablespoons sugar
2 tablespoons miso paste
1 teaspoon salt

1. In a small saucepan, combine the vinegar, water, sugar, miso paste, and salt. Bring to a boil over medium heat, stirring until the sugar and miso paste are dissolved.

2. Place the sliced onion in a clean, sterilized ball jar. Pour the hot vinegar mixture over the onions, making sure to completely cover them.

3. Let the jar cool to room temperature, then seal it with a lid and refrigerate for at least 2 hours. The longer the onions sit, the more flavorful they will become.

4. Serve the pickled onions as a topping for sandwiches or salads or enjoy them as a snack on their own. They will keep in the fridge for up to 1 month. Enjoy!

"SPICY PICKLED ONION AND LEMON"

This recipe for pickled onions and lemon is a tangy and spicy twist on a classic pickling technique. The combination of sweet onions and tart lemons is perfectly balanced by the addition of red pepper flakes and mustard seeds. These pickles are the perfect addition to sandwiches, salads, or as a topping for grilled meats.

---

1 large red onion, thinly sliced

1 lemon, thinly sliced

1 cup white vinegar

1 cup water

2 tablespoons sugar

1 teaspoon salt

1 teaspoon red pepper flakes

1 teaspoon mustard seeds

2 cloves garlic, minced

2 ball jars with lids

1. In a small saucepan, combine the vinegar, water, sugar, salt, red pepper flakes, and mustard seeds. Bring to a boil over medium heat, stirring occasionally until the sugar and salt have dissolved.
2. Meanwhile, divide the onion slices and lemon slices evenly between the two ball jars.
3. Once the brine has come to a boil, pour it over the onions and lemon slices in the ball jars.
4. Add a clove of minced garlic to each jar.
5. Close the lids tightly and let the jars cool to room temperature.
6. Once cooled, transfer the jars to the refrigerator and let them pickle for at least 24 hours before serving. The pickles will keep in the refrigerator for up to 3 weeks.

"ZESTY PICKLED ONIONS AND GARLIC"

Looking for a tangy and flavorful addition to your sandwiches or salads? These pickled onions and garlic are just the thing! The combination of red onions and garlic, pickled in a mixture of vinegar, sugar, and spices, adds a burst of flavor to any dish. Plus, they're super easy to make and can be stored in a ball jar in the refrigerator for several weeks. So, let's get pickling!

---

1 red onion, thinly sliced
4 cloves of garlic, thinly sliced
1 cup of white vinegar
1 tablespoon of sugar
1 teaspoon of salt
1 teaspoon of black peppercorns
1 bay leaf

1. Begin by sterilizing a medium-sized ball jar and its lid. Wash the jar and lid with hot, soapy water, then rinse and dry thoroughly. Place the jar and lid in a large pot of boiling water for at least 10 minutes to sterilize.

2. In a small saucepan, combine the vinegar, sugar, salt, peppercorns, and bay leaf. Heat over medium heat until the sugar has dissolved, stirring occasionally.

3. Remove the jar from the boiling water and carefully place the sliced onions and garlic inside. Pour the vinegar mixture over the onions and garlic, making sure to fully cover them.

4. Secure the lid on the jar and place it in the refrigerator to cool. The pickled onions and garlic will be ready to eat in about 24 hours, but they will taste even better if you let them sit for a week or so.

5. Enjoy your pickled onions and garlic on sandwiches, salads, or as a flavorful addition to any dish. They will keep in the refrigerator for several weeks.

DELICIOUSLY PICKLED PAPAYA AND RED PEPPER

There's nothing quite like the tangy and sweet flavor of pickled papaya and red pepper. And what better way to preserve them than by using a classic ball jar? This recipe is easy to follow and will result in a tasty condiment that you'll love to have on hand in your pantry.

1 medium papaya, peeled and sliced into 1/4-inch slices

1 red bell pepper, seeded and sliced into thin strips

1 cup white vinegar

1 cup water

1/2 cup sugar

1 tablespoon kosher salt

1 tablespoon mustard seeds

1 teaspoon red pepper flakes (optional)

1. In a medium saucepan, combine the vinegar, water, sugar, salt, mustard seeds, and red pepper flakes (if using). Bring to a boil, stirring until the sugar has dissolved.

2. Place the papaya and red pepper slices into a clean ball jar. Pour the hot pickling liquid over the top, making sure to fully cover the fruit and peppers.

3. Place the lid on the jar and let it cool to room temperature. Once cooled, store in the fridge for at least 3 days before using to allow the flavors to fully develop.

4. Serve as a condiment with sandwiches, burgers, or on top of salads. The pickled papaya and red pepper will last for up to 1 month in the fridge.

"TROPICAL PICKLED PAPAYA WITH THYME"

This pickled papaya recipe is a unique and delicious way to preserve the sweet, tropical flavors of papaya. The addition of thyme adds an earthy, aromatic touch that complements the fruit perfectly. Serve these pickled papayas as a garnish for cocktails, a topping for salads, or as an interesting addition to a cheese plate.

2 medium papayas, peeled and sliced into wedges

1 cup white vinegar

1 cup water

1/2 cup sugar

2 tablespoons thyme leaves

1 tablespoon salt

4 small ball jars with lids

1. In a small saucepan, combine the vinegar, water, sugar, thyme, and salt. Bring to a boil over medium heat, stirring occasionally, until the sugar has dissolved.

2. Meanwhile, divide the sliced papaya among the four ball jars.

3. Once the vinegar mixture has come to a boil, pour it over the papaya slices in the jars, filling the jars to the top.

4. Secure the lids on the jars and place them in the refrigerator for at least 24 hours before serving. The pickled papaya will keep in the refrigerator for up to 2 weeks.

PICKLED PAPAYA AND TURMERIC

If you're a fan of tropical flavors and colorful dishes, then this recipe is for you! The combination of sweet, juicy papaya and the warm, earthy flavor of turmeric creates a pickle that is both unique and delicious. These pickles are perfect for adding a burst of flavor to sandwiches, salads, or as a snack on their own.

1 medium papaya, peeled, seeded, and cut into 1/4-inch slices
1 cup distilled white vinegar
1 cup water
1/2 cup granulated sugar
2 teaspoons salt
1 tablespoon turmeric
1 tablespoon mustard seeds
1 cinnamon stick
4 whole cloves

1. In a medium saucepan, combine the vinegar, water, sugar, salt, turmeric, mustard seeds, cinnamon stick, and cloves. Bring to a boil over medium heat, stirring occasionally, until the sugar and salt have dissolved.

2. Place the papaya slices in a clean, sterilized ball jar. Pour the hot pickling liquid over the papaya slices, making sure to fully cover them.

3. Secure the lid on the ball jar and let the jar cool to room temperature. Once cooled, transfer the jar to the refrigerator and let the pickles sit for at least 24 hours before serving.

4. The pickled papaya will keep in the refrigerator for up to 3 months. Enjoy!

"ZESTY PICKLED PAPRIKA AND ONION RELISH"

This tangy and flavorful relish is a perfect addition to any sandwich or burger. The combination of sweet and spicy paprika, along with the crunch of the onions, make it a tasty condiment that's sure to be a hit at any barbecue or potluck.

2 cups paprika, finely chopped
1 cup onions, finely chopped
1 cup vinegar
1/2 cup sugar
1 tsp salt
1 tsp mustard seeds
1 tsp celery seeds

1. In a small saucepan, combine the paprika, onions, vinegar, sugar, salt, mustard seeds, and celery seeds.
2. Bring the mixture to a boil, then reduce the heat to a simmer.
3. Cook the mixture for 10-15 minutes, or until the onions are soft and the mixture has thickened slightly.
4. Allow the mixture to cool completely.
5. Once cooled, transfer the mixture to a clean ball jar.
6. Seal the jar and store in the refrigerator for up to 1 month.
7. Enjoy the relish on sandwiches, burgers, or as a topping for grilled chicken or pork.

"GRANDMA'S PICKLED PARSLEY AND ONION RELISH"

Growing up, my grandma always had a batch of this relish in her pantry. She would serve it on sandwiches, burgers, and even as a topping for baked potatoes. It adds a tangy, flavorful kick to any dish. Now, I like to keep a jar of it in my own pantry for those times when I'm feeling nostalgia for my grandma's cooking. Here's how you can make your own batch of pickled parsley and onion relish.

1 cup parsley, finely chopped
1 cup onion, finely chopped
1/2 cup vinegar
1/4 cup sugar
1/2 tsp salt
1/2 tsp black pepper

1. In a small saucepan, combine the vinegar, sugar, salt, and black pepper. Bring to a boil over medium heat, stirring constantly until the sugar has dissolved.
2. Place the parsley and onion in a clean ball jar.
3. Pour the vinegar mixture over the parsley and onion, making sure to completely cover them.
4. Place the lid on the ball jar and let it cool to room temperature.
5. Once the relish has cooled, store it in the fridge until ready to use. It will keep for up to 3 weeks.
6. Enjoy the relish on sandwiches, burgers, or as a topping for any dish you'd like to add some extra flavor to.

DELICIOUSLY PICKLED PARSNIP AND GARLIC

Growing up, my grandma always had a jar of pickled parsnips and garlic in her pantry. She would serve them as a tangy and crunchy side dish at family dinners, and they quickly became a favorite of mine. This recipe is a slightly adapted version of my grandma's classic pickle, and I hope you enjoy it as much as my family does!

1-pound parsnips, peeled and sliced into thin rounds

4 cloves garlic, peeled and sliced thin

1 cup white vinegar

1 cup water

2 tablespoons sugar

1 tablespoon kosher salt

1 teaspoon black peppercorns

1 teaspoon dill seeds

1 bay leaf

1. Prepare a large ball jar by sterilizing it in boiling water for at least 10 minutes.
2. In a medium saucepan, combine the vinegar, water, sugar, salt, peppercorns, dill seeds, and bay leaf. Bring to a boil over high heat, stirring to dissolve the sugar and salt.
3. Add the parsnip slices and garlic to the ball jar. Pour the hot vinegar mixture over the parsnips and garlic, making sure to cover them completely.
4. Place the lid on the ball jar and let it cool to room temperature. Once cooled, store the jar in the refrigerator for at least 24 hours before serving. The pickled parsnips and garlic will keep in the refrigerator for up to 2 weeks. Enjoy!

"ZESTY PICKLED PARSNIP AND ONION RELISH"

Growing up, my grandma always had a jar of pickled parsnip and onion relish on the shelf in her pantry. She would serve it up as a tangy condiment on sandwiches or as a topping for burgers and hot dogs. This recipe is my version of her classic, with a little extra kick from some spicy peppers.

---

3 parsnips, peeled and thinly sliced

1 large onion, thinly sliced

1 jalapeno pepper, thinly sliced

1 red bell pepper, thinly sliced

1/2 cup white vinegar

1/2 cup water

2 tablespoons sugar

1 tablespoon pickling salt

1 tablespoon mustard seeds

1 teaspoon celery seeds

1. Sterilize a ball jar by boiling it in hot water for 10 minutes.
2. In a medium saucepan, combine the vinegar, water, sugar, pickling salt, mustard seeds, celery seeds, and turmeric. Bring to a boil over medium heat, stirring occasionally.
3. Once the mixture is boiling, add the parsnips, onion, jalapeno, and red bell pepper. Return to a boil, then remove from heat.
4. Using a slotted spoon, carefully transfer the vegetables to the sterilized ball jar, making sure to pack them in tightly.
5. Pour the hot pickling liquid over the vegetables, filling the jar until it is almost full. Leave about 1/2 inch of headspace at the top.
6. Wipe the rim of the jar with a clean cloth to remove any excess liquid, then place the lid on the jar and tighten it down.

"ROSEMARY AND PICKLED PARSNIP DELIGHTS"

This recipe is perfect for those who love the combination of sweet and savory flavors. The pickled parsnip has a slightly sweet taste, while the rosemary adds a hint of earthiness. These pickles are great on their own or as a topping for sandwiches and salads.

1-pound parsnips, peeled and sliced into thin rounds

2 sprigs fresh rosemary

1 cup white vinegar

1 cup water

2 tablespoons sugar

1 tablespoon salt

2 cloves garlic, minced

1. In a medium saucepan, combine the vinegar, water, sugar, and salt. Bring to a boil, stirring occasionally.
2. Place the parsnip slices and rosemary sprigs into a clean and sterilized ball jar.
3. Once the vinegar mixture has come to a boil, pour it over the parsnips and rosemary in the jar.
4. Add the minced garlic to the jar.
5. Secure the lid on the ball jar and let it cool to room temperature.
6. Once cooled, store the ball jar in the refrigerator for at least 24 hours before serving. These pickles will keep in the refrigerator for up to 3 weeks. Enjoy!

"ZESTY PICKLED PASSIONFRUIT AND GINGER"

This tangy and spicy pickled passionfruit and ginger is the perfect addition to any dish. Whether you're looking to add some flair to a salad or sandwich, or want a unique topping for your favorite protein, these pickles will not disappoint. The combination of sweet passionfruit and spicy ginger is a match made in heaven, and the addition of vinegar and spices only enhances the flavors.

---

1 cup passionfruit pulp
1/2 cup white vinegar
1/2 cup water
1/4 cup sugar
1 tablespoon freshly grated ginger
1 teaspoon mustard seeds
1 teaspoon whole peppercorns
1/2 teaspoon salt
1 bay leaf
1 ball jar with a tight-fitting lid

1. In a small saucepan, combine the vinegar, water, sugar, ginger, mustard seeds, peppercorns, salt, and bay leaf. Bring to a boil over medium heat, stirring occasionally.

2. Reduce the heat to low and simmer for 5 minutes, or until the sugar has dissolved and the mixture has thickened slightly.

3. Remove the saucepan from the heat and add the passionfruit pulp. Stir to combine.

4. Pour the mixture into the ball jar, making sure to leave about 1 inch of headspace at the top.

5. Secure the lid on the jar and refrigerate for at least 24 hours before serving. The pickles will keep in the refrigerator for up to 1 month. Enjoy!

"SUMMERTIME BLISS IN A BALL JAR: PICKLED PEACH AND CINNAMON"

As the summer heat starts to fade and the leaves begin to change, there's nothing like the comfort of a sweet and spicy pickled peach to bring back memories of lazy days spent lounging in the sun. This recipe is a twist on the traditional pickled fruit, with the addition of cinnamon adding a warmth and depth to the flavor. It's the perfect way to preserve a bit of summer for those chilly fall and winter days.

4 cups sliced peaches

1 cup apple cider vinegar

1 cup water

1 cup white sugar

2 cinnamon sticks

1 tsp whole cloves

1 tsp whole allspice

1. In a medium saucepan, combine the vinegar, water, sugar, cinnamon sticks, cloves, and allspice. Bring to a boil and stir until the sugar has dissolved.
2. Add the sliced peaches to the mixture and reduce the heat to a simmer. Cook for 5 minutes or until the peaches are tender.
3. Remove the pan from the heat and let it cool to room temperature.
4. Using a slotted spoon, transfer the peaches and spices to a clean, sterilized ball jar.
5. Pour the pickling liquid over the peaches, making sure to leave at least 1/2 inch of headspace at the top of the jar.
6. Secure the lid and store in the refrigerator for at least 3 days before serving. The pickled peaches will keep in the refrigerator for up to 2 weeks. Enjoy as a topping for ice cream, a condiment for grilled pork, or as a sweet and spicy snack on their own.

"SUN-RIPENED PICKLED PEACHES WITH A HINT OF LEMON"

Summertime brings with it an abundance of fresh peaches, and what better way to preserve their sweet, juicy flavor than by pickling them? This recipe combines the classic taste of pickled peaches with a twist of lemon for a unique and delicious treat.

---

4 cups peeled and sliced peaches

2 cups white vinegar

1 cup sugar

2 tablespoons lemon zest

1 teaspoon salt

4 cinnamon sticks

8 cloves

4 ball jars with lids

1. In a medium saucepan, combine the vinegar, sugar, lemon zest, salt, cinnamon sticks, and cloves. Bring to a boil, stirring occasionally, until the sugar has dissolved.
2. Meanwhile, pack the sliced peaches into the ball jars.
3. Once the pickling liquid has come to a boil, carefully pour it over the peaches in the ball jars, leaving about 1/2 inch of headspace.
4. Wipe the rims of the ball jars clean and securely fasten the lids.
5. Place the ball jars in a large pot of boiling water and process for 10 minutes.
6. Remove the ball jars from the pot and let them cool on the counter. Once cooled, store the pickled peaches in the refrigerator for up to 3 months. Enjoy as a tasty accompaniment to sandwiches or as a sweet and tangy snack on their own.

"SUMMER IN A JAR: PICKLED PEACH AND ONION RELISH"

This recipe is a perfect way to preserve the flavors of summer for a taste of sunshine on a cold winter day. The combination of sweet peaches and tangy onions creates a unique and flavorful relish that can be used on sandwiches, burgers, or as a condiment for grilled meats.

---

4 cups sliced peaches

2 cups diced onions

1 cup white vinegar

1 cup white sugar

1 tsp mustard seeds

1 tsp salt

1. In a large saucepan, combine the peaches, onions, vinegar, sugar, mustard seeds, and salt.

2. Bring the mixture to a boil, then reduce the heat to a simmer and let it cook for 10 minutes.

3. Using a slotted spoon, transfer the pickled peach and onion mixture into a sterilized ball jar, making sure to leave at least 1 inch of space at the top.

4. Close the jar tightly and store it in the refrigerator for at least 24 hours before serving to allow the flavors to meld together.

5. The relish will keep in the fridge for up to 2 weeks or can be canned for longer shelf life. Enjoy!

"SUMMERTIME SWEETNESS: PICKLED PEACH AND THYME"

This recipe is a perfect way to capture the sweetness of summer peaches and preserve them for a delicious treat all year round. The addition of thyme gives these pickled peaches a unique and savory twist. Serve them alongside a cheese platter or as a topping for a salad.

---

4 peaches, peeled and sliced
1 cup white vinegar
1 cup water
1/2 cup sugar
2 tablespoons pickling salt
1 teaspoon thyme leaves
4 ball jars, sterilized

1. In a medium saucepan, combine the vinegar, water, sugar, and pickling salt. Bring to a boil, stirring until the sugar and salt have dissolved.
2. Add the thyme leaves to the ball jars.
3. Pack the sliced peaches into the ball jars, leaving about 1/2 inch of headspace.
4. Pour the hot vinegar mixture over the peaches, making sure to cover all of the slices.
5. Wipe the rims of the ball jars with a clean cloth and seal with the lids.
6. Process the ball jars in a boiling water bath for 10 minutes.
7. Remove the ball jars from the water bath and allow to cool completely before storing in the pantry for up to 1 year. Enjoy!

SWEET AND SPICY PICKLED PEACHES"

Growing up, my grandma would always make a batch of these pickled peaches in the summer when the fruit was at its peak. She would pack them into ball jars and they would last all winter long, providing a tangy and slightly spicy treat to enjoy with a meal or as a snack. These pickled peaches are the perfect balance of sweet and spicy and are a unique addition to any meal.

4 cups sliced peaches

2 cups white vinegar

1 cup sugar

2 tablespoons mustard seeds

1 teaspoon ground cinnamon

1 teaspoon ground cloves

1 teaspoon ground allspice

4 cloves garlic, minced

2 jalapeno peppers, thinly sliced

1. Wash and slice the peaches into thin wedges.
2. In a medium saucepan, combine the vinegar, sugar, mustard seeds, cinnamon, cloves, allspice, garlic, and jalapeno peppers. Bring to a boil over medium heat.
3. Once boiling, add the sliced peaches to the mixture and stir to coat.
4. Remove the pan from the heat and let the mixture cool for 5 minutes.
5. Using a slotted spoon, transfer the peaches to a clean ball jar, making sure to pack them in tightly.
6. Pour the remaining liquid from the saucepan over the peaches, making sure to leave about 1 inch of headspace at the top of the jar.
7. Close the jar tightly and let it sit at room temperature for at least 24 hours before refrigerating. The pickled peaches will last for several weeks in the refrigerator. Enjoy as a tasty condiment or snack.

"GINGER-INFUSED PICKLED PEACHES"

These pickled peaches are the perfect summertime treat, with a spicy kick from the ginger. They're perfect as a side dish or topping for a salad.

4 cups water

2 cups white vinegar

1 cup sugar

1 tsp salt

2 lbs peaches, peeled and sliced

1 inch piece of ginger, thinly sliced

2 cinnamon sticks

1. In a large saucepan, bring the water, vinegar, sugar, and salt to a boil.
2. Add the peaches, ginger, and cinnamon sticks to a ball jar.
3. Pour the hot liquid over the peaches in the jar, making sure to cover them completely.
4. Secure the lid on the jar and let it cool to room temperature.
5. Once cooled, place the jar in the refrigerator for at least 3 hours before serving. The pickled peaches will keep in the refrigerator for up to 2 weeks. Enjoy!

"SUMMER IN A JAR: PICKLED PEACHES"

When the summer sun is at its peak, there's nothing quite like a juicy, ripe peach to satisfy your sweet tooth. But when the season ends and the peaches are gone, how can you hold onto that taste of summer? One way is to pickle them! These pickled peaches are sweet and tangy, with a little bit of spice from the ginger and cloves. They're perfect for topping a salad, adding to a cheese plate, or just snacking on straight from the jar.

4 cups peaches, peeled and sliced
1 cup white vinegar
1 cup water
1 cup sugar
1 tsp salt
1 tsp whole cloves
1 tsp whole allspice
1 tsp ground ginger
2-3 cinnamon sticks

1. Begin by sterilizing your ball jar(s). Wash the jar(s) and lid(s) in hot soapy water, then rinse and place on a baking sheet. Heat your oven to 250°F and place the jar(s) in the oven for at least 10 minutes. This will help to kill any bacteria that may be present on the jar(s).

2. In a medium saucepan, combine the vinegar, water, sugar, salt, cloves, allspice, and ginger. Bring to a boil over medium heat, stirring occasionally to dissolve the sugar.

3. Place the sliced peaches in the sterilized jar(s) and add the cinnamon sticks. Pour the hot vinegar mixture over the peaches, making sure to cover them completely.

4. Seal the jar(s) tightly and allow to cool to room temperature. Once cooled, store in the refrigerator for at least 1 week before enjoying. The pickled peaches will last for up to 3 months in the refrigerator.

"GINGER-INFUSED PICKLED PEARS"

Pickling fruit is a fun and easy way to preserve your harvest for later use. These pickled pears are infused with a spicy kick of ginger, making them a unique and flavorful addition to any dish.

4 cups white vinegar

2 cups water

1 cup sugar

2 tablespoons salt

4-5 slices of fresh ginger

4-5 firm pears, peeled and sliced

2-3 cinnamon sticks

1 tablespoon whole cloves

1. In a large saucepan, combine the vinegar, water, sugar, and salt. Bring to a boil, stirring until the sugar and salt have dissolved.
2. Add the ginger slices, pears, cinnamon sticks, and cloves to a clean, sterilized ball jar.
3. Pour the hot vinegar mixture over the pears, making sure to fully cover them.
4. Tightly seal the jar and let it sit at room temperature for 24 hours.
5. Transfer the jar to the refrigerator and allow the pears to pickle for at least a week before serving.
6. Enjoy the pickled pears as a topping for sandwiches, salads, or charcuterie boards.

"SWEET AND SPICY PICKLED PEAR AND ONION RELISH"

This pickled pear and onion relish is the perfect addition to any sandwich or charcuterie board. The sweetness of the pears pairs perfectly with the spicy kick from the onions, making it a unique and tasty condiment.

---

2 pears, peeled and diced

1 medium onion, sliced

1 cup apple cider vinegar

1/2 cup white sugar

1 teaspoon mustard seeds

1/2 teaspoon red pepper flakes

1/4 teaspoon salt

1. In a small saucepan, combine the apple cider vinegar, sugar, mustard seeds, red pepper flakes, and salt. Bring to a boil, stirring occasionally, until the sugar has dissolved.

2. Place the diced pears and sliced onions in a medium bowl. Pour the hot vinegar mixture over the top and stir to combine.

3. Transfer the mixture to a clean ball jar and let cool to room temperature.

4. Once cooled, seal the jar and store in the refrigerator for at least 2 hours before serving. The pickled relish will keep in the refrigerator for up to 3 weeks. Enjoy!

DELICIOUSLY PICKLED PEARS WITH THYME

This recipe for pickled pears and thyme is the perfect way to preserve the flavors of fall. The sweet, juicy pears are perfectly balanced with the savory thyme and the tangy vinegar pickling liquid. These pickled pears are great on sandwiches, as a topping for salads, or simply enjoyed on their own as a tasty snack.

---

4 cups pear slices (peeled and cored)

2 cups white vinegar

1 cup water

1/2 cup sugar

4 sprigs fresh thyme

4 ball jars

1. Wash and sterilize the ball jars and lids.
2. In a large pot, bring the vinegar, water, and sugar to a boil.
3. Add the pear slices to the pot and reduce the heat to medium.
4. Add the thyme sprigs to the pot and simmer for 5 minutes.
5. Carefully remove the ball jars from the pot and fill with the pear slices, thyme sprigs, and pickling liquid.
6. Close the lids and place the ball jars in the pot, ensuring that they are covered with water.
7. Bring the pot to a boil and boil for 10 minutes.
8. Carefully remove the ball jars from the pot and allow them to cool.
9. Store the ball jars in a cool, dry place for up to 6 months. Enjoy!

"VANILLA-INFUSED PICKLED PEARS"

If you're a fan of sweet and savory combinations, these vanilla-infused pickled pears are sure to be a hit. The pears are pickled in a mixture of white vinegar, sugar, and vanilla beans, giving them a delightful balance of tart and sweet flavors. They make a great addition to cheese boards, as well as a tasty topping for sandwiches and salads.

4 firm, ripe pears

2 cups white vinegar

1 cup sugar

2 vanilla beans, split lengthwise

2 cinnamon sticks

4 whole cloves

1. Begin by preparing your pears. Wash them thoroughly and cut off the stems. Slice the pears into thin wedges and set aside.
2. In a medium saucepan, combine the vinegar, sugar, vanilla beans, cinnamon sticks, and cloves. Bring the mixture to a boil, stirring occasionally to dissolve the sugar.
3. Once the mixture has reached a boil, add the pear slices to the pot. Reduce the heat to low and simmer the pears for 5 minutes.
4. Remove the saucepan from the heat and let the pears cool in the liquid for 30 minutes.
5. While the pears are cooling, sterilize your ball jars. You can do this by washing the jars in hot, soapy water and then rinsing them well. Place the clean jars on a baking sheet and put them in the oven at 225°F for 10 minutes.
6. Once the pears have cooled and the jars have been sterilized, use a slotted spoon to transfer the pears to the jars, dividing them evenly. Pour the pickling liquid over the pears, making sure to leave about 1/2 inch of headspace at the top of each jar.
7. Wipe the rim of the jars with a clean, damp cloth to remove any stray bits of food. Place the lids on the jars and screw on the rings until they are tightened, but not too tightly.

"HONEYED PICKLED PEARS"

These honeyed pickled pears are the perfect balance of sweet and tangy. They are a great addition to cheese boards or can be enjoyed on their own as a unique snack. The best part is that they are incredibly easy to make and can be stored in a ball jar in the fridge for up to a month.

4 firm pears, peeled and sliced into wedges
1 cup white vinegar
1 cup water
1/2 cup honey
1 cinnamon stick
5 cloves
1 teaspoon whole peppercorns
1 teaspoon salt

1. In a small saucepan, combine the vinegar, water, honey, cinnamon stick, cloves, peppercorns, and salt. Bring the mixture to a boil, stirring to dissolve the honey.

2. Place the pear slices in a ball jar. Pour the hot pickling liquid over the pears, making sure they are fully submerged.

3. Let the pears cool to room temperature, then seal the jar and refrigerate for at least 24 hours before serving.

4. Serve the pickled pears as a snack or use them to add a tangy twist to cheese boards and other dishes. Enjoy!

"HONEY-SWEETENED PICKLED PEARS"

These pickled pears are the perfect balance of sweet and tangy. The honey adds a touch of warmth and depth to the brine, making them a unique and delightful addition to any charcuterie board or as a topping for salads and sandwiches.

---

4 pears, peeled, cored, and sliced into wedges
1 cup white vinegar
1 cup water
1/2 cup honey
1 tablespoon pickling spices
1/2 teaspoon salt

1. In a small saucepan, bring the vinegar, water, honey, pickling spices, and salt to a boil.
2. Place the pear slices in a clean and sterilized ball jar.
3. Pour the hot brine over the pears, making sure to completely cover them.
4. Close the jar tightly and place it in the fridge to cool.
5. Allow the pears to pickle for at least 24 hours before enjoying.
6. Store the pickled pears in the fridge for up to 2 weeks.

"SPICY PICKLED PEPPERS"

There's nothing like a jar of spicy pickled peppers to add a little kick to your meals. Whether you're using them as a topping for sandwiches, as a side dish, or just snacking on them straight from the jar, these peppers are sure to satisfy your cravings for heat. Plus, they're easy to make and can last for several months in the pantry. Here's how to make your own batch of spicy pickled peppers.

1-pound fresh peppers (such as jalapenos or serranos)
1 cup white vinegar
1 cup water
2 tablespoons sugar
1 tablespoon salt
2 cloves garlic, peeled and thinly sliced
1 teaspoon mustard seeds
1 teaspoon coriander seeds

1. Wash and dry the peppers. Cut off the stems and slice the peppers into thin rings or leave them whole, depending on your preference.
2. In a small saucepan, combine the vinegar, water, sugar, and salt. Bring to a boil, stirring until the sugar and salt are dissolved.
3. Place the peppers, garlic, mustard seeds, and coriander seeds in a clean ball jar. Pour the hot vinegar mixture over the peppers, making sure to fully cover them.
4. Seal the jar tightly and let it cool to room temperature. Once cooled, store the jar in the pantry for at least a week before opening and using the peppers. The peppers will keep for several months in the pantry. Enjoy!

"TROPICAL PARADISE PICKLED PINEAPPLE"

This pickled pineapple recipe is a great way to add a sweet and tangy twist to your meals. It's a great addition to sandwiches and salads, or as a topping for grilled meats. The pineapples are preserved in a mixture of vinegar, sugar, and spices, giving them a delicious, pickled flavor. Plus, the bright yellow color adds a pop of color to any dish.

---

1 pineapple, peeled, cored, and cut into chunks

1 cup white vinegar

1 cup water

1 cup sugar

2 cinnamon sticks

2-star anise

1 teaspoon whole cloves

1 teaspoon mustard seeds

1. In a medium saucepan, combine the vinegar, water, sugar, cinnamon sticks, star anise, cloves, and mustard seeds. Bring to a boil, stirring until the sugar has dissolved.

2. Add the pineapple chunks to a clean and sterilized ball jar.

3. Pour the hot vinegar mixture over the pineapple, making sure to cover the fruit completely.

4. Allow the jar to cool to room temperature, then seal with a lid and store in the refrigerator for at least 1 week before serving.

5. The pickled pineapple will keep in the refrigerator for up to 3 months. Enjoy as a topping for sandwiches, salads, or grilled meats, or simply as a snack on its own.

"TROPICAL TWIST PICKLED PINEAPPLE WITH BLACK PEPPER"

This unique pickled pineapple recipe is sure to be a hit at your next barbecue or potluck. The combination of sweet pineapple and spicy black pepper creates a balance of flavors that is both tangy and refreshing. Plus, the use of a ball jar makes it easy to store and transport the finished product.

---

1 medium pineapple, peeled, cored, and cut into 1-inch chunks

1 cup white vinegar

1 cup water

1/2 cup sugar

1 tablespoon black peppercorns

1 tablespoon mustard seeds

1 tablespoon coriander seeds

1 teaspoon salt

4 cloves garlic, peeled and smashed

4 small, dried chilies, or 1 teaspoon red pepper flakes (optional)

1. In a medium saucepan, combine the vinegar, water, sugar, peppercorns, mustard seeds, coriander seeds, salt, garlic, and chilies (if using). Bring to a boil over medium heat, stirring occasionally to dissolve the sugar.

2. Place the pineapple chunks in a clean ball jar. Pour the hot vinegar mixture over the pineapple, making sure to cover the pineapple completely.

3. Let the jar cool to room temperature, then seal the jar and refrigerate for at least 24 hours before serving. The pickled pineapple will keep for up to 1 month in the refrigerator.

4. Serve the pickled pineapple as a condiment or snack or use it to add a tropical twist to sandwiches and salads. Enjoy!

"SPICY PICKLED PINEAPPLE"

This recipe is a perfect balance of sweet and spicy. The pineapple adds a touch of tropical flavor, and the chili adds a kick of heat. The pickling process helps to preserve the fruit and adds an extra tangy flavor. This recipe is great as a topping for tacos, sandwiches, or as a snack on its own.

---

1 fresh pineapple, peeled and sliced into wedges

1 cup white vinegar

1 cup water

1/2 cup sugar

1 tablespoon salt

2-3 chili peppers, sliced (use your favorite variety and adjust the number to your desired level of heat)

2 cloves garlic, minced

1 teaspoon mustard seeds

1. In a small saucepan, combine the vinegar, water, sugar, and salt. Bring the mixture to a boil, stirring occasionally, until the sugar and salt have dissolved.

2. Place the pineapple wedges, chili peppers, garlic, and mustard seeds in a clean 1-quart Ball jar.

3. Pour the hot vinegar mixture over the pineapple and chili peppers. Make sure the pineapple is fully submerged in the liquid.

4. Place the lid on the Ball jar and let it cool to room temperature.

5. Once cool, store the jar in the refrigerator for at least 24 hours before serving. The pickled pineapple will keep in the refrigerator for up to 1 month. Enjoy!

"TROPICAL TWIST PICKLED PINEAPPLE AND GARLIC"

This pickled pineapple and garlic recipe is a unique and flavorful addition to any meal. The sweet and tangy pineapple pairs perfectly with the pungent garlic, creating a taste sensation that will have your taste buds dancing. It's a great way to add some excitement to your meals and is perfect for topping sandwiches, salads, and more. Plus, it's super easy to make and can be stored in a Ball jar for later use.

---

1 cup pineapple chunks
1 cup pineapple juice
1/2 cup white vinegar
1/4 cup sugar
1 tablespoon salt
5 cloves garlic, minced
1 teaspoon red pepper flakes (optional)

1. In a small saucepan, combine the pineapple juice, vinegar, sugar, and salt. Bring to a boil, stirring to dissolve the sugar and salt.
2. Place the pineapple chunks and minced garlic in a sterilized Ball jar.
3. Pour the hot vinegar mixture over the pineapple and garlic, making sure to fully cover the fruit.
4. Allow the jar to cool to room temperature before sealing and storing in the refrigerator for at least 24 hours before enjoying. The pickled pineapple and garlic will last for up to 2 weeks in the refrigerator.

"TROPICAL TWIST PICKLED PINEAPPLE AND GINGER"

This pickled pineapple and ginger recipe is the perfect combination of sweet and spicy. The pineapples are pickled in a mixture of vinegar, sugar, and spices, giving them a tangy and flavorful taste. The addition of ginger adds a spicy kick that balances out the sweetness of the pineapple. These pickled pineapples are great as a condiment for grilled meats or as a topping for salads and sandwiches.

1 large pineapple, peeled and cut into 1-inch chunks
1 cup white vinegar
1 cup water
1 cup granulated sugar
2 tablespoons fresh ginger, thinly sliced
2 teaspoons mustard seeds
1 teaspoon coriander seeds
1/2 teaspoon red pepper flakes (optional)
3-4 Ball jars with lids

1. In a medium saucepan, combine the vinegar, water, sugar, ginger, mustard seeds, coriander seeds, and red pepper flakes (if using). Bring to a boil, stirring occasionally, until the sugar has dissolved.

2. Place the pineapple chunks in the Ball jars. Pour the hot vinegar mixture over the pineapple, making sure to cover the pineapple completely.

3. Let the jars cool to room temperature, then seal the lids and refrigerate for at least 24 hours before serving. The pickled pineapples will keep in the refrigerator for up to 2 weeks. Enjoy!

"SWEET AND SPICY PICKLED PINEAPPLE WITH A HINT OF NUTMEG"

This pickled pineapple recipe is a unique twist on the traditional pickling method. The addition of nutmeg adds a warm and aromatic flavor to the sweet and spicy brine, making it a perfect accompaniment to any savory dish. It's a great way to preserve pineapple for the winter months and adds a pop of flavor to your meals.

---

1 pineapple, peeled and cut into bite-sized chunks
2 cups white vinegar
1 cup water
1 cup sugar
2 tablespoons salt
2 tablespoons mustard seeds
1 tablespoon red pepper flakes
1 teaspoon nutmeg
2 cinnamon sticks
4 whole cloves
4 garlic cloves, minced
4 ball jars with lids

1. In a large saucepan, combine the vinegar, water, sugar, salt, mustard seeds, red pepper flakes, nutmeg, cinnamon sticks, and cloves. Bring to a boil, stirring until the sugar and salt are dissolved.

2. Add the pineapple chunks to the saucepan and bring the mixture back to a boil. Reduce the heat to a simmer and cook for 5 minutes.

3. Add the minced garlic to the saucepan and cook for an additional 2 minutes.

4. Using tongs, carefully transfer the pineapple chunks and brine to the ball jars, leaving about 1/2 inch of headspace at the top of each jar.

5. Place the lids on the jars and tighten until snug.

6. Place the jars in a large pot of boiling water and process for 10 minutes.

7. Carefully remove the jars from the pot and let them cool to room temperature.

"TROPICAL TWIST PICKLED PINEAPPLE AND ONION"

If you're looking for a unique and flavorful addition to your pantry, this pickled pineapple and onion recipe is sure to satisfy your taste buds. With sweet and tangy flavors, these pickled pineapples and onions are perfect for adding to sandwiches, salads, or as a topping for tacos.

---

1 medium pineapple, peeled and cut into small chunks

1 medium onion, thinly sliced

1 cup white vinegar

1 cup water

1/2 cup sugar

1 tablespoon pickling spices

2 teaspoons salt

1. In a small saucepan, bring the vinegar, water, sugar, pickling spices, and salt to a boil.
2. Place the pineapple and onion in a clean ball jar.
3. Pour the hot vinegar mixture over the pineapple and onion, making sure to cover the ingredients completely.
4. Seal the ball jar and let it cool to room temperature.
5. Once cooled, store the ball jar in the refrigerator for at least 24 hours before serving to allow the flavors to fully develop.
6. These pickled pineapples and onions will keep in the refrigerator for up to 2 weeks. Enjoy!

PICKLED PINEAPPLE AND ONION RELISH

This pickled pineapple and onion relish is the perfect blend of sweet and savory flavors. It's great as a topping for burgers, sandwiches, or even as a side dish. The pineapple adds a touch of tropical flavor, while the onions give it a bit of a kick. It's easy to make and can be stored in a ball jar in the refrigerator for a few weeks.

---

1 small pineapple, peeled and diced
1 medium red onion, thinly sliced
1 cup white vinegar
1/2 cup sugar
1 tablespoon salt
1 teaspoon mustard seeds
1 teaspoon coriander seeds
1/2 teaspoon black peppercorns
1/2 teaspoon red pepper flakes (optional)

1. In a large saucepan, combine the vinegar, sugar, salt, mustard seeds, coriander seeds, black peppercorns, and red pepper flakes (if using). Bring to a boil over medium heat, stirring occasionally until the sugar and salt have dissolved.

2. Add the pineapple and onion to the saucepan and stir to combine. Reduce the heat to low and simmer for 5 minutes.

3. Remove the saucepan from the heat and let the mixture cool for 10 minutes.

4. Transfer the pickled pineapple and onion mixture to a ball jar, making sure to pack it tightly. Cover the jar with a lid and refrigerate for at least 1 hour before serving. The pickled pineapple and onion relish will keep in the refrigerator for up to 2 weeks. Enjoy!

"TROPICAL TWIST PICKLED PINEAPPLE AND SAGE"

If you're looking to add some tropical flair to your pickled creations, this recipe is for you! The combination of sweet pineapple and savory sage creates a unique and delicious flavor that is sure to be a hit at your next gathering.

---

1 medium pineapple, peeled and cut into 1-inch chunks
1 cup white vinegar
1 cup water
1/2 cup sugar
2 tablespoons salt
1 tablespoon whole black peppercorns
2 cloves garlic, minced
1 tablespoon chopped fresh sage
1 teaspoon mustard seeds
2 small hot chili peppers, sliced (optional)

1. In a small saucepan, combine the vinegar, water, sugar, salt, peppercorns, garlic, sage, mustard seeds, and chili peppers (if using). Bring to a boil over medium heat, stirring until the sugar and salt have dissolved.

2. Place the pineapple chunks in a clean and sterilized ball jar. Pour the hot pickling liquid over the pineapple, making sure to fully cover the fruit.

3. Seal the jar and let it cool to room temperature. Once cool, store the jar in the refrigerator for at least 24 hours before serving. The pickled pineapple will keep in the refrigerator for up to 1 month. Enjoy!

"TANGY PICKLED PLUM AND GARLIC DELIGHT"

Pickling is a great way to preserve the abundance of summer produce and add flavor to your meals. This pickled plum and garlic recipe is a delicious addition to any charcuterie board or as a condiment for sandwiches and salads. The combination of sweet and savory will have your taste buds singing.

1-pound plums, halved and pitted
1 cup apple cider vinegar
1 cup water
1/2 cup granulated sugar
1 tablespoon pickling salt
5 cloves garlic, peeled
1 teaspoon black peppercorns
1 teaspoon mustard seeds
1 dried chili pepper (optional)

1. In a small saucepan, bring the vinegar, water, sugar, and pickling salt to a boil. Stir until the sugar and salt are dissolved.
2. Pack the plums and garlic into a clean, quart-sized Ball jar. Add the peppercorns, mustard seeds, and chili pepper (if using).
3. Pour the hot vinegar mixture over the plums and garlic, making sure to fully submerge the fruit.
4. Place the lid on the jar and let cool to room temperature. Once cooled, transfer the jar to the refrigerator to chill for at least 24 hours before serving. The pickled plums and garlic will keep in the refrigerator for up to 2 weeks. Enjoy!

"TANGY PICKLED PLUM AND ONION RELISH"

This pickled plum and onion relish is a sweet and tangy condiment that is perfect for adding a pop of flavor to sandwiches, burgers, and more. It's easy to make and can be stored in a ball jar in the fridge for up to a few months.

---

4 cups chopped red onions

2 cups chopped plums

1 cup white vinegar

1 cup sugar

1 tablespoon salt

1 teaspoon mustard seeds

1 teaspoon ground coriander

1. In a large saucepan, combine the onions, plums, vinegar, sugar, salt, mustard seeds, and coriander.

2. Bring the mixture to a boil over medium heat, stirring frequently.

3. Reduce the heat to low and simmer for 20 minutes, or until the onions are tender and the mixture has thickened slightly.

4. Remove the saucepan from the heat and let the relish cool to room temperature.

5. Transfer the relish to a ball jar and store in the fridge until ready to use. Enjoy!

THYME-INFUSED PICKLED PLUMS"

This recipe for pickled plums is a delicious and easy way to preserve the summer fruit for enjoyment throughout the year. The addition of thyme adds a unique and aromatic twist to the traditional pickling process.

1-pound plums, halved and pitted
1 cup apple cider vinegar
1 cup water
1/2 cup sugar
2 tablespoons salt
4 sprigs thyme

1. In a small saucepan, bring the vinegar, water, sugar, and salt to a boil over medium heat, stirring until the sugar and salt have dissolved.
2. Place the plums in a sterilized ball jar, along with the thyme sprigs.
3. Pour the vinegar mixture over the plums, making sure to fully cover them.
4. Seal the jar and let it sit at room temperature for at least 24 hours before storing in the refrigerator.
5. The pickled plums will keep in the refrigerator for up to 1 month. Enjoy as a tangy and flavorful condiment on sandwiches or as a topping for cheese plates.

"SPICED PICKLED PLUMS"

Pickled plums are a traditional Japanese snack that have a sweet and sour flavor. They are often served as a side dish or used as a condiment for dishes like sushi or rice bowls. This recipe adds a touch of warm spices, like cloves and cinnamon, to give the pickled plums a unique and flavorful twist.

1-pound plums, halved and pitted
1 cup rice vinegar
1 cup water
1/2 cup sugar
1 cinnamon stick
5 whole cloves
1 tablespoon salt

1. In a small saucepan, bring the vinegar, water, sugar, cinnamon stick, and cloves to a boil. Reduce the heat to low and simmer for 5 minutes.
2. Meanwhile, pack the plums into a clean and sterilized ball jar.
3. Pour the hot vinegar mixture over the plums, making sure to cover them completely.
4. Close the jar tightly and let it cool to room temperature.
5. Once cooled, store the jar in the refrigerator for at least a week before serving. The pickled plums will keep for up to 2 months in the refrigerator.
6. Serve the pickled plums as a side dish or use as a condiment for other dishes. Enjoy!

DELICIOUSLY SWEET PICKLED PLUMS AND VANILLA

Pickled plums are a traditional Japanese snack that are sweet and tangy. They are a great way to use up plums that are a little past their prime, and the addition of vanilla gives them a unique and delicious flavor.

1-pound plums

1 cup water

1 cup white vinegar

1 cup sugar

1 vanilla bean

1 ball jar

1. Wash the plums and remove the pits. Cut the plums into quarters and place them in the ball jar.

2. In a small saucepan, combine the water, vinegar, and sugar. Split the vanilla bean in half lengthwise and scrape the seeds into the saucepan. Bring the mixture to a boil, stirring until the sugar is dissolved.

3. Pour the hot liquid over the plums in the jar, making sure to cover the plums completely.

4. Seal the jar and let it cool to room temperature. Once cooled, store the jar in the refrigerator for at least a week before eating, to allow the flavors to develop.

5. Enjoy the pickled plums as a snack or use them as a topping for ice cream or yogurt. They will keep in the refrigerator for several weeks.

SPICED PICKLED POMEGRANATE AND CINNAMON DELIGHT"

This recipe for pickled pomegranate and cinnamon is a unique and tasty twist on traditional pickling recipes. The combination of sweet and tangy flavors creates a delectable condiment that is perfect for adding a burst of flavor to sandwiches, salads, and more.

2 cups pomegranate seeds
1 cinnamon stick
1 cup white vinegar
1 cup water
1/2 cup sugar
1 tablespoon pickling salt
2 ball jars with lids

1. In a small saucepan, combine the vinegar, water, sugar, and pickling salt. Bring the mixture to a boil, stirring until the sugar and salt are fully dissolved.
2. Meanwhile, divide the pomegranate seeds and cinnamon stick evenly between the two ball jars.
3. Once the pickling liquid has come to a boil, carefully pour it over the pomegranate seeds and cinnamon stick in the ball jars, making sure to leave about 1/2 inch of headspace.
4. Secure the lids on the ball jars and place them in the refrigerator to cool.
5. Allow the pickled pomegranate and cinnamon to marinate in the refrigerator for at least 24 hours before serving.
6. These pickles will keep in the refrigerator for up to 2 weeks. Enjoy!

"POMEGRANATE MINT PICKLES"

These pickles are the perfect combination of sweet and sour, with the refreshing flavors of pomegranate and mint. They're a unique and delicious addition to any charcuterie board or sandwich. Plus, by canning them in a ball jar, you can enjoy them all year round.

2 cups pomegranate seeds

1 cup white vinegar

1 cup water

1/2 cup sugar

1 tablespoon pickling salt

1 tablespoon chopped fresh mint

1 clove garlic, minced

1 teaspoon mustard seeds

1 teaspoon coriander seeds

1. In a small saucepan, combine the vinegar, water, sugar, and pickling salt. Bring to a boil, stirring until the sugar and salt are dissolved.

2. Meanwhile, divide the pomegranate seeds, mint, garlic, mustard seeds, and coriander seeds evenly among the ball jars.

3. Once the pickling liquid has come to a boil, carefully pour it over the ingredients in the ball jars, leaving about 1/2 inch of headspace at the top.

4. Wipe the rim of the ball jars with a damp cloth and place the lids on top.

5. Place the ball jars in a boiling water bath and process for 10 minutes.

6. Remove the ball jars from the boiling water bath and allow them to cool completely before storing in the refrigerator. The pickles will be ready to eat after a few hours, but they will taste even better after a day or two. Enjoy!

"ZESTY POMEGRANATE AND ORANGE PICKLES"

These colorful pickles are a fun and unique twist on traditional pickled fruits. The combination of sweet oranges and tart pomegranate arils creates a balance of flavors that is both refreshing and satisfying. They are a great addition to any charcuterie board or as a topping for salads and sandwiches.

1 pomegranate, seeds removed

3 oranges, peeled and sliced

1 cup white vinegar

1 cup water

1/2 cup sugar

1 tablespoon salt

2 cinnamon sticks

1 tablespoon whole cloves

1 tablespoon whole allspice

1 tablespoon mustard seeds

1. In a small saucepan, combine the vinegar, water, sugar, salt, cinnamon sticks, cloves, allspice, and mustard seeds. Bring to a boil, then reduce the heat and simmer for 5 minutes.
2. Place the pomegranate seeds and orange slices in a sterilized ball jar.
3. Pour the hot vinegar mixture over the fruit, making sure to completely cover the fruit with the liquid.
4. Secure the lid on the ball jar and let the pickles cool to room temperature.
5. Once cool, place the jar in the refrigerator and let the pickles marinate for at least 24 hours before serving.
6. The pickles will keep in the refrigerator for up to 2 weeks. Enjoy!

"SPICED QUINCE PICKLES"

Pickled quince is a unique and delicious way to preserve the sweet-tart flavor of quince fruit. The addition of cinnamon adds a warm, aromatic touch to these pickles, making them perfect for fall and winter snacking.

4 quinces, peeled, cored, and cut into wedges
1 cinnamon stick
2 cups apple cider vinegar
1 cup water
1 cup sugar
1 tablespoon salt
2 cloves
2 allspice berries
2 cardamom pods

1. In a small saucepan, combine the vinegar, water, sugar, salt, cloves, allspice, and cardamom. Bring to a boil and simmer for 5 minutes.
2. Place the quince wedges and cinnamon stick in a clean ball jar. Pour the hot pickling liquid over the quince, making sure to fully cover the fruit.
3. Close the jar tightly and store in the refrigerator for at least 3 days before serving, to allow the flavors to fully develop. Enjoy the pickled quince as a condiment or snack, or use them as a topping for sandwiches and salads.

"ZESTY PICKLED RADISHES WITH FRESH DILL"

This recipe is a quick and easy way to preserve the crisp, refreshing flavor of radishes and the aromatic herbs of dill. It's the perfect condiment to add a pop of flavor to sandwiches, salads, and more.

1-pound radishes, thinly sliced
1 cup water
1 cup white vinegar
1 tablespoon sugar
1 tablespoon salt
1 teaspoon mustard seeds
1 teaspoon peppercorns
1/2 teaspoon dill seeds
1 sprig fresh dill
1 ball jar

1. In a small saucepan, bring the water, vinegar, sugar, salt, mustard seeds, peppercorns, and dill seeds to a boil.
2. Place the radish slices and fresh dill sprig in the ball jar.
3. Pour the hot vinegar mixture over the radishes, making sure to cover them completely.
4. Seal the jar tightly and let it cool to room temperature.
5. Once cooled, place the jar in the refrigerator for at least 24 hours before serving. The pickled radishes will keep in the refrigerator for up to 1 month.

"SPICY PICKLED RADISH AND GARLIC"

Pickling is a great way to preserve the crispness and flavor of radishes and garlic, and this recipe gives them a spicy kick. It's perfect for adding some zing to sandwiches, salads, or as a garnish for cocktails.

---

1 cup white vinegar

1 cup water

2 tablespoons sugar

1 tablespoon salt

1 teaspoon red pepper flakes

1-pound radishes, thinly sliced

4 cloves garlic, thinly sliced

2 ball jars (16 ounces each) with lids

1. In a small saucepan, combine the vinegar, water, sugar, salt, and red pepper flakes. Bring to a boil over medium heat, stirring occasionally until the sugar and salt have dissolved.
2. Meanwhile, divide the radishes and garlic evenly between the two ball jars.
3. Once the brine is boiling, carefully pour it over the radishes and garlic in the ball jars, making sure to cover them completely.
4. Allow the jars to cool to room temperature, then seal with the lids and store in the refrigerator for at least 24 hours before serving. The pickled radishes and garlic will keep for up to 2 weeks in the refrigerator.

Enjoy your spicy pickled radish and garlic on sandwiches, salads, or as a garnish for cocktails. The pickled radishes and garlic will add a pop of flavor and crunch to any dish.

"GINGER-INFUSED PICKLED RADISHES"

Pickling is a great way to preserve the crisp, refreshing flavor of radishes. The added ginger gives these pickled radishes a spicy kick that pairs well with a variety of dishes. Whether you're serving them as a condiment or snacking on them straight from the jar, these pickled radishes are sure to be a hit.

---

1 cup water
1 cup white vinegar
1/4 cup sugar
1 tablespoon kosher salt
1/2 teaspoon whole black peppercorns
1/2 teaspoon mustard seeds
4 cloves garlic, thinly sliced
1 tablespoon grated ginger
4-6 small radishes, thinly sliced

1. In a small saucepan, combine the water, vinegar, sugar, salt, peppercorns, and mustard seeds. Bring to a boil over medium heat, stirring occasionally to dissolve the sugar and salt.
2. Once the mixture has boiled, remove it from the heat and add the garlic and ginger. Let it cool for a few minutes.
3. While the pickling liquid is cooling, thinly slice the radishes.
4. Once the pickling liquid has cooled slightly, place the sliced radishes in a clean and sterilized ball jar. Pour the pickling liquid over the radishes, making sure they are fully submerged.
5. Seal the jar and let it sit at room temperature for at least 2 hours, or until the radishes have reached your desired level of pickelness
6. Once the radishes are pickled to your liking, store the jar in the refrigerator for up to 2 weeks. Enjoy as a condiment or snack.

"ZESTY PICKLED RADISH AND LEMON"

This pickled radish and lemon recipe is a bright and refreshing addition to any meal. The combination of tangy lemon and spicy radish creates a unique and flavorful pickle. Serve these pickles as a side dish or use them to add some pep to sandwiches and salads.

1 bunch of radishes, thinly sliced

1 lemon, thinly sliced

1 cup water

1 cup white vinegar

2 tbsp sugar

2 tsp salt

1 tsp whole black peppercorns

1 tsp mustard seeds

2 cloves garlic, minced

1 small sprig of fresh dill

1. In a small saucepan, combine the water, vinegar, sugar, salt, peppercorns, mustard seeds, and garlic. Bring to a boil over medium heat, stirring to dissolve the sugar and salt.
2. Place the sliced radishes and lemon in a clean, sterilized ball jar.
3. Pour the hot pickling liquid over the radishes and lemon, making sure to fully submerge them.
4. Add the sprig of fresh dill to the jar.
5. Close the jar tightly and allow it to cool to room temperature.
6. Transfer the jar to the refrigerator and let it sit for at least 24 hours before serving to allow the flavors to fully develop.
7. These pickles will keep in the refrigerator for up to 2 weeks. Enjoy!

"ZESTY PICKLED RADISH AND MUSTARD"

Pickling is a great way to preserve and add flavor to your vegetables. This recipe combines the crunch of radishes with the tanginess of mustard for a unique and tasty pickled treat. Perfect for topping sandwiches or adding to a charcuterie board, these pickled radishes are sure to be a hit with your friends and family.

1-pound radishes, thinly sliced
1 cup water
1 cup white vinegar
2 tablespoons sugar
1 tablespoon mustard seeds
1 tablespoon sea salt
2 cloves garlic, minced
1 teaspoon black peppercorns
1 teaspoon dill seeds

1. In a medium saucepan, combine the water, vinegar, sugar, mustard seeds, sea salt, garlic, peppercorns, and dill seeds. Bring to a boil over medium heat, stirring until the sugar has dissolved.

2. Place the sliced radishes in a clean, sterilized ball jar. Pour the hot pickling liquid over the radishes, making sure to cover them completely.

3. Allow the jar to cool to room temperature, then seal it with a lid and store it in the refrigerator. The pickled radishes will be ready to eat after 24 hours and will keep for up to 2 weeks in the refrigerator.

4. Serve the pickled radishes as a topping for sandwiches, or as a flavorful addition to a charcuterie board. Enjoy!

"ZESTY PICKLED RADISH AND ONION RELISH"

This pickled radish and onion relish is a tangy and refreshing addition to any sandwich or charcuterie board. It's quick and easy to make and can be stored in the refrigerator for up to a month.

1 cup thinly sliced radishes

1 cup thinly sliced onion

1 cup vinegar (either white vinegar or apple cider vinegar will work)

1 tablespoon sugar

1 teaspoon salt

1/2 teaspoon mustard seeds

1/2 teaspoon black peppercorns

1/4 teaspoon red pepper flakes (optional)

1. In a small saucepan, combine the vinegar, sugar, salt, mustard seeds, peppercorns, and red pepper flakes (if using). Bring to a boil over medium heat, stirring until the sugar and salt have dissolved.

2. Place the radishes and onions in a sterilized ball jar. Pour the hot vinegar mixture over the top, making sure to cover the vegetables completely.

3. Let the jar sit at room temperature for at least 30 minutes to allow the flavors to meld.

4. Once cooled, seal the jar and store it in the refrigerator for up to a month. The pickled radish and onion relish is ready to use once it has chilled in the refrigerator for at least an hour. Enjoy!

"ZESTY PICKLED RED ONIONS WITH FRESH CILANTRO"

These pickled red onions are the perfect addition to any Mexican-inspired dish, adding a burst of flavor and a pop of color. The combination of red onions, cilantro, and a spicy vinegar marinade creates a tangy and refreshing condiment. Plus, they're super easy to make and can be stored in the fridge for weeks, making them a great pantry staple to have on hand.

---

1 large red onion, thinly sliced
1 cup white vinegar
1 cup water
1 tablespoon sugar
1 tablespoon salt
1 teaspoon chili flakes (optional)
1/2 cup fresh cilantro, roughly chopped
1 ball jar

1. Begin by thinly slicing your red onion. You can use a mandolin or a sharp knife to achieve thin, even slices.
2. In a small saucepan, bring the vinegar, water, sugar, salt, and chili flakes (if using) to a boil. Stir to dissolve the sugar and salt.
3. Place the sliced red onions in a ball jar and add the fresh cilantro on top.
4. Pour the hot vinegar mixture over the onions and cilantro, making sure to completely cover the onions.
5. Let the jar sit at room temperature for at least an hour, or until the onions have cooled down.
6. Once cooled, close the jar with a lid and store in the refrigerator. The pickled red onions will be ready to eat in about an hour, but they will taste even better after a day or two in the fridge. Enjoy!

"GRANDMA'S PICKLED RED CABBAGE AND APPLES"

This recipe for pickled red cabbage and apples was passed down from my grandma, who always had a batch of these tangy and slightly sweet pickles in her pantry. She used to serve them as a side dish with roast pork or as a topping for sandwiches. The combination of red cabbage and apples gives these pickles a unique and delicious flavor that is sure to become a family favorite.

---

1 small head of red cabbage, thinly sliced
2 apples, cored and thinly sliced
1/2 cup apple cider vinegar
1/2 cup granulated sugar
1 tablespoon kosher salt
1 cinnamon stick
5 whole cloves
5 whole allspice berries

1. In a large bowl, combine the cabbage and apples.
2. In a small saucepan, combine the vinegar, sugar, salt, cinnamon stick, cloves, and allspice berries. Bring to a boil over medium heat, stirring to dissolve the sugar.
3. Pour the hot vinegar mixture over the cabbage and apples, stirring to combine.
4. Transfer the mixture to a large ball jar and press down to compact the pickles. Make sure the pickles are completely covered with the vinegar mixture.
5. Let the jar cool to room temperature, then cover and refrigerate for at least 24 hours before serving. The pickles will keep in the refrigerator for up to 1 month.

"ZINGY PICKLED GINGER AND WASABI"

This recipe combines two classic Japanese condiments - pickled ginger and wasabi - into one tangy and spicy treat. Perfect for adding a burst of flavor to sushi rolls, sandwiches, or even just snacking on straight from the jar.

1 cup peeled and thinly sliced ginger
1/4 cup rice vinegar
1 tablespoon sugar
1 teaspoon salt
1/4 cup water
2 tablespoons wasabi paste

1. In a small saucepan, combine the rice vinegar, sugar, salt, and water. Bring to a boil, stirring until the sugar and salt have dissolved.
2. Place the sliced ginger in a sterilized ball jar. Pour the hot vinegar mixture over the ginger, making sure to fully cover the ginger.
3. Allow the ginger to cool to room temperature, then seal the jar and refrigerate for at least 24 hours before serving.
4. When ready to serve, mix the wasabi paste into the pickled ginger. Enjoy!

"SWEET AND TANGY PICKLED RASPBERRY VANILLA CURD"

This recipe combines the tartness of pickled raspberries with the creamy richness of vanilla curd to create a truly unique and flavorful preserve. The result is a sweet and tangy spread that is perfect for slathering on toast, spooning over ice cream, or using as a filling for cakes and tarts.

---

1 cup raspberries, fresh or frozen
1/2 cup white vinegar
1/2 cup granulated sugar
1 cinnamon stick
1 vanilla bean, split and scraped
3 egg yolks
1/2 cup granulated sugar
1/4 cup butter, softened
1/4 cup lemon juice

1. In a small saucepan, combine the raspberries, vinegar, sugar, and cinnamon stick. Bring to a boil over medium heat, stirring frequently to dissolve the sugar. Reduce the heat to low and simmer for 5 minutes.

2. Remove the pan from the heat and stir in the vanilla bean seeds. Allow the mixture to cool to room temperature.

3. In a medium saucepan, whisk together the egg yolks and sugar until well combined. Add the butter and lemon juice, and cook over medium heat, stirring constantly, until the mixture thickens and coats the back of a spoon.

4. Remove the pan from the heat and strain the curd through a fine mesh sieve to remove any lumps. Discard the solids.

5. Transfer the curd to a ball jar and refrigerate until chilled.

6. To serve, spoon the pickled raspberry vanilla curd over toast, or ice cream

"RUBY RASPBERRY ROSE JAM"

This pickled raspberry and rose jam is the perfect combination of sweet and tart. The raspberries provide a burst of flavor, while the rose adds a floral, aromatic touch. It's a unique and sophisticated spread that's sure to impress.

2 cups raspberries
1 cup granulated sugar
2 tablespoons rose water
1/4 cup apple cider vinegar
1/4 teaspoon salt

1. In a medium saucepan, combine the raspberries, sugar, and rose water. Cook over medium heat, stirring occasionally, until the raspberries have broken down and the mixture has thickened, about 10 minutes.

2. Add the vinegar and salt, stirring to combine.

3. Transfer the mixture to a clean ball jar and let cool to room temperature.

4. Seal the jar and store in the refrigerator for up to 2 weeks. Enjoy on toast, biscuits, or as a topping for ice cream or cheesecake.

"TANGY PICKLED RASPBERRY AND LIME DELIGHT"

This recipe combines the sweetness of raspberries with the tartness of lime to create a unique and flavorful pickled fruit. It's a perfect addition to any charcuterie board or as a topping for a refreshing summer salad.

1-pint fresh raspberries

1 lime, sliced into thin rounds

1 cup white vinegar

1 cup water

1/2 cup sugar

1 tablespoon pickling salt

2 cloves garlic, sliced

1 teaspoon mustard seeds

1 teaspoon black peppercorns

1 dried chili pepper (optional)

1. Wash and sterilize a 16-ounce Ball jar and lid.
2. In a small saucepan, combine the vinegar, water, sugar, and pickling salt. Bring to a boil and stir until the sugar and salt are dissolved.
3. Add the garlic, mustard seeds, peppercorns, and chili pepper (if using) to the Ball jar.
4. Add the raspberries and lime slices to the Ball jar.
5. Pour the hot vinegar mixture over the fruit in the Ball jar, making sure to cover all of the fruit.
6. Place the lid on the Ball jar and allow to cool to room temperature.
7. Once cooled, transfer the Ball jar to the refrigerator and allow the fruit to pickle for at least 24 hours before serving. The pickled fruit will keep for up to 2 weeks in the refrigerator. Enjoy!

"SPICY PICKLED RASPBERRY DELIGHT"

This recipe for pickled raspberry and black pepper is a unique and flavorful twist on traditional pickled fruit. The combination of sweet raspberries and spicy black pepper creates a balance of flavors that is sure to surprise and delight your taste buds. These pickled raspberries are perfect as a garnish for cocktails, as a topping for cheese plates, or as a condiment for meats.

1-pint fresh raspberries

1 cup white vinegar

1 cup water

1/2 cup sugar

1 tablespoon black peppercorns

1 teaspoon salt

1 ball jar with a lid

1. Wash and dry the raspberries.
2. In a small saucepan, combine the vinegar, water, sugar, black peppercorns, and salt. Bring the mixture to a boil over medium heat, stirring until the sugar and salt have dissolved.
3. Place the raspberries in the ball jar.
4. Pour the hot vinegar mixture over the raspberries, making sure to completely cover them.
5. Place the lid on the ball jar and allow the raspberries to cool to room temperature.
6. Once cooled, refrigerate the ball jar for at least 24 hours before serving to allow the flavors to meld.
7. The pickled raspberries will keep in the refrigerator for up to 1 month. Enjoy!

"SUMMER'S SWEETEST PICKLED RASPBERRIES AND LEMON"

If you're looking for a unique and flavorful twist on traditional pickled vegetables, give these pickled raspberries and lemon a try! They make a delicious addition to a cheese platter or charcuterie board or can be served alongside grilled meats for a pop of tangy flavor.

1-pint fresh raspberries

1 lemon, sliced into thin rounds

1 cup white vinegar

1 cup water

1/2 cup sugar

1 teaspoon sea salt

1 cinnamon stick

4 cloves

2 allspice berries

1 Ball jar with a lid

1. Rinse the raspberries and set aside.

2. In a small saucepan, combine the vinegar, water, sugar, salt, cinnamon stick, cloves, and allspice berries. Bring to a boil over medium heat, stirring to dissolve the sugar.

3. Once the mixture has come to a boil, remove it from the heat and let it cool for 5 minutes.

4. Place the raspberries and lemon slices into the Ball jar. Pour the vinegar mixture over the top, making sure to completely cover the raspberries and lemon.

5. Tightly close the lid on the Ball jar and let the pickles cool to room temperature.

6. Once cooled, place the Ball jar in the refrigerator for at least 24 hours before serving. The pickled raspberries and lemon will keep in the refrigerator for up to 2 weeks. Enjoy!

"SPICY PICKLED RAMBUTAN"

If you're a fan of sweet and sour flavors, you'll love this recipe for pickled rambutan and chili. Rambutan is a tropical fruit native to Southeast Asia, with a sweet and slightly sour flavor. When pickled, it takes on a delicious tangy taste that pairs perfectly with the heat of the chili. These pickled rambutan are great as a snack or topping for sandwiches and salads.

---

1 cup rambutan, peeled and seeded
1 cup white vinegar
1 cup water
1/2 cup sugar
1 tablespoon kosher salt
2 cloves garlic, minced
2 dried chili peppers
1 ball jar with a lid

1. In a small saucepan, combine the vinegar, water, sugar, salt, and minced garlic. Bring to a boil over medium heat, stirring until the sugar and salt are dissolved.
2. Place the dried chili peppers in the bottom of the ball jar.
3. Pack the peeled and seeded rambutan into the jar, fitting as many as you can while still leaving some headspace.
4. Pour the hot vinegar mixture over the rambutan, making sure to fully cover the fruit.
5. Place the lid on the jar and let it cool to room temperature.
6. Once cooled, transfer the jar to the refrigerator and let it pickle for at least 24 hours before serving. The pickled rambutan will keep in the refrigerator for up to 2 weeks. Enjoy!

"ZESTY PICKLED RED ONION AND LIME"

These pickled red onions are a perfect addition to any Mexican dish or as a topping for a sandwich or burger. The lime adds a bright and refreshing flavor, making these onions a standout condiment.

---

1 red onion, thinly sliced

1 lime, thinly sliced

1 cup white vinegar

1 cup water

2 tbsp sugar

1 tsp salt

1 tsp black peppercorns

1. In a small saucepan, bring the vinegar, water, sugar, salt, and peppercorns to a boil.
2. In a sterilized ball jar, pack the sliced red onion and lime.
3. Pour the hot vinegar mixture over the onions and lime, ensuring they are fully submerged.
4. Let the jar cool to room temperature before sealing and storing in the fridge. These pickled onions will be ready to eat after 24 hours and will last up to a month in the fridge. Enjoy!

"SPICY AND TANGY PICKLED RED ONION"

For those who love the sharp and distinct taste of pickled onions, this recipe is for you! These pickled red onions are made with a mixture of vinegar, mustard, and spices, giving them a unique and flavorful twist. Perfect for adding some extra zing to sandwiches, salads, or even just snacking on their own.

---

1 red onion, thinly sliced

1 cup white vinegar

1/4 cup water

1 tablespoon mustard seeds

1 teaspoon salt

1/2 teaspoon black peppercorns

1/2 teaspoon cumin seeds

1/2 teaspoon chili flakes (optional)

1 ball jar

1. Start by slicing the red onion into thin rings and placing them in a bowl.

2. In a small saucepan, combine the vinegar, water, mustard seeds, salt, black peppercorns, cumin seeds, and chili flakes (if using). Bring the mixture to a boil over high heat.

3. Once the mixture is boiling, pour it over the sliced onions in the bowl. Let the onions sit in the mixture for at least 20 minutes to allow them to pickle.

4. Once the onions have pickled, transfer them to a clean ball jar using a slotted spoon. Make sure to leave enough room at the top of the jar to allow for the onions to be fully submerged in the pickling liquid.

5. Close the jar and store in the refrigerator for at least a week before serving. The pickled onions will keep for up to 3 months in the refrigerator. Enjoy!

"SPICY AND SWEET PICKLED RED ONIONS"

This recipe is perfect for adding a pop of flavor to sandwiches, salads, or even as a topping for tacos. The combination of sweet and spicy will have your taste buds dancing.

1 red onion, thinly sliced

1 cup white vinegar

1 cup water

1/2 cup sugar

2 tbsp sesame seeds

1 tsp red pepper flakes

1 tsp salt

1. In a small saucepan, combine vinegar, water, sugar, sesame seeds, red pepper flakes, and salt. Bring to a boil, stirring occasionally until the sugar has dissolved.
2. Place the sliced onion in a ball jar.
3. Pour the vinegar mixture over the onions, making sure to cover them completely.
4. Let the jar sit at room temperature for at least an hour to allow the flavors to meld.
5. Once the onions have cooled, seal the jar and store in the refrigerator for up to a month.
6. Serve as desired and enjoy the spicy and sweet flavor of these pickled red onions.

DELICIOUS PICKLED RED ONION AND TARRAGON

Growing up, my mom always kept a jar of pickled red onions in the fridge. They were the perfect addition to sandwiches, salads, and even just eaten on their own as a snack. This recipe combines the tangy flavor of pickled onions with the fresh, anise-like taste of tarragon, creating a unique and flavorful condiment. These pickled onions are easy to make and can be stored in a ball jar in the fridge for up to two months.

---

1 large red onion, thinly sliced

1 cup white vinegar

1 cup water

2 tbsp sugar

1 tbsp salt

1 tsp black peppercorns

1 tsp tarragon leaves

1 ball jar with lid

1. In a small saucepan, combine the vinegar, water, sugar, salt, and peppercorns. Bring to a boil, stirring until the sugar and salt have dissolved.

2. Place the sliced onion and tarragon leaves in the ball jar. Pour the hot vinegar mixture over the onions, making sure to fully cover them.

3. Secure the lid on the ball jar and allow to cool to room temperature.

4. Once cooled, store in the fridge for at least 24 hours before using to allow the flavors to meld together.

5. Use in sandwiches, salads, or as a snack on their own. Enjoy!

DELICIOUSLY PICKLED RED ONION AND THYME

When I was first learning how to cook, my grandma taught me the importance of preserving ingredients. One of her go-to recipes was pickled red onion and thyme. The combination of sweet onions and earthy thyme creates a tangy and savory flavor that is perfect for adding to sandwiches, salads, or even just as a tasty snack. Follow this recipe to learn how to make your own pickled red onion and thyme in a ball jar.

1 large red onion, thinly sliced
1 cup white vinegar
1 cup water
2 tbsp sugar
1 tsp salt
1 tsp thyme leaves

1. In a small saucepan, combine the vinegar, water, sugar, and salt. Bring to a boil, stirring occasionally until the sugar and salt are fully dissolved.
2. Place the sliced red onions in a clean ball jar.
3. Pour the hot vinegar mixture over the onions, making sure to fully cover the onions.
4. Add the thyme leaves to the jar.
5. Secure the lid on the ball jar and place in the refrigerator for at least 24 hours before serving.
6. These pickled red onions will last in the refrigerator for up to 2 weeks. Enjoy on sandwiches, salads, or as a tasty snack.

"SPICY PICKLED RED ONIONS"

These pickled red onions are the perfect addition to any sandwich or salad. The spicy kick from the jalapenos and red pepper flakes will give your dish an extra pop of flavor. These onions can be stored in a ball jar for up to 1 month in the refrigerator.

1 large red onion, thinly sliced

1 jalapeno, thinly sliced

1/2 tsp red pepper flakes

1/2 cup vinegar (white or apple cider)

1/2 cup water

2 tbsp sugar

1 tsp salt

1. In a small saucepan, combine vinegar, water, sugar, and salt. Heat over medium heat until the sugar and salt have dissolved.

2. Place the sliced onions and jalapeno in a ball jar.

3. Pour the vinegar mixture over the onions and jalapeno, making sure they are fully covered.

4. Let the jar sit at room temperature for at least 1 hour.

5. Once the onions have pickled to your desired level of tanginess, place the jar in the refrigerator. The onions will continue to pickle as they cool.

6. Serve the pickled onions on sandwiches, salads, or as a garnish for cocktails. Enjoy!

SPICY PICKLED RED PEPPER AND GARLIC

This recipe is inspired by my love for all things spicy and pickled. Red peppers and garlic are two of my favorite ingredients, and when pickled together they create the perfect balance of flavor and heat. These pickled peppers and garlic are great on sandwiches, in salads, or as a garnish for cocktails.

---

1 cup red pepper, thinly sliced
1 cup garlic cloves, peeled
1 cup white vinegar
1 cup water
1 tablespoon sugar
1 tablespoon salt
1 teaspoon red pepper flakes
1 teaspoon black peppercorns

1. In a small saucepan, combine the vinegar, water, sugar, salt, red pepper flakes, and black peppercorns. Bring to a boil, stirring until the sugar and salt are dissolved.
2. Place the sliced red pepper and garlic cloves in a clean ball jar. Pour the hot pickling liquid over the peppers and garlic, making sure to fully submerge them.
3. Let the jar cool to room temperature before sealing with a lid and storing in the refrigerator.
4. These pickled red pepper and garlic will be ready to eat in about 24 hours, and will keep in the refrigerator for up to 1 month. Enjoy!

"ZESTY PICKLED RED PEPPER AND ONION RELISH"

When I first tasted this pickled red pepper and onion relish, I was immediately taken aback by the bold, tangy flavors. It's the perfect condiment to add a little kick to sandwiches, burgers, or even scrambled eggs. The best part? It's super easy to make and can be stored in a ball jar in the fridge for weeks to come.

2 red bell peppers, seeded and finely diced

1 red onion, finely diced

1 cup white vinegar

1/2 cup granulated sugar

1 teaspoon salt

1 teaspoon dried oregano

1/2 teaspoon red pepper flakes

1. In a medium saucepan, combine the red bell peppers, red onion, vinegar, sugar, salt, oregano, and red pepper flakes.

2. Bring the mixture to a boil over medium heat, stirring occasionally.

3. Reduce the heat to low and simmer for 5 minutes, until the vegetables are tender.

4. Remove the saucepan from the heat and let the mixture cool to room temperature.

5. Once cooled, transfer the pickled red pepper and onion relish to a ball jar and seal tightly.

6. Store the jar in the refrigerator for at least 24 hours before serving to allow the flavors to develop.

7. Serve the pickled red pepper and onion relish on sandwiches, burgers, or as a condiment for any dish that needs a little kick. Enjoy!

"ZESTY PICKLED RED PEPPERS WITH A TOUCH OF THYME"

This recipe is a perfect way to preserve the abundance of red peppers from your summer garden. The combination of vinegar and thyme add a delightful zing to the peppers, making them the perfect addition to any sandwich or charcuterie board.

---

4 red peppers, sliced
1 cup white vinegar
1 cup water
1 tablespoon sugar
1 tablespoon salt
2 cloves garlic, minced
1 teaspoon thyme
1 ball jar with a lid

1. Begin by slicing the red peppers into thin strips.
2. In a small saucepan, bring the vinegar, water, sugar, and salt to a boil.
3. Add the minced garlic and thyme to the mixture, stirring to combine.
4. Once the mixture has come to a boil, add the sliced red peppers to the ball jar.
5. Pour the vinegar mixture over the peppers, making sure to completely cover them.
6. Place the lid on the ball jar and let the peppers sit at room temperature for at least 2 hours.
7. Once the peppers have cooled, store them in the refrigerator for up to 2 months. Enjoy!

DELICIOUSLY TART PICKLED RHUBARB

When I was growing up, my grandma always had a stash of pickled rhubarb in the pantry. She would serve it as a tangy condiment with grilled chicken or pork, and it was always a hit at summer barbecues. This recipe is my interpretation of my grandma's classic pickled rhubarb, and I think it's just as delicious as the original.

1 pound fresh rhubarb, trimmed and sliced into 1/2 inch pieces

1 cup apple cider vinegar

1 cup water

1/2 cup granulated sugar

1 tablespoon mustard seeds

2 teaspoons salt

1 cinnamon stick

5 whole cloves

1. In a medium saucepan, bring the vinegar, water, sugar, mustard seeds, salt, cinnamon stick, and cloves to a boil over medium heat.
2. Add the sliced rhubarb to the pot and stir to combine.
3. Reduce the heat to low and simmer for 5 minutes.
4. Remove the pot from the heat and allow the mixture to cool for a few minutes.
5. Using a slotted spoon, transfer the pickled rhubarb to a clean ball jar.
6. Pour the pickling liquid over the rhubarb, making sure it is fully covered.
7. Close the jar and refrigerate for at least 24 hours before serving. The pickled rhubarb will keep in the refrigerator for up to 1 month. Enjoy!

"SPICY PICKLED RHUBARB AND GINGER DELIGHT"

If you're a fan of sweet and sour flavors, this pickled rhubarb and ginger recipe is for you! The combination of spicy ginger and tangy rhubarb is perfect for adding some zest to your sandwiches or as a topping for grilled meats. Plus, using a ball jar means you can easily store and preserve this delicious condiment.

---

2 cups diced rhubarb

1 cup white vinegar

1 cup water

1/2 cup sugar

2 tablespoons grated ginger

2 cloves garlic, minced

1 teaspoon red pepper flakes

2 teaspoons salt

1. In a small saucepan, combine the vinegar, water, sugar, ginger, garlic, red pepper flakes, and salt. Bring to a boil and stir until the sugar has dissolved.
2. Place the diced rhubarb in a sterilized ball jar.
3. Pour the hot vinegar mixture over the rhubarb, making sure to completely cover the rhubarb.
4. Seal the ball jar and let it cool to room temperature.
5. Once cooled, store the jar in the refrigerator for at least 24 hours before serving. The pickled rhubarb and ginger will keep in the refrigerator for up to 2 weeks. Enjoy!

DELICIOUS PICKLED RHUBARB AND MINT

Introducing a unique and refreshing twist on traditional pickled vegetables - pickled rhubarb and mint. This recipe is perfect for those who love the tartness of pickled vegetables, but are looking for something a little more unexpected.

1 pound fresh rhubarb, cut into small pieces
1/2 cup white vinegar
1/2 cup water
1/4 cup sugar
1 tablespoon pickling salt
1 teaspoon black peppercorns
3 sprigs fresh mint

1. Combine the vinegar, water, sugar, pickling salt, and black peppercorns in a small saucepan. Bring to a boil over medium heat, stirring until the sugar and salt are dissolved.
2. Place the rhubarb and mint in a clean ball jar. Pour the hot vinegar mixture over the top, making sure to fully cover the rhubarb.
3. Secure the lid on the ball jar and allow the mixture to cool to room temperature.
4. Once cooled, transfer the jar to the refrigerator to allow the pickling process to complete. The pickled rhubarb and mint will be ready to enjoy in about 24 hours, but will taste even better after a few days in the refrigerator.
5. Serve the pickled rhubarb and mint as a unique side dish, or add it to sandwiches and salads for a burst of flavor. Enjoy!

"ZESTY PICKLED SALSIFY AND ONION RELISH"

Looking for a unique and flavorful condiment to add to your sandwiches, burgers, or even just to enjoy on its own? Look no further than this pickled salsify and onion relish! Salsify, also known as "oyster plant," is a root vegetable with a slightly sweet and nutty flavor, and when paired with tangy onions and a variety of spices, it creates a relish that will elevate any dish.

---

2 salsify roots, peeled and thinly sliced

1 large onion, thinly sliced

2 cups white vinegar

1 cup water

1/4 cup sugar

1 tbsp salt

1 tsp mustard seeds

1 tsp coriander seeds

1 tsp black peppercorns

1/2 tsp allspice berries

1 bay leaf

2 cloves garlic, minced

2 ball jars, sterilized

1. In a medium pot, combine the vinegar, water, sugar, salt, mustard seeds, coriander seeds, peppercorns, allspice berries, bay leaf, and minced garlic. Bring to a boil, stirring occasionally.

2. Once the mixture is boiling, add in the sliced salsify and onion. Reduce heat to a simmer and cook for an additional 5 minutes.

3. Using a slotted spoon, carefully transfer the salsify and onion to the sterilized ball jars, packing them in tightly.

4. Pour the pickling liquid over the salsify and onion in the jars, leaving about 1/2 inch of headspace.

5. Wipe the rim of the jars with a damp cloth and seal the jars with their lids.

6. Place the jars in a pot filled with water, making sure the water level is at least 1 inch above the top of the jars. Bring the water to a boil and process the jars for 10 minutes.

7. Remove the jars from the pot and allow them to cool completely. The relish will keep in the refrigerator for up to 3 months. Enjoy!

"SWEET AND SPICY PICKLED SHALLOT AND GARLIC"

This pickled shallot and garlic recipe is a perfect blend of sweet and spicy flavors. It's a great addition to any sandwich or salad, and it's also great as a condiment for grilled meats.

1 cup white vinegar

1 cup sugar

1 tablespoon red pepper flakes

1 tablespoon black peppercorns

1 tablespoon mustard seeds

4 cloves garlic, thinly sliced

1 large shallot, thinly sliced

2 ball jars

1. In a medium saucepan, combine the vinegar, sugar, red pepper flakes, peppercorns, and mustard seeds. Bring to a boil, stirring occasionally, until the sugar is dissolved.

2. Divide the garlic and shallot slices between the two ball jars.

3. Carefully pour the vinegar mixture over the garlic and shallots in the ball jars, making sure to cover them completely.

4. Close the ball jars and allow them to cool to room temperature.

5. Once cooled, place the ball jars in the refrigerator and allow them to pickle for at least 3 days before serving. The pickled shallot and garlic will keep in the refrigerator for up to 2 weeks.

"ZESTY PICKLED SHALLOT AND LEMON"

Pickling is a great way to preserve the flavors of fresh produce and add a burst of tanginess to dishes. This recipe for pickled shallots and lemon is perfect for adding a pop of flavor to sandwiches, salads, or as a topping for grilled meats.

1 pound shallots, thinly sliced

2 lemons, thinly sliced

2 cups white vinegar

1 cup water

2 tablespoons sugar

1 tablespoon salt

1 teaspoon black peppercorns

1 teaspoon mustard seeds

2 bay leaves

2 cloves garlic, smashed

1. In a small saucepan, combine the vinegar, water, sugar, salt, peppercorns, mustard seeds, bay leaves, and garlic. Bring to a boil over medium heat, stirring occasionally until the sugar and salt have dissolved.

2. In a large ball jar, layer the shallots and lemon slices. Pour the hot vinegar mixture over the shallots and lemons, making sure they are fully submerged.

3. Allow the jar to cool to room temperature, then seal and store in the refrigerator for at least 24 hours before using. The pickled shallots and lemon will last for up to 2 months in the refrigerator.

4. To use, simply remove the desired amount of pickled shallots and lemon from the jar and add to your desired dish. Enjoy!

"ZESTY PICKLED SHALLOT AND ONION RELISH"

This pickled shallot and onion relish is the perfect addition to any sandwich or charcuterie board. The combination of sweet onions and tangy shallots pairs well with a variety of meats and cheeses. Plus, the colorful jar of pickled vegetables makes for a beautiful display on any table.

---

1 cup sliced shallots

1 cup sliced onions

1 cup apple cider vinegar

1 cup water

1 tablespoon sugar

1 teaspoon salt

2 cloves garlic, minced

1 teaspoon mustard seeds

1 teaspoon peppercorns

1. In a small saucepan, combine the apple cider vinegar, water, sugar, and salt. Bring to a boil and then reduce to a simmer.

2. Place the shallots, onions, garlic, mustard seeds, and peppercorns in a clean ball jar.

3. Pour the hot vinegar mixture over the vegetables in the jar, making sure to cover them completely.

4. Secure the lid on the jar and let it cool to room temperature.

5. Once cool, store in the refrigerator for at least 1 hour before serving. The pickled shallot and onion relish will last up to 2 weeks in the fridge.

6. Serve alongside sandwiches or on a charcuterie board with meats and cheeses of your choice. Enjoy!

"TANTALIZING THYME AND PICKLED SHALLOT DELIGHT"

If you're a fan of bold and savory flavors, you'll love this recipe for pickled shallot and thyme. The combination of sweet and tangy shallots with the woodsy, aromatic flavor of thyme is truly something special. Plus, this recipe is super easy to make and can be stored in a ball jar for weeks, making it a great addition to any pantry.

1 cup white vinegar

1 cup water

1/4 cup sugar

1 tsp salt

2 large shallots, thinly sliced

3 sprigs of thyme

1 ball jar

1. In a small saucepan, combine the vinegar, water, sugar, and salt. Bring to a boil and stir until the sugar and salt have dissolved.

2. Place the sliced shallots and thyme sprigs in the ball jar.

3. Pour the vinegar mixture over the shallots and thyme, making sure to cover them completely.

4. Let the jar cool to room temperature, then seal and store in the refrigerator for at least a week before enjoying.

5. These pickled shallots and thyme are a great addition to sandwiches, salads, and even as a topping for grilled meats. Enjoy!

DELICIOUSLY SPICY PICKLED CARROTS AND JALAPENO

These pickled carrots and jalapeno are the perfect addition to any Mexican-inspired dish or as a tasty snack on their own. The spicy kick from the jalapeno pairs perfectly with the crispness of the carrots, making for a flavorful and addicting treat.

---

1 lb carrots, peeled and cut into thin slices
2 jalapeno peppers, thinly sliced
1 cup white vinegar
1 cup water
2 tbsp sugar
2 tsp salt
1 tsp black peppercorns
2 cloves garlic, minced

1. In a small saucepan, bring the vinegar, water, sugar, salt, and peppercorns to a boil.
2. Once boiling, remove from heat and add the garlic.
3. Place the carrots and jalapeno slices in a clean ball jar.
4. Pour the hot vinegar mixture over the carrots and jalapeno, making sure they are fully covered.
5. Seal the jar and allow it to cool completely.
6. Once cooled, store in the refrigerator for at least 24 hours before enjoying. These pickled carrots and jalapeno will last for up to two weeks in the refrigerator.

SPICY PICKLED CARROTS AND RADISHES

These spicy pickled carrots and radishes are the perfect addition to any sandwich or salad. The combination of sweet carrots and spicy radishes is a match made in heaven. The vinegar and spices give these veggies a tangy kick that will have you coming back for more.

---

1 cup vinegar

1 cup water

1 tablespoon sugar

1 teaspoon salt

1 teaspoon red pepper flakes

1 clove garlic, minced

1 cup carrots, thinly sliced

1 cup radishes, thinly sliced

1. In a small saucepan, combine the vinegar, water, sugar, salt, red pepper flakes, and minced garlic. Bring to a boil.
2. Place the thinly sliced carrots and radishes in a sterilized ball jar.
3. Pour the hot vinegar mixture over the carrots and radishes in the jar, making sure to fully cover the veggies.
4. Close the jar tightly and allow to cool.
5. Place the jar in the refrigerator for at least 24 hours before serving. These pickled carrots and radishes will keep in the refrigerator for up to one month.

"ZESTY PICKLED GREEN BEANS"

Growing up, my grandma always had a jar of these spicy pickled green beans in her pantry. They were the perfect addition to any sandwich or burger, adding a crunchy and tangy bite. Now, I like to make a batch of my own to keep in my own pantry. This recipe makes enough to fill a quart-sized ball jar.

---

1 pound green beans, trimmed

1 cup white vinegar

1 cup water

2 teaspoons sugar

1 teaspoon salt

2 cloves garlic, minced

1 teaspoon mustard seeds

1 teaspoon coriander seeds

1/2 teaspoon red pepper flakes

1. In a small saucepan, bring the vinegar, water, sugar, and salt to a boil.

2. While the brine is heating up, pack the green beans into the ball jar.

3. Add the garlic, mustard seeds, coriander seeds, and red pepper flakes to the jar.

4. Once the brine has come to a boil, pour it over the green beans in the jar, making sure to fully cover them.

5. Close the jar tightly and let it cool to room temperature.

6. Once cooled, store the jar in the fridge for at least 24 hours before serving. The pickled green beans will last in the fridge for up to 2 weeks. Enjoy!

SPICY PICKLED GREEN TOMATOES

Growing up, my family always had a huge garden in the summertime. One year, we decided to try growing green tomatoes and ended up with a surplus. My mom came up with this recipe for pickled green tomatoes and they have been a family favorite ever since. The heat from the jalapenos pairs perfectly with the tanginess of the vinegar. These spicy pickled green tomatoes are perfect on sandwiches, in salads, or as a snack on their own.

---

4 cups green tomatoes, sliced into wedges

2 jalapeno peppers, sliced into thin rounds

2 cloves garlic, sliced

1 cup vinegar

1 cup water

2 tablespoons sugar

1 tablespoon salt

1 tablespoon black peppercorns

1. Sterilize a large ball jar by boiling it in a pot of water for 10 minutes.
2. In a small saucepan, bring the vinegar, water, sugar, salt, and peppercorns to a boil.
3. Place the green tomato wedges, jalapeno slices, and garlic slices in the sterilized ball jar.
4. Pour the hot vinegar mixture over the vegetables, making sure to completely cover them.
5. Close the jar and allow to cool to room temperature.
6. Store in the refrigerator for at least 2 days before serving. These pickled green tomatoes will last for up to 3 months in the refrigerator. Enjoy!

"SPICY PICKLED SPINACH AND GARLIC DELIGHT"

When I was traveling through the Mediterranean, I discovered the delicious combination of pickled spinach and garlic. The tangy and spicy flavors were the perfect complement to so many dishes. I knew I had to recreate this recipe at home, and now it's a staple in my kitchen. Try it as a topping for sandwiches or salads, or add it to your charcuterie board for an extra kick of flavor.

---

1 pound fresh spinach

1 cup white vinegar

2 cloves garlic, minced

1 teaspoon salt

1 teaspoon sugar

1 teaspoon red pepper flakes

1. Wash and dry the spinach leaves, then roughly chop them into bite-sized pieces.

2. In a small saucepan, combine the vinegar, garlic, salt, sugar, and red pepper flakes. Bring the mixture to a boil, then reduce the heat to a simmer.

3. Add the chopped spinach to the saucepan and stir until the leaves are fully coated in the pickling liquid.

4. Remove the saucepan from the heat and let the spinach cool to room temperature.

5. Once cooled, transfer the spinach and pickling liquid to a clean ball jar. Make sure to pack the spinach tightly into the jar.

6. Place the lid on the jar and store it in the refrigerator for at least 24 hours before serving. The pickled spinach will keep in the refrigerator for up to 2 weeks.

"GRANDMA'S FAMOUS PICKLED SQUASH"

Growing up, my grandma always had a jar of pickled squash in the pantry. She would make it every summer using the freshest zucchini and yellow squash from her garden. It was a staple at every family gathering and now, I carry on her tradition with this recipe.

---

3 medium zucchini, thinly sliced

3 medium yellow squash, thinly sliced

1 large onion, thinly sliced

1 cup white vinegar

1 cup water

1 tablespoon sugar

1 tablespoon salt

1 tablespoon pickling spice

1. In a large bowl, combine the sliced zucchini, yellow squash, and onion.
2. In a small saucepan, bring the vinegar, water, sugar, salt, and pickling spice to a boil.
3. Pour the hot liquid over the vegetables in the bowl and stir to combine.
4. Transfer the mixture to a large ball jar, making sure to pack the vegetables tightly.
5. Allow the jar to cool to room temperature, then refrigerate for at least 24 hours before serving.
6. The pickled squash will keep for up to a month in the refrigerator. Enjoy as a side dish or add to sandwiches and salads for a burst of flavor.

DELICIOUS PICKLED SQUASH AND ONION RELISH

This recipe for pickled squash and onion relish is perfect for those hot summer days when you want to add a little something extra to your burger or sandwich. The combination of sweet and tangy flavors is sure to be a hit with your friends and family.

2 cups diced squash

1 cup diced onions

1 cup vinegar

1 cup sugar

1 tablespoon mustard seeds

1 teaspoon salt

1 ball jar

1. In a small saucepan, combine the vinegar, sugar, mustard seeds, and salt. Bring to a boil and stir until the sugar is dissolved.

2. In a bowl, combine the diced squash and onions. Pour the hot vinegar mixture over the top and stir to combine.

3. Place the mixture in the ball jar and close the lid. Let the jar sit at room temperature for at least 24 hours before serving.

4. Enjoy your pickled squash and onion relish on sandwiches, burgers, or as a topping for grilled vegetables. It will keep in the refrigerator for up to 2 weeks.

"VANILLA AND STARFRUIT PICKLES - A TROPICAL TWIST ON CLASSIC PICKLES"

Growing up, I loved the classic dill pickles that my mom would make every summer. However, as I've gotten older and started experimenting with different flavors, I've come to love the unique taste of pickled starfruit and vanilla. The sweetness of the vanilla pairs perfectly with the tanginess of the starfruit, creating a truly delicious pickle that is perfect for any summer barbecue or just as a snack.

1 pound starfruit, thinly sliced

1 cup white vinegar

1 cup water

1/2 cup sugar

1 tablespoon pickling salt

2 cinnamon sticks

4 whole cloves

1 vanilla bean, split lengthwise

4 ball jars

1. Wash and sterilize the ball jars and lids.
2. In a small saucepan, combine the vinegar, water, sugar, pickling salt, cinnamon sticks, and cloves. Bring to a boil over medium heat, stirring occasionally to dissolve the sugar and salt.
3. Add the sliced starfruit to the boiling liquid and return to a boil. Reduce the heat to low and simmer for 5 minutes.
4. Meanwhile, scrape the seeds out of the vanilla bean and add them to the pot. Discard the bean.
5. Using tongs, carefully transfer the starfruit slices to the prepared ball jars, making sure to evenly distribute the spices and vanilla seeds.
6. Pour the hot liquid over the starfruit, filling the jars to within 1/2 inch of the top. Wipe the rims clean and screw on the lids.
7. Process the jars in a hot water bath for 10 minutes.

DELICIOUSLY PICKLED STRAWBERRY AND BALSAMIC VINEGAR

This recipe is inspired by a trip to the local farmer's market where I found the most beautiful, ripe strawberries. I wanted to find a way to preserve them, and came up with this recipe for pickled strawberries in balsamic vinegar. It's a sweet and tangy treat that's perfect for topping salads, cheese plates, or even for enjoying on their own as a snack.

1 pint strawberries, hulled and quartered

1/2 cup balsamic vinegar

1/4 cup sugar

1/4 cup water

1 cinnamon stick

2 whole cloves

1 ball jar (quart size)

1. In a small saucepan, combine the balsamic vinegar, sugar, water, cinnamon stick, and cloves. Bring to a boil over medium heat, stirring occasionally, until the sugar has dissolved.

2. Place the quartered strawberries in the ball jar. Pour the hot vinegar mixture over the strawberries, making sure to fully submerge them.

3. Let the jar cool to room temperature, then seal and store in the refrigerator. The pickled strawberries will be ready to eat in about 2 days, and will keep in the refrigerator for up to a month.

4. Serve the pickled strawberries on top of salads, cheese plates, or enjoy them as a snack. Enjoy!

"SWEET AND TART PICKLED STRAWBERRIES WITH A HINT OF BASIL"

These pickled strawberries are a unique and tasty addition to any charcuterie board or cheese plate. The combination of sweet and tart flavors, paired with the aromatic basil, make for a truly delightful snack. And the best part? They're super easy to make and can be stored in a beautiful ball jar for up to a month in the fridge.

---

1 pint fresh strawberries, hulled and halved
1/2 cup white vinegar
1/2 cup water
1/4 cup granulated sugar
1 tablespoon pickling salt
1/4 teaspoon red pepper flakes (optional)
8-10 basil leaves

1. In a small saucepan, combine the vinegar, water, sugar, pickling salt, and red pepper flakes (if using). Bring to a boil over medium heat, stirring until the sugar and salt are fully dissolved.

2. Place the strawberries in a clean and sterile ball jar. Add the basil leaves on top.

3. Pour the hot vinegar mixture over the strawberries, making sure to fully cover them.

4. Let the jar cool to room temperature, then seal and store in the refrigerator for at least 1 day before serving. The pickled strawberries will keep in the fridge for up to 1 month.

5. Serve the pickled strawberries as part of a charcuterie board or cheese plate, or use them as a topping for salads or desserts. Enjoy!

"SPICY AND SWEET PICKLED STRAWBERRIES"

If you're a fan of sweet and savory combinations, these pickled strawberries are sure to become a new favorite. The combination of strawberries and black pepper might sound odd, but trust us, it works. The pepper adds a subtle kick to the sweetness of the strawberries, making for a truly unique and delicious treat.

---

1 pint fresh strawberries, hulled and quartered
1 cup white vinegar
1 cup water
1/2 cup sugar
1 tablespoon black peppercorns
1 teaspoon salt

1. In a small saucepan, combine the vinegar, water, sugar, peppercorns, and salt. Bring to a boil, stirring occasionally, until the sugar has dissolved.

2. Place the strawberries in a sterilized ball jar. Pour the hot vinegar mixture over the strawberries, making sure to completely cover the fruit.

3. Let the jar cool to room temperature, then seal the lid and store in the refrigerator for at least 24 hours before serving. The strawberries will keep in the refrigerator for up to 2 weeks.

4. Serve the pickled strawberries as a topping for salads, sandwiches, or cheese plates, or simply enjoy them on their own as a tasty snack. Enjoy!

"ELEGANT PICKLED STRAWBERRIES WITH LAVENDER"

This recipe is a unique twist on traditional pickled fruit, using the floral flavors of lavender to elevate the sweetness of the strawberries. Perfect for a summertime appetizer or a gift for a foodie friend, these pickled strawberries are sure to impress.

---

1 pint fresh strawberries, hulled and halved

1 cup white vinegar

1 cup water

1/2 cup sugar

2 tablespoons dried lavender

2 cloves garlic, peeled and lightly smashed

1 teaspoon kosher salt

1 bay leaf

2 whole cloves

1 small cinnamon stick

1. In a medium saucepan, combine the vinegar, water, sugar, lavender, garlic, salt, bay leaf, cloves, and cinnamon stick. Bring the mixture to a boil over medium-high heat, stirring until the sugar has dissolved.

2. Add the strawberries to a clean and sterilized ball jar, packing them in tightly.

3. Pour the hot pickling liquid over the strawberries, making sure to cover them completely.

4. Close the ball jar tightly and let it cool to room temperature.

5. Once cooled, transfer the jar to the refrigerator and let it sit for at least 24 hours before serving. The pickled strawberries will keep for up to 2 weeks in the refrigerator.

6. Serve the pickled strawberries as an appetizer, on a cheese board, or alongside grilled meats. Enjoy!

"SWEET AND TART PICKLED STRAWBERRIES AND LEMONS"

This recipe for pickled strawberries and lemons is the perfect balance of sweet and tart. The combination may seem unusual, but the flavors complement each other perfectly. The pickled fruit can be served as a unique condiment or topping for salads, desserts, or even cocktails.

---

1 pint strawberries, hulled and halved
1 lemon, thinly sliced
1 cup white vinegar
1 cup water
1/2 cup sugar
1 teaspoon salt
1 cinnamon stick
4 whole cloves

1. In a medium saucepan, combine the vinegar, water, sugar, salt, cinnamon stick, and cloves. Bring to a boil, stirring to dissolve the sugar and salt.
2. Place the strawberries and lemon slices in a clean ball jar.
3. Pour the hot vinegar mixture over the fruit, making sure to cover it completely.
4. Seal the jar and let it cool to room temperature.
5. Transfer the jar to the refrigerator and let it pickle for at least 2 days before serving. The pickled fruit will last up to 2 weeks in the refrigerator.

DELICIOUS PICKLED STRAWBERRY AND ONION RELISH

This pickled strawberry and onion relish is the perfect balance of sweet and savory. It's a unique condiment that will add flavor to any dish.

---

1 pint fresh strawberries, hulled and quartered
1 small red onion, thinly sliced
1/2 cup white vinegar
1/2 cup sugar
1/2 teaspoon salt
1/4 teaspoon black pepper

1. In a small saucepan, combine the vinegar, sugar, salt, and pepper. Bring to a boil over medium heat, stirring until the sugar has dissolved.
2. In a sterilized ball jar, layer the strawberries and onion slices.
3. Pour the hot vinegar mixture over the strawberries and onions, making sure to completely cover the fruit.
4. Close the jar tightly and let it cool to room temperature.
5. Once cooled, store the jar in the refrigerator for at least 24 hours to allow the flavors to meld.
6. The pickled strawberry and onion relish will keep in the refrigerator for up to 1 month. Enjoy!

"SWEET AND TANGY PICKLED STRAWBERRIES WITH A HINT OF ROSE"

These pickled strawberries are the perfect balance of sweet and tangy, with a hint of floral rose flavor. They make a delightful addition to a cheese platter or can be used as a topping for ice cream or yogurt. The recipe is simple and the results are truly delicious.

---

1 pint strawberries, hulled and quartered

1 cup white vinegar

1 cup water

1/2 cup granulated sugar

1 teaspoon rose water

1/2 teaspoon salt

1 cinnamon stick

4 whole cloves

1. In a medium saucepan, combine the vinegar, water, sugar, rose water, salt, cinnamon stick, and cloves. Bring to a boil over medium heat, stirring until the sugar is dissolved.

2. Add the strawberries to a clean, sterilized ball jar. Pour the hot pickling liquid over the strawberries, making sure to fully cover the fruit.

3. Let the jar cool to room temperature, then seal and refrigerate for at least 24 hours before serving. The pickled strawberries will keep in the refrigerator for up to 2 weeks. Enjoy!

"SWEET AND SAVORY PICKLED STRAWBERRIES WITH ROSEMARY"

These pickled strawberries are the perfect balance of sweet and savory, with a hint of rosemary for an added depth of flavor. They make a unique addition to a cheese board or charcuterie spread, and are also delicious on their own as a snack. Plus, they're super easy to make and can be stored in the fridge for up to a month, making them a great option for preserving the taste of summer strawberries long after they're out of season.

---

1 pint fresh strawberries, hulled and quartered

1 cup apple cider vinegar

1 cup water

1/2 cup granulated sugar

2 tablespoons honey

2 sprigs fresh rosemary

2 teaspoons whole black peppercorns

2 teaspoons kosher salt

1 small shallot, thinly sliced

1. In a medium saucepan, combine the vinegar, water, sugar, honey, rosemary, peppercorns, and salt. Bring to a boil over medium-high heat, stirring until the sugar and salt have dissolved.

2. Add the strawberries and shallot to a clean and sterilized ball jar. Pour the hot vinegar mixture over the top of the strawberries, making sure to completely cover them.

3. Let the jar cool to room temperature, then seal and store in the fridge for at least 24 hours before enjoying. The pickled strawberries will keep in the fridge for up to a month.

BALL JAR BEAUTY: PICKLED SWEET AND SOUR RED ONIONS"

Pickled red onions are a tangy and colorful addition to any dish. They add a pop of flavor and texture to sandwiches, salads, and more. These sweet and sour pickled red onions are easy to make and can be stored in the fridge for up to a month.

1 large red onion, thinly sliced

1 cup white vinegar

1 cup water

2 tablespoons granulated sugar

1 teaspoon salt

2 bay leaves

2 whole cloves

1 cinnamon stick

1. In a medium saucepan, combine the vinegar, water, sugar, salt, bay leaves, cloves, and cinnamon stick. Bring the mixture to a boil over high heat, stirring occasionally.

2. Once boiling, add the sliced onions to the mixture and stir to combine. Reduce the heat to low and simmer for 5 minutes.

3. Remove the saucepan from the heat and let the onions cool in the pickling liquid for about 20 minutes.

4. Using a slotted spoon, transfer the pickled onions to a clean and sterilized ball jar. Pour the pickling liquid over the onions, making sure to cover them completely.

5. Tightly seal the ball jar and store it in the refrigerator for at least 24 hours before using. The pickled onions will keep in the fridge for up to a month.

"TANGY AND SWEET PICKLED RED PEPPERS"

These pickled red peppers are the perfect combination of tangy and sweet, with a satisfying crunch in every bite. They are a great addition to sandwiches, salads, or as a topping for tacos and nachos. Plus, the red peppers add a pop of color to any dish.

---

2 cups red bell peppers, sliced
1 cup white vinegar
1 cup water
1/2 cup sugar
1 tablespoon salt
2 cloves garlic, minced
1 teaspoon mustard seeds
1 teaspoon coriander seeds
1 teaspoon black peppercorns
1 ball jar (1 quart size)

1. In a small saucepan, combine the vinegar, water, sugar, salt, garlic, mustard seeds, coriander seeds, and black peppercorns. Bring to a boil, stirring occasionally until the sugar and salt have dissolved.

2. Meanwhile, prepare the red peppers by slicing them into thin strips.

3. Place the red pepper strips into the ball jar.

4. Once the vinegar mixture has come to a boil, pour it over the red peppers in the ball jar, making sure to cover the peppers completely.

5. Close the ball jar with a lid and let it cool to room temperature. Once cooled, place the jar in the refrigerator for at least 24 hours before serving.

6. These pickled red peppers will last for up to 2 weeks in the refrigerator. Enjoy!

"SUN-RIPENED PICKLED TOMATOES WITH BASIL"

There's nothing quite like the taste of a sun-ripened tomato fresh off the vine. But if you find yourself with an abundance of tomatoes and don't think you'll be able to eat them all before they go bad, pickling is a great way to preserve their delicious flavor for later. These pickled tomatoes are infused with the bright, fresh taste of basil, making them a tasty addition to sandwiches, salads, and more.

2 cups white vinegar

1 cup water

2 tablespoons sugar

2 tablespoons kosher salt

1 tablespoon peppercorns

1 teaspoon mustard seeds

4 cloves garlic, peeled

4 sprigs fresh basil

4 cups cherry tomatoes, halved

1. In a small saucepan, bring the vinegar, water, sugar, salt, peppercorns, and mustard seeds to a boil. Stir until the sugar and salt are dissolved.

2. Place the garlic and basil sprigs in the bottom of a clean, sterilized ball jar.

3. Pack the cherry tomato halves into the jar, fitting them in as tightly as possible.

4. Pour the hot vinegar mixture over the tomatoes, making sure to completely cover them.

5. Place the lid on the jar and let it cool to room temperature.

6. Once cooled, transfer the jar to the refrigerator and let it sit for at least 24 hours before serving. The pickled tomatoes will last for up to a month in the refrigerator. Enjoy!

ZESTY PICKLED TOMATOES WITH A KICK OF BLACK PEPPER"

These pickled tomatoes are the perfect addition to any sandwich or charcuterie board. The combination of sweet, tangy, and spicy flavors is sure to please the palate. And the best part? They're super easy to make! All you need is a few simple ingredients and a ball jar.

2 lbs tomatoes, cored and quartered

1 cup white vinegar

1 cup water

1/4 cup sugar

2 tsp black peppercorns

2 cloves garlic, sliced

1 tsp salt

1. In a small saucepan, bring the vinegar, water, sugar, peppercorns, garlic, and salt to a boil. Stir until the sugar is dissolved.

2. Place the tomatoes in a sterilized ball jar. Pour the vinegar mixture over the tomatoes, making sure to cover them completely.

3. Let the jar cool to room temperature, then seal and refrigerate for at least 24 hours before serving. The pickled tomatoes will keep for up to a month in the refrigerator.

4. Serve the pickled tomatoes as a condiment on sandwiches or as a topping for burgers and salads. Enjoy!

"FIRE-ROASTED PICKLED TOMATO AND CHILI"

If you're a fan of spicy and tangy flavors, these fire-roasted pickled tomatoes and chilis are sure to be a hit. They're the perfect addition to any sandwich or salad, or can be served as a spicy appetizer. The fire-roasting adds a smoky depth to the tomatoes and chilis, while the pickling process preserves them for long-term storage in the fridge or pantry.

---

2 lbs Roma tomatoes

4 jalapeno peppers

4 serrano peppers

2 cloves garlic, minced

2 tbsp olive oil

1 cup white vinegar

1 cup water

2 tbsp sugar

1 tsp salt

1 tsp black peppercorns

4 sprigs fresh thyme

4 sprigs fresh oregano

1. Preheat your grill to high heat.
2. Cut the tomatoes in half lengthwise and place them cut side down on the grill. Grill for 5-7 minutes, or until the skin is blackened and blistered.
3. While the tomatoes are grilling, place the jalapeno and serrano peppers on the grill. Grill for 3-4 minutes, or until the skin is blackened and blistered.
4. Remove the grilled vegetables from the grill and place them in a bowl. Cover the bowl with foil or plastic wrap and let the vegetables sit for 10-15 minutes.
5. Peel the skin off of the tomatoes and peppers, and chop them into small pieces.
6. In a small saucepan, combine the vinegar, water, sugar, salt, peppercorns, thyme, and oregano. Bring to a boil, then reduce the heat and simmer for 5 minutes.
7. Place the chopped tomatoes and peppers in a large jar or several smaller jars. Pour the hot vinegar mixture over the vegetables, making sure to cover them completely.
8. Let the jar(s) cool to room temperature, then seal and refrigerate for at least 24 hours before serving. These pickled tomatoes and chilis will keep in the fridge for up to 2 weeks.

"ZESTY PICKLED TOMATO AND GARLIC"

If you love the tangy, briny flavor of pickled vegetables, then you'll definitely want to give this recipe a try. The combination of ripe tomatoes and pungent garlic is a match made in heaven, and the result is a flavorful and addictive condiment that will add a pop of flavor to any dish. Whether you're a fan of canning or just looking for a new way to use up an excess of tomatoes, this recipe is sure to become a new favorite.

4 cups cherry tomatoes, quartered

4 cloves garlic, minced

1 cup white vinegar

1 cup water

2 tablespoons sugar

2 teaspoons salt

1 teaspoon black peppercorns

1 teaspoon dried oregano

1 teaspoon dried basil

1. In a small saucepan, combine the vinegar, water, sugar, salt, peppercorns, oregano, and basil. Bring to a boil over medium heat, stirring to dissolve the sugar and salt.
2. Meanwhile, place the quartered tomatoes and minced garlic in a large ball jar.
3. Once the brine has come to a boil, pour it over the tomatoes and garlic in the jar. Make sure the vegetables are fully submerged in the brine.
4. Secure the lid on the ball jar and let the pickled tomatoes and garlic cool to room temperature.
5. Once cooled, transfer the jar to the refrigerator and let the pickles marinate for at least 24 hours before serving. The pickled tomatoes and garlic will last for up to 2 weeks in the refrigerator. Enjoy!

"SUMMERTIME BLISS: PICKLED TOMATO AND ONION RELISH"

This pickled tomato and onion relish is the perfect condiment to add a little zing to your summertime barbecue. It's easy to make and can be stored in a ball jar in the fridge for up to a few months, so you can enjoy it all season long.

2 cups diced tomatoes

1 cup diced onions

1/2 cup white vinegar

1/4 cup sugar

1 tsp salt

1/2 tsp black pepper

1 tsp mustard seeds

1/2 tsp coriander seeds

1/2 tsp celery seeds

1/2 tsp red pepper flakes (optional for a little extra heat)

1. In a medium saucepan, combine the diced tomatoes, onions, vinegar, sugar, salt, pepper, mustard seeds, coriander seeds, celery seeds, and red pepper flakes (if using).

2. Bring the mixture to a boil, then reduce the heat to a simmer and let cook for about 5 minutes, until the vegetables are slightly softened.

3. Remove the saucepan from the heat and let the mixture cool slightly.

4. Transfer the pickled tomato and onion relish to a ball jar, making sure to leave about 1 inch of headspace at the top.

5. Secure the lid on the ball jar and store in the fridge for at least a few hours, or up to a few months.

6. Serve the pickled tomato and onion relish alongside your favorite grilled meats or as a topping for burgers and sandwiches. Enjoy!

DELICIOUS PICKLED TOMATOES WITH OREGANO

This recipe for pickled tomatoes with oregano is a delicious and easy way to preserve the taste of summer tomatoes for year-round enjoyment. The oregano adds a lovely depth of flavor to the pickled tomatoes, making them the perfect addition to sandwiches, salads, and more.

4 cups diced tomatoes

2 tablespoons oregano, fresh or dried

1 cup vinegar

1 cup water

2 tablespoons sugar

1 tablespoon salt

4 cloves garlic, peeled

4 sprigs fresh thyme

4 sprigs fresh oregano

4 ball jars with lids

1. Begin by sterilizing your ball jars and lids. To do this, wash the jars and lids in hot, soapy water and then place them in a large pot of boiling water for 10 minutes. Remove the jars and lids from the pot and set them aside to cool.
2. In a small saucepan, combine the vinegar, water, sugar, and salt. Bring the mixture to a boil, stirring occasionally, until the sugar and salt have dissolved.
3. Place the diced tomatoes, oregano, garlic, thyme, and oregano sprigs in the sterilized ball jars.
4. Carefully pour the vinegar mixture over the tomatoes, leaving about 1/2 inch of headspace at the top of the jar.
5. Wipe the rim of the jar with a clean, damp cloth and place the lid on top, securing it tightly.
6. Place the jars in a large pot of boiling water and process for 15 minutes.
7. Remove the jars from the pot and set them aside to cool. As the jars cool, you should hear a popping sound, indicating that the jars are sealing properly.
8. Once the jars are completely cooled, label and store them in a cool, dark place for up to 1 year. Enjoy your pickled tomatoes with oregano on sandwiches, salads, and more.

"SUMMERTIME IN A JAR: PICKLED TOMATOES WITH ROSEMARY"

This recipe is the perfect way to preserve the taste of summertime all year round. The combination of tangy pickled tomatoes and fragrant rosemary creates a unique and flavorful condiment that can be enjoyed on sandwiches, salads, or as a topping for grilled meats. Plus, the use of a Ball jar means you can easily store and transport these pickled tomatoes for any occasion.

---

1 pint cherry tomatoes, halved

1 sprig fresh rosemary

1 clove garlic, peeled and minced

1 teaspoon whole black peppercorns

1 teaspoon sea salt

1 cup white vinegar

1 cup water

1. Wash and dry a pint-sized Ball jar and its lid.
2. In the jar, combine the cherry tomatoes, rosemary sprig, garlic, peppercorns, and salt.
3. In a small saucepan, bring the vinegar and water to a boil.
4. Pour the hot vinegar mixture over the ingredients in the jar, making sure to cover all of the tomatoes.
5. Place the lid on the jar and seal it tightly.
6. Allow the jar to cool to room temperature, then store it in the refrigerator for at least 24 hours before serving. The pickled tomatoes will last for up to a week in the refrigerator.

"TANGY THYME TOMATO PICKLES"

If you love the flavor of sun-ripened tomatoes but are looking for a new way to enjoy them, these pickled tomato and thyme snacks are the perfect solution. They're easy to make and add a delightful tanginess to any meal.

---

2 cups white vinegar

1 cup water

1 tablespoon sugar

2 teaspoons salt

2 tablespoons fresh
thyme leaves

2 pounds small
tomatoes, cut into
wedges

1. In a small saucepan, combine the vinegar, water, sugar, and salt. Bring to a boil, stirring until the sugar and salt have dissolved.

2. Pack the tomato wedges into a clean ball jar. Add the thyme leaves to the jar.

3. Pour the hot vinegar mixture over the tomatoes, making sure to cover them completely.

4. Seal the jar and place it in the refrigerator for at least 24 hours before serving. The pickles will keep in the refrigerator for up to 2 weeks.

5. Serve the pickled tomatoes as a tangy addition to sandwiches, salads, or as a snack on their own. Enjoy!

"SPICY PICKLED TURNIPS WITH A KICK"

Pickled turnips are a common condiment in Middle Eastern cuisine, and adding chili gives them a spicy kick. These pickled turnips are great as a topping for sandwiches or as a side dish to serve with grilled meats.

---

1 medium turnip, peeled and thinly sliced
1 small red chili pepper, thinly sliced
1 clove garlic, thinly sliced
1 teaspoon salt
1/2 teaspoon sugar
1/2 cup white vinegar
1/2 cup water

1. Place the turnip slices, chili pepper slices, and garlic slices in a small bowl. Sprinkle the salt and sugar over the top.
2. In a separate small saucepan, bring the vinegar and water to a boil.
3. Pour the hot vinegar mixture over the turnip mixture and let it sit for at least 30 minutes to allow the flavors to meld.
4. Transfer the pickled turnips to a clean, sterilized ball jar.
5. Store the jar in the refrigerator for at least 24 hours before serving to allow the flavors to fully develop. The pickled turnips will keep in the refrigerator for up to 2 weeks.

Note: Be sure to use a clean, sterilized ball jar to store the pickled turnips. This will help prevent the growth of harmful bacteria and ensure that the pickled turnips stay fresh and safe to eat.

"TANGY PICKLED TURNIP AND GARLIC DELIGHT"

Pickled turnip is a common ingredient in Middle Eastern cuisine, and adding garlic to the mix takes the flavor to a whole new level. This recipe is a quick and easy way to preserve turnips and infuse them with the bold flavors of garlic and vinegar. The result is a tangy and crunchy condiment that pairs well with a variety of dishes, from sandwiches to salads.

1 pound small turnips, peeled and thinly sliced
4 cloves garlic, thinly sliced
1 cup white vinegar
1 cup water
1 tablespoon sugar
1 tablespoon kosher salt
1 teaspoon peppercorns
1 bay leaf
1 ball jar with a tight-fitting lid

1. In a small saucepan, combine the vinegar, water, sugar, salt, peppercorns, and bay leaf. Bring to a boil, stirring to dissolve the sugar and salt.

2. Meanwhile, pack the turnip slices and garlic slices into the ball jar.

3. Pour the hot vinegar mixture over the turnips and garlic, making sure to cover them completely.

4. Close the lid tightly and let the jar sit at room temperature for at least 2 hours to allow the flavors to meld.

5. Transfer the jar to the refrigerator and let it sit for at least 3 days before serving, to allow the pickled turnip and garlic to fully develop in flavor.

6. Serve the pickled turnip and garlic as a condiment or topping for sandwiches, salads, or any other dish of your choice. Enjoy!

"TANGY TURNIP AND ONION RELISH"

This pickled turnip and onion relish is a flavorful and tangy addition to any meal. It's perfect for adding a burst of flavor to sandwiches, burgers, or hot dogs. The best part is that it's easy to make and can be stored in the refrigerator for up to a month.

2 cups diced turnips

1 cup diced onions

1 cup white vinegar

1/2 cup sugar

1 tablespoon salt

1 teaspoon mustard seeds

1/2 teaspoon celery seeds

1/2 teaspoon turmeric

1. In a medium saucepan, combine the turnips, onions, vinegar, sugar, salt, mustard seeds, celery seeds, and turmeric.

2. Bring the mixture to a boil over high heat, stirring occasionally.

3. Reduce the heat to low and simmer for 5 minutes.

4. Remove the pan from the heat and let the mixture cool slightly.

5. Transfer the mixture to a ball jar or other glass jar with a tight-fitting lid.

6. Refrigerate the jar for at least 24 hours before serving to allow the flavors to meld.

7. Serve the relish chilled or at room temperature as a condiment or topping for sandwiches, burgers, or hot dogs. Enjoy!

"SAGE-INFUSED PICKLED TURNIPS"

Pickled turnips are a traditional Middle Eastern condiment that adds a tangy, crunchy bite to sandwiches and grain bowls. This recipe infuses the turnips with the earthy flavor of sage, making for a unique and flavorful twist on the classic condiment.

---

1 pound small turnips, peeled and thinly sliced
1 cup water
1 cup white vinegar
1 tablespoon sugar
1 tablespoon salt
4-5 sage leaves
1 small garlic clove, minced

1. In a small saucepan, combine the water, vinegar, sugar, and salt. Bring to a boil and stir until the sugar and salt are dissolved.
2. Place the turnip slices, sage leaves, and minced garlic in a clean, sterilized ball jar.
3. Pour the hot pickling liquid over the turnips, making sure to fully submerge them.
4. Seal the jar and let it cool to room temperature.
5. Once cooled, place the jar in the refrigerator and let it pickle for at least 3 days before serving. The pickled turnips will last for up to 3 months in the refrigerator.
6. Serve the pickled turnips as a condiment for sandwiches, grain bowls, or as a snack on their own. Enjoy!

DELICIOUSLY SPICED PLUM CHUTNEY

This plum chutney is the perfect accompaniment to any cheese platter or as a condiment for grilled meats. The combination of sweet plums and savory spices creates a complex and satisfying flavor. Plus, it's super easy to make and can be canned and preserved in a ball jar for future use.

3 lbs plums, pitted and roughly chopped
1 cup white vinegar
1 cup sugar
1 medium onion, finely diced
1 tbsp grated ginger
1 tsp mustard seeds
1 tsp ground cinnamon
1 tsp ground cumin
1 tsp ground coriander
1/2 tsp ground cloves
1/2 tsp ground allspice
Pinch of salt

1. In a large pot, combine the plums, vinegar, sugar, onion, ginger, mustard seeds, and spices.

2. Bring the mixture to a boil, then reduce the heat to a simmer and cook for 20-30 minutes, stirring occasionally, until the plums are soft and the mixture has thickened.

3. Using a slotted spoon, transfer the chutney to a ball jar, leaving about 1 inch of headspace.

4. Secure the lid and process the jar in a boiling water bath for 15 minutes.

5. Allow the jar to cool completely before storing in the pantry for up to 1 year. Enjoy!

"GLORIOUS POMEGRANATE AND MINT JAM"

This recipe was inspired by a trip to the Mediterranean, where the abundance of fresh pomegranates and mint left a lasting impression on my taste buds. Combining the tartness of the pomegranate with the refreshing hint of mint creates a jam that is both sweet and savory, perfect for spreading on toast or topping a cheesecake.

---

4 cups pomegranate seeds
1 cup white sugar
1/2 cup water
1/2 cup fresh mint leaves, finely chopped
1 tsp lemon juice

1. In a large saucepan, combine the pomegranate seeds, sugar, and water. Bring to a boil, stirring constantly to dissolve the sugar.
2. Reduce the heat to medium-low and add the mint leaves. Simmer for 30 minutes, stirring occasionally.
3. Remove from heat and stir in the lemon juice.
4. Ladle the jam into sterilized ball jars, leaving about 1/4 inch of headspace. Wipe the rims of the jars with a damp cloth and place the lids on top.
5. Process the jars in a boiling water bath for 10 minutes.
6. Remove the jars from the water and allow to cool on a towel. The jam will keep in the refrigerator for up to 2 weeks or can be stored in the pantry for up to a year. Enjoy!

"GOLDEN QUINCE CHUTNEY: A SWEET AND SAVORY TREAT"

Growing up, my grandma would always make quince chutney during the fall when the fruit was in season. She would preserve it in ball jars and we would enjoy it all year long on sandwiches, with cheese plates, or even mixed into rice dishes. This recipe is my version of her delicious chutney, with a mix of sweet and savory flavors that will make your taste buds dance.

---

4 quince, peeled and diced
1 cup apple cider vinegar
1 cup brown sugar
1 onion, diced
1 cup raisins
1 tablespoon mustard seeds
1 teaspoon ground ginger
1 teaspoon ground cinnamon
1/2 teaspoon ground cloves

1. In a large pot, combine the quince, vinegar, brown sugar, and onion. Bring to a boil, then reduce heat to a simmer.
2. Add the raisins, mustard seeds, ginger, cinnamon, and cloves. Stir to combine.
3. Let the chutney simmer for about 1 hour, stirring occasionally, until the quince is tender and the mixture has thickened.
4. Use a ladle to spoon the chutney into sterilized ball jars, leaving about 1/2 inch of headspace.
5. Process the jars in a boiling water bath for 15 minutes to ensure proper sealing.
6. Allow the jars to cool completely before storing in a cool, dry place. The chutney will keep for up to 1 year.

"TANGY RADISH AND ONION RELISH"

This relish is the perfect accompaniment to any grilled meat or sandwich. It adds a burst of flavor with its combination of spicy radishes and tangy onions. Plus, it's easy to make and can be stored in a ball jar for later use.

1 cup radishes, finely diced
1/2 cup red onions, finely diced
1/4 cup white vinegar
1/4 cup sugar
1 tsp salt
1 tsp black pepper
1/4 tsp red pepper flakes (optional for added heat)

1. In a medium-sized saucepan, combine the diced radishes, onions, vinegar, sugar, salt, pepper, and red pepper flakes (if using).
2. Bring the mixture to a boil, then reduce the heat and simmer for 10 minutes.
3. Allow the mixture to cool, then transfer it to a clean ball jar.
4. Seal the jar and store in the refrigerator for up to 2 weeks.
5. Serve as a condiment on sandwiches or with grilled meats. Enjoy!

"RASPBERRY ROSE BLISS JAM"

This jam is a perfect blend of sweet and floral flavors. The fresh raspberries are paired with the delicate aroma of rose water to create a unique and delicious spread. It's perfect for spreading on toast or adding to cakes and pastries.

4 cups fresh raspberries

1 1/2 cups granulated sugar

2 tablespoons rose water

2 tablespoons lemon juice

1 pouch liquid pectin

1. In a large pot, combine the raspberries, sugar, and rose water. Bring to a boil over medium heat, stirring constantly.
2. Once boiling, add the lemon juice and pectin. Bring to a full rolling boil and let boil for 1 minute.
3. Remove from heat and skim off any foam that has formed on the top of the jam.
4. Ladle the jam into clean and sterilized ball jars, leaving about 1/4 inch of headspace.
5. Wipe the rims of the jars with a clean cloth and seal with the lids and rings.
6. Process the jars in a boiling water bath for 10 minutes.
7. Remove the jars from the water bath and let cool completely. The lids should make a popping sound as they seal.
8. Store in a cool, dry place for up to one year. Enjoy!

"SPICY SWEET RED PEPPER AND ONION RELISH"

This red pepper and onion relish is the perfect accompaniment to any barbecue or sandwich. The combination of sweet red peppers and tangy onions is perfectly balanced by a kick of spice. It's easy to make and can be stored in a ball jar in the fridge for up to a month.

---

4 red peppers, seeded and diced

2 onions, finely diced

1 cup sugar

1 cup white vinegar

1 tsp red pepper flakes

1 tsp salt

1. In a large saucepan, combine the red peppers, onions, sugar, vinegar, red pepper flakes, and salt.
2. Bring the mixture to a boil over medium heat, stirring frequently.
3. Reduce the heat to low and simmer for 45 minutes, or until the peppers and onions are tender and the relish has thickened.
4. Let the relish cool slightly before transferring it to a clean ball jar.
5. Store in the fridge for up to a month. Serve chilled or at room temperature with your favorite barbecue or sandwich. Enjoy!

"HEARTY, SMOKY, AND OH-SO-MAPLE: SMOKED MAPLE-JUNIPER BACON"

Growing up in the mountains of Vermont, bacon was a staple in my family's kitchen. We always had a few slabs in the fridge, ready to be fried up and added to break-fast dishes or used as a flavorful addition to dinner recipes. But my all-time favorite bacon recipe is this smoked maple-juniper bacon. The combination of smoky flavors from the grill and the sweetness of maple syrup is heavenly, and the juniper adds a unique twist that takes this bacon to the next level. Trust me, once you try this recipe,

---

1 pound bacon

1/2 cup maple syrup

2 tablespoons juniper berries, crushed

2 teaspoons smoked paprika

1 teaspoon garlic powder

1/2 teaspoon black pepper

1. Preheat your grill to medium-high heat.

2. In a small bowl, mix together the maple syrup, juniper berries, smoked paprika, garlic powder, and black pepper.

3. Lay the bacon on a baking sheet and brush each slice with the maple syrup mixture.

4. Place the bacon on the grill and cook for 5-7 minutes on each side, or until it reaches your desired level of crispness.

5. Remove the bacon from the grill and let it cool on a paper towel-lined plate.

6. Once the bacon is cool, place it in a ball jar and seal the lid tightly. The bacon will last in the fridge for up to a week or in the freezer for up to 3 months.

7. Serve the bacon in your favorite dishes or enjoy it as a tasty snack on its own.

"TROPICAL PARADISE PINEAPPLE CHUTNEY"

Are you looking for a new and exciting way to use up that canned pineapple sitting in your pantry? Look no further! This pineapple chutney is a sweet and tangy condiment that pairs perfectly with grilled meats or as a topping for burgers and sandwiches. Plus, it's super easy to make and can be stored in a ball jar for future use.

---

1 20-ounce can of pineapple chunks, drained

1 red bell pepper, finely chopped

1 small red onion, finely chopped

1 jalapeno pepper, seeded and finely chopped

1/2 cup white vinegar

1/2 cup sugar

1 tablespoon mustard seeds

1 teaspoon ground ginger

1/2 teaspoon salt

1. In a medium saucepan, combine the pineapple, bell pepper, red onion, jalapeno pepper, vinegar, sugar, mustard seeds, ginger, and salt.

2. Bring the mixture to a boil over medium heat, stirring occasionally.

3. Reduce the heat to low and simmer for 20-30 minutes, or until the chutney has thickened and the vegetables are tender.

4. Allow the chutney to cool before transferring it to a ball jar or other airtight container.

5. Store the chutney in the refrigerator for up to 2 weeks. Enjoy!

"TROPICAL SUNRISE PINEAPPLE AND TURMERIC JAM"

This sweet and savory jam is the perfect blend of tropical pineapple and earthy turmeric. It's a unique and flavorful spread for toast or biscuits, and adds a special touch to any charcuterie board. Plus, it's so easy to make and can be canned and preserved for later use.

4 cups diced fresh pineapple

1 cup granulated sugar

2 tablespoons lemon juice

1 teaspoon ground turmeric

1/4 teaspoon salt

1. In a large saucepan, combine the pineapple, sugar, lemon juice, turmeric, and salt. Bring the mixture to a boil over medium heat, stirring occasionally.

2. Reduce the heat to medium-low and simmer for 20-25 minutes, or until the mixture has thickened and the pineapple is soft.

3. Using a potato masher or immersion blender, mash or blend the mixture until it reaches your desired consistency.

4. Ladle the jam into clean, sterilized ball jars, leaving about 1/4 inch of headspace at the top.

5. Wipe the rims of the jars with a clean, damp cloth and place the lids on top, screwing on the bands until they are fingertip tight.

6. Place the jars in a large pot of boiling water, making sure they are fully submerged. Boil for 10-15 minutes to process the jars.

7. Remove the jars from the pot and allow them to cool completely. The lids should pop down, indicating that they are properly sealed. If any of the lids do not seal, store those jars in the refrigerator and use within 3 weeks. Otherwise, store the sealed jars in a cool, dry place for up to 1 year. Enjoy!

"ZESTY PICKLED ZUCCHINI"

If you have a surplus of zucchini from your garden or just want to try something new, these pickled zucchinis are the perfect solution. They are tangy, crunchy, and add a unique flavor to any dish. Plus, they are super easy to make and can be stored in the pantry or fridge for months.

2 cups white vinegar

1 cup water

2 tbsp sugar

2 tsp salt

1 tsp mustard seeds

1 tsp dill seeds

1 tsp black peppercorns

4 cloves garlic, thinly sliced

4 small zucchini, thinly sliced

1. In a small saucepan, combine the vinegar, water, sugar, salt, mustard seeds, dill seeds, and peppercorns. Bring to a boil over medium heat, stirring occasionally.

2. Once the mixture has come to a boil, add the sliced garlic and zucchini to a clean and sterilized ball jar.

3. Pour the hot vinegar mixture over the zucchini and garlic, making sure to cover all of the vegetables.

4. Close the jar tightly and let it cool to room temperature. Once cooled, transfer the jar to the fridge to let the zucchini pickle for at least a week before eating.

5. The pickled zucchini will keep in the fridge for up to 3 months. Enjoy as a condiment or snack on their own.

"ZESTY PICKLED ZUCCHINI AND THYME"

If you have a surplus of zucchini from your garden or farmers market, try pickling them for a tangy and flavorful snack or side dish. The addition of thyme adds an aromatic and earthy note to the pickling liquid. These pickled zucchinis are perfect for topping sandwiches or salads, or just eating on their own.

2 medium zucchinis, sliced into 1/4 inch rounds
1 cup white vinegar
1 cup water
2 tablespoons sugar
1 teaspoon salt
2 sprigs fresh thyme
1 garlic clove, sliced
1/2 teaspoon mustard seeds
1/2 teaspoon black peppercorns
1 ball jar

1. Wash the zucchini slices and set aside.
2. In a small saucepan, combine the vinegar, water, sugar, and salt. Bring to a boil, stirring to dissolve the sugar and salt.
3. Add the thyme, garlic, mustard seeds, and peppercorns to the ball jar.
4. Pack the zucchini slices into the ball jar, making sure to leave about 1 inch of headspace at the top.
5. Pour the hot pickling liquid over the zucchini, making sure to cover all of the slices.
6. Seal the jar and let it cool to room temperature. Once cooled, store the jar in the refrigerator for at least 24 hours before serving to allow the flavors to develop. The pickled zucchini will keep in the refrigerator for up to 2 weeks.

"ZESTY PICKLED ZUCCHINI WITH A KICK OF OREGANO"

If you have an abundance of zucchini from your summer garden or farmer's market, this pickled zucchini recipe is the perfect way to preserve them for a tasty snack or addition to sandwiches and salads. The oregano adds a unique and flavorful twist to the classic pickled vegetable.

---

4 medium zucchini, thinly sliced
2 cloves of garlic, minced
2 tablespoons dried oregano
1 cup white vinegar
1 cup water
2 tablespoons sugar
2 teaspoons salt
4 ball jars with lids

1. In a small saucepan, bring the vinegar, water, sugar, and salt to a boil. Stir until the sugar and salt have dissolved.

2. In each ball jar, place a few slices of zucchini, a pinch of minced garlic, and a sprinkle of oregano.

3. Pour the hot vinegar mixture over the zucchini in the jars, leaving about 1/2 inch of headspace at the top.

4. Close the jars tightly and let them cool to room temperature.

5. Once cooled, store the jars in the refrigerator for at least 3 days before serving to allow the flavors to fully develop.

6. The pickled zucchini will keep in the refrigerator for up to 3 months. Enjoy as a snack or use as a topping for sandwiches and salads.

"GRANDMA'S FAMOUS PICKLED ZUCCHINI AND ONION RELISH"

This recipe is a family favorite passed down through generations. It's a delicious accompaniment to any barbecue or summertime gathering. The pickled zucchini and onion add a tangy and refreshing flavor to any dish. Plus, the use of a Ball jar makes for easy storage and a beautiful presentation.

3 cups thinly sliced zucchini

1 cup thinly sliced onion

1 cup white vinegar

1 cup sugar

1 tsp salt

1 tsp mustard seeds

1 tsp celery seeds

1. Wash and sterilize a Ball jar and its lid.
2. In a medium saucepan, combine the vinegar, sugar, salt, mustard seeds, and celery seeds. Bring to a boil over medium heat, stirring until the sugar has dissolved.
3. Place the sliced zucchini and onion in the Ball jar.
4. Pour the vinegar mixture over the zucchini and onion, making sure to cover the vegetables completely.
5. Tightly seal the Ball jar and let it cool to room temperature.
6. Once cooled, place the Ball jar in the refrigerator and let it sit for at least 24 hours before serving. This will allow the flavors to meld together and the vegetables to fully pickle.
7. Serve the pickled zucchini and onion relish as a side to any meal or use it as a topping for burgers, sandwiches, or hot dogs. Enjoy!

"ZESTY PICKLED ZUCCHINI AND ONION"

This recipe is a great way to use up an abundance of zucchini and onions from the garden. The pickling process not only adds flavor, but also extends the shelf life of the vegetables. These pickled zucchini and onions are a delicious addition to sandwiches, salads, and charcuterie boards.

3 small zucchini, thinly sliced

1 medium onion, thinly sliced

1 cup white vinegar

1 cup water

2 tablespoons sugar

1 tablespoon salt

1 teaspoon mustard seeds

1 teaspoon dill seeds

1 teaspoon peppercorns

2 cloves garlic, minced

1. In a small saucepan, combine the vinegar, water, sugar, salt, mustard seeds, dill seeds, peppercorns, and garlic. Bring to a boil over medium heat, stirring occasionally to dissolve the sugar and salt.
2. Pack the sliced zucchini and onion into a clean, sterilized ball jar.
3. Pour the hot vinegar mixture over the vegetables, making sure to completely cover them.
4. Place the lid on the jar and let it cool to room temperature.
5. Once cooled, store the jar in the refrigerator for at least a day before serving to allow the flavors to develop. These pickled zucchini and onions will last up to two weeks in the refrigerator. Enjoy!

"REFRESHING PICKLED ZUCCHINI AND MINT"

Are you tired of the same old veggies in your salads and sandwiches? This pickled zucchini and mint recipe is the perfect way to add some variety and zing to your meals. The combination of tangy vinegar, aromatic mint, and crunchy zucchini is truly mouthwatering. Plus, it's super easy to make and can be stored in a ball jar in the fridge for weeks. Give it a try and elevate your salads, sandwiches, and more to the next level!

---

1 large zucchini, thinly sliced
1 cup white vinegar
1 cup water
2 tablespoons sugar
1 teaspoon salt
1/2 cup fresh mint leaves

1. In a small saucepan, combine the vinegar, water, sugar, and salt. Bring to a boil over medium heat, stirring until the sugar and salt have dissolved.
2. Meanwhile, place the zucchini slices and mint leaves in a medium bowl.
3. Once the vinegar mixture has come to a boil, pour it over the zucchini and mint. Let it cool to room temperature.
4. Transfer the pickled zucchini and mint to a ball jar and seal tightly. Place in the refrigerator for at least 24 hours before serving, to allow the flavors to develop.
5. Serve the pickled zucchini and mint as a topping for sandwiches, salads, or as a refreshing snack. Enjoy!

"ZESTY PICKLED ZUCCHINI AND GARLIC"

Pickled vegetables are a staple in many cuisines and are a great way to add flavor and crunch to any meal. This recipe for pickled zucchini and garlic is a delicious and easy way to preserve your summer zucchini harvest, or to enjoy a taste of summer all year round. The combination of zucchini and garlic is zesty and flavorful, and the pickling process helps to soften the zucchini while also enhancing its taste.

2 cups white vinegar

1 cup water

2 tablespoons sugar

2 tablespoons pickling salt

2 cloves garlic, thinly sliced

2 small zucchini, thinly sliced

2 ball jars with lids

1. In a small saucepan, combine the vinegar, water, sugar, and pickling salt. Bring to a boil and stir to dissolve the sugar and salt.
2. Divide the sliced garlic and zucchini evenly between the two ball jars.
3. Pour the hot vinegar mixture over the vegetables in the jars, leaving about 1/2 inch of headspace at the top of the jar.
4. Seal the jars and let them cool to room temperature.
5. Once cooled, place the jars in the refrigerator and let them pickle for at least 24 hours before serving.
6. The pickled zucchini and garlic will last for up to 2 weeks in the refrigerator. Enjoy as a condiment on sandwiches or as a topping for salads and bowls.

"SUN-RIPENED PICKLED YELLOW PEPPERS WITH THYME"

These pickled yellow peppers are the perfect addition to any charcuterie board or sandwich. The combination of sweet peppers and earthy thyme is elevated by the tangy vinegar brine. These pickles are easy to make and only require a few simple ingredients.

3-4 yellow peppers, thinly sliced

2 sprigs of thyme

1 cup white vinegar

1 cup water

1 tablespoon sugar

1 tablespoon salt

1 garlic clove, sliced

1 teaspoon black peppercorns

1. Wash and sterilize a 16 oz ball jar.
2. In a small saucepan, combine the vinegar, water, sugar, and salt. Bring to a boil, stirring until the sugar and salt have dissolved.
3. Place the sliced peppers, thyme, garlic, and peppercorns in the sterilized ball jar.
4. Pour the hot vinegar mixture over the peppers, making sure to fully cover them.
5. Close the ball jar and let it sit at room temperature for at least 1 hour to allow the flavors to meld.
6. Store the pickled peppers in the refrigerator for up to 1 month. Enjoy as a topping for sandwiches or as a garnish for cocktails.

"TANGY PICKLED YELLOW PEPPERS AND FRESH PARSLEY"

If you're looking for a unique and flavorful pickle to add to your charcuterie board or to serve as a tangy condiment on sandwiches, this recipe for pickled yellow peppers and parsley is a must-try. The combination of sweet and sour flavors from the vinegar and sugar, and the bright, fresh taste of the parsley, make these pickles a tasty and visually appealing addition to any dish.

---

2 cups white vinegar

1 cup water

1/2 cup sugar

1 tablespoon kosher salt

1 teaspoon black peppercorns

2 cloves garlic, peeled

1 small bunch fresh parsley, washed and trimmed

4 yellow bell peppers, cored, seeded, and sliced into thin strips

1. In a small saucepan, combine the vinegar, water, sugar, salt, peppercorns, and garlic. Bring to a boil over high heat, stirring until the sugar and salt are dissolved. Remove from heat and let cool for 10 minutes.
2. Meanwhile, place the parsley and pepper strips in a large bowl.
3. Pour the cooled pickling liquid over the peppers and parsley. Stir to combine.
4. Transfer the mixture to a large ball jar or several smaller jars, making sure to pack the peppers and parsley tightly.
5. Cover the jars with their lids and let them sit at room temperature for at least 3 hours to allow the flavors to develop.
6. Transfer the jars to the refrigerator and let them pickle for at least 3 days before serving. The pickles will keep in the refrigerator for up to 1 month. Enjoy!

"TANGY YELLOW PEPPER AND ONION RELISH"

This pickled relish is the perfect accompaniment to any barbecue or grilled meat. The combination of sweet yellow peppers and tangy onions pairs well with the vinegar and spice blend, creating a flavorful condiment that will elevate any dish.

---

2 yellow peppers, thinly sliced

1 large onion, thinly sliced

1 cup white vinegar

1/2 cup sugar

1 tablespoon salt

1 teaspoon mustard seeds

1/2 teaspoon celery seeds

1/2 teaspoon black peppercorns

1. In a medium saucepan, combine the vinegar, sugar, salt, mustard seeds, celery seeds, and peppercorns. Bring to a boil, stirring until the sugar and salt have dissolved.
2. In a large glass jar (such as a Ball jar), layer the sliced yellow peppers and onions.
3. Pour the vinegar mixture over the peppers and onions, making sure to cover them completely.
4. Tightly seal the jar and place in the refrigerator for at least 24 hours before serving. The relish will keep for up to 2 weeks in the refrigerator.
5. Serve chilled, as a condiment for grilled meats or sandwiches. Enjoy!

"SPICY PICKLED WHITE ONIONS WITH MUSTARD SEEDS"

These pickled white onions are the perfect addition to any sandwich or charcuterie board. The mustard seeds add a lovely depth of flavor and a little bit of heat, making them irresistible.

---

1 large white onion, thinly sliced

1 cup white vinegar

1 cup water

1 tablespoon mustard seeds

1 tablespoon sugar

1 tablespoon salt

1 teaspoon red pepper flakes (optional)

1. In a small saucepan, combine the vinegar, water, mustard seeds, sugar, salt, and red pepper flakes (if using). Bring to a boil, stirring until the sugar and salt are dissolved.

2. Place the sliced onions in a clean, sterilized ball jar. Pour the pickling liquid over the onions, making sure to fully cover them.

3. Close the ball jar and let it sit at room temperature for at least 1 hour before transferring to the refrigerator.

4. The pickled onions will be ready to eat after 1 hour, but they will taste even better if left to pickle for at least 24 hours. They will keep in the refrigerator for up to 1 month.

"FIESTA-READY PICKLED WATERMELON RIND"

If you've ever found yourself with a surplus of watermelon and not sure what to do with the rind, this recipe is for you! Pickled watermelon rind may sound unusual, but trust us, it's a tasty and unique addition to any meal. Whether you're looking to spruce up a charcuterie board or add some tang to your tacos, this pickled watermelon rind is the way to go.

4 cups watermelon rind, cut into 1-inch cubes

1 cup white vinegar

1 cup water

1/2 cup granulated sugar

1 tablespoon pickling salt

1 teaspoon mustard seeds

1 teaspoon coriander seeds

1/2 teaspoon red pepper flakes (optional)

2 cloves garlic, peeled and thinly sliced

2 sprigs fresh dill

2 ball jars with lids

1. In a medium saucepan, combine the vinegar, water, sugar, pickling salt, mustard seeds, coriander seeds, and red pepper flakes (if using). Bring to a boil over medium heat, stirring to dissolve the sugar and salt.

2. Add the watermelon rind, garlic, and dill to the saucepan. Reduce the heat to low and simmer for 5 minutes.

3. Using a slotted spoon, transfer the watermelon rind and other ingredients to the ball jars.

4. Pour the pickling liquid over the watermelon rind, leaving about 1/2 inch of headspace at the top of the jar.

5. Wipe the rim of the jar clean and secure the lid.

6. Place the jars in the refrigerator and let them sit for at least 24 hours before serving. The pickled watermelon rind will keep for up to 2 weeks in the refrigerator. Enjoy!

"SUMMERTIME SWEET AND SOUR PICKLED WATERMELON AND ONION RELISH"

This pickled watermelon and onion relish is the perfect combination of sweet and sour, making it the perfect addition to any summertime barbecue or picnic. It's a unique twist on traditional pickle recipes and adds a pop of color to any dish. Plus, it's super easy to make and can be stored in a ball jar in the fridge for up to a month.

1 medium watermelon, rind removed and diced into small pieces

1 large red onion, thinly sliced

1 cup apple cider vinegar

1 cup granulated sugar

1 tsp mustard seeds

1 tsp coriander seeds

1 tsp salt

1/2 tsp red pepper flakes (optional for a little extra spice)

1. In a large saucepan, combine the watermelon, onion, vinegar, sugar, mustard seeds, coriander seeds, salt, and red pepper flakes (if using).

2. Bring the mixture to a boil, then reduce the heat to a simmer and let cook for about 10 minutes, or until the watermelon and onion are tender.

3. Remove the saucepan from the heat and let the mixture cool for a few minutes.

4. Once cooled, transfer the pickled watermelon and onion relish to a ball jar or other airtight container.

5. Store in the refrigerator for at least 24 hours before serving, as the flavors will need time to develop and meld together.

6. Serve as a condiment with grilled meats, in sandwiches, or as a topping for salads and other dishes. Enjoy!

DELICIOUS PICKLED WATERMELON AND MINT RECIPE

Pickled watermelon may sound strange, but trust us, it's a refreshing and unique twist on traditional pickled vegetables. The combination of sweet watermelon and refreshing mint creates a balance of flavors that will have you coming back for more. This recipe is perfect for summer barbecues or as a unique addition to a charcuterie board.

1 small seedless watermelon, cut into bite-sized pieces

1 cup white vinegar

1 cup water

1/2 cup sugar

2 tablespoons salt

1 tablespoon whole peppercorns

1 small bunch fresh mint leaves

3 cloves garlic, sliced

1 small jalapeno pepper, sliced (optional)

1. In a medium saucepan, combine the vinegar, water, sugar, salt, and peppercorns. Bring to a boil over high heat, stirring occasionally to dissolve the sugar and salt.

2. Place the watermelon pieces, mint leaves, garlic, and jalapeno (if using) in a large ball jar.

3. Pour the hot vinegar mixture over the top of the watermelon and mint. Make sure the watermelon is completely covered by the liquid.

4. Let the jar cool to room temperature, then seal and refrigerate for at least 24 hours before serving.

5. The pickled watermelon will keep in the refrigerator for up to 2 weeks. Serve chilled or at room temperature as a side dish or topping for salads and sandwiches. Enjoy!

"ZESTY PICKLED TURNIPS"

Pickled turnips are a traditional Middle Eastern condiment that add a burst of flavor to any dish. This recipe will show you how to make your own zesty pickled turnips at home using simple pantry ingredients.

1 pound small turnips, peeled and thinly sliced

1 cup white vinegar

1 cup water

2 teaspoons sugar

1 teaspoon salt

1 tablespoon pickling spices (such as mustard seeds, coriander seeds, and peppercorns)

1 garlic clove, minced

1. In a small saucepan, combine the vinegar, water, sugar, salt, pickling spices, and minced garlic. Bring to a boil, stirring until the sugar and salt have dissolved.

2. Place the sliced turnips in a 1-quart Ball jar. Pour the hot vinegar mixture over the turnips, making sure they are fully covered.

3. Let the jar sit at room temperature for at least 2 hours before serving, or refrigerate for up to 1 month.

4. Serve the pickled turnips as a condiment alongside your favorite dishes, or use them to add flavor to sandwiches and salads. Enjoy!

"ZESTY PICKLED TURNIP AND THYME DELIGHT"

Pickling is a great way to preserve vegetables and add some tangy flavor to your meals. These pickled turnips are the perfect addition to any sandwich or charcuterie board. The thyme adds a lovely aromatic touch to the pickling liquid, making these turnips extra special.

---

1 pound small turnips, peeled and sliced into ¼ inch rounds
1 cup white vinegar
1 cup water
2 tablespoons sugar
1 tablespoon kosher salt
1 teaspoon black peppercorns
2 cloves garlic, peeled and smashed
3 sprigs fresh thyme
1 dried red chili pepper (optional)

1. In a medium saucepan, combine the vinegar, water, sugar, salt, peppercorns, garlic, thyme, and chili pepper (if using). Bring to a boil over medium-high heat, stirring occasionally until the sugar and salt have dissolved.

2. Place the turnip slices in a clean 1 quart Ball jar. Pour the hot pickling liquid over the turnips, making sure to fully submerge them.

3. Let the jar cool to room temperature, then seal and refrigerate for at least 24 hours before serving. The pickled turnips will last for up to 2 weeks in the refrigerator.

4. Serve the pickled turnips as a tangy condiment or snack. Enjoy!

"TANGY TURNIP AND TARRAGON PICKLES"

If you're looking for a unique pickle recipe to add some flavor to your sandwiches and charcuterie boards, these tangy turnip and tarragon pickles are a must-try. The combination of sweet and sour flavors, combined with the anise-like flavor of tarragon, creates a pickle that is both refreshing and satisfying. Plus, they're super easy to make and can be stored in the refrigerator for up to a month.

1 pound small turnips, peeled and sliced into thin rounds

1 cup white vinegar

1 cup water

1/4 cup sugar

1 tablespoon salt

1 teaspoon black peppercorns

1 tablespoon tarragon leaves

1. In a small saucepan, combine the vinegar, water, sugar, salt, and peppercorns. Bring to a boil, stirring occasionally, until the sugar and salt have dissolved. Remove from heat and let cool slightly.

2. Place the turnip slices in a clean, sterilized ball jar. Add the tarragon leaves on top of the turnips.

3. Pour the vinegar mixture over the turnips, making sure they are completely submerged.

4. Close the jar tightly and store in the refrigerator for at least 24 hours before serving. The pickles will keep in the refrigerator for up to a month.

"SAGE-INFUSED PICKLED TURNIPS"

Pickling is a great way to preserve the crisp, fresh flavor of turnips, and adding sage gives them an extra layer of flavor. These pickled turnips are perfect for adding a tangy crunch to sandwiches, salads, and more.

2 cups thinly sliced turnips
1 cup apple cider vinegar
1 cup water
2 tablespoons sugar
1 tablespoon salt
1 teaspoon black peppercorns
5 fresh sage leaves

1. Wash and sterilize a 1-quart Ball jar and its lid.
2. In a small saucepan, combine the vinegar, water, sugar, salt, and peppercorns. Bring to a boil over medium heat, stirring until the sugar and salt are dissolved.
3. Meanwhile, place the turnip slices and sage leaves in the sterilized Ball jar.
4. Pour the hot vinegar mixture over the turnips, making sure to completely cover them.
5. Let the jar cool to room temperature, then seal with the lid.
6. Store in the refrigerator for at least 24 hours before serving, to allow the flavors to fully develop. These pickled turnips will keep in the refrigerator for up to 2 months. Enjoy!

"TANGY TURNIP AND ONION RELISH"

This pickled turnip and onion relish is a delicious and tangy addition to any sandwich or burger. It's easy to make and can be stored in the fridge for up to a month. Plus, it's a great way to use up any excess turnips or onions you may have on hand.

---

1 cup white vinegar

1 cup water

1 tablespoon sugar

1 tablespoon pickling salt

1 medium turnip, peeled and diced

1 medium onion, diced

1/2 teaspoon mustard seeds

1/2 teaspoon celery seeds

1. In a small saucepan, combine the vinegar, water, sugar, and pickling salt. Bring to a boil over medium heat, stirring until the sugar and salt are dissolved.

2. Meanwhile, place the turnip and onion in a medium bowl. Add the mustard seeds and celery seeds.

3. Once the vinegar mixture has come to a boil, pour it over the turnip and onion mixture. Stir to combine.

4. Transfer the mixture to a clean ball jar and let cool to room temperature.

5. Once cooled, seal the jar and store in the refrigerator for at least 24 hours before serving to allow the flavors to meld. The relish will keep in the fridge for up to a month.

SPICY PICKLED TURNIP AND GARLIC"

Pickled turnip and garlic is a popular condiment in many Middle Eastern cuisines. It adds a tangy and spicy flavor to sandwiches, falafel, and other dishes. This recipe combines pickled turnip with pungent garlic and a blend of aromatic spices to create a delicious condiment that will add a burst of flavor to any meal.

4 cups thinly sliced turnip

4 cloves garlic, thinly sliced

1 teaspoon cumin seeds

1 teaspoon coriander seeds

1 teaspoon mustard seeds

1 teaspoon fennel seeds

1/2 teaspoon red pepper flakes

2 cups white vinegar

1 cup water

1 tablespoon sugar

2 teaspoons salt

2 Ball jars with lids

1. In a small pan, toast the cumin, coriander, mustard, and fennel seeds over medium heat until fragrant, about 1-2 minutes.
2. In a small bowl, mix together the vinegar, water, sugar, and salt until the sugar and salt are dissolved.
3. Place the turnip and garlic slices in the Ball jars.
4. Pour the vinegar mixture over the turnip and garlic, making sure to cover all the slices.
5. Add the toasted seeds and red pepper flakes to the Ball jars.
6. Close the lids tightly and shake the jars to distribute the spices evenly.
7. Let the jars sit at room temperature for at least 24 hours before refrigerating. The pickled turnip and garlic will be ready to eat after 24 hours, but the flavor will continue to develop over time. Enjoy!

"ZESTY PICKLED TURNIP AND CHILI"

Pickled turnip is a popular condiment in Middle Eastern cuisine, and adding chili to the mix gives it a spicy kick. This recipe is easy to make and can be enjoyed as a side dish or added to sandwiches and wraps for added flavor.

1 medium turnip, peeled and thinly sliced

1 small red chili, thinly sliced

1 clove of garlic, thinly sliced

1 teaspoon mustard seeds

1 teaspoon coriander seeds

1 cup white vinegar

1 cup water

1 tablespoon sugar

1 teaspoon salt

1 Ball jar with a tight-fitting lid

1. Begin by preparing the turnip and chili. Peel the turnip and slice it thinly, then slice the chili and garlic into thin slices as well.

2. In a small saucepan, combine the vinegar, water, sugar, and salt. Bring the mixture to a boil, stirring to dissolve the sugar and salt.

3. Place the turnip slices, chili slices, and garlic slices in the Ball jar. Add the mustard seeds and coriander seeds to the jar as well.

4. Once the vinegar mixture has come to a boil, carefully pour it over the vegetables in the jar, making sure to cover them completely.

5. Close the lid tightly and allow the jar to cool to room temperature. Once cooled, store the jar in the refrigerator for at least 24 hours to allow the flavors to meld.

6. The pickled turnip and chili can be enjoyed immediately, or stored in the refrigerator for up to 2 weeks. Enjoy as a side dish or add to sandwiches and wraps for added flavor.

"SUN-RIPENED PICKLED TOMATOES WITH THYME"

Introducing our delicious pickled tomato and thyme recipe! These tangy, flavorful tomatoes are the perfect addition to any charcuterie board, sandwich, or salad. They're also great for gifting to friends and family as a unique, homemade present.

---

1 pound cherry or grape tomatoes, halved

2 sprigs fresh thyme

1 clove garlic, thinly sliced

1/2 teaspoon mustard seeds

1/2 teaspoon coriander seeds

1/2 teaspoon peppercorns

1/2 cup white vinegar

1/2 cup water

2 tablespoons sugar

1 tablespoon kosher salt

1 ball jar with a tight-fitting lid

1. Wash and dry the cherry or grape tomatoes, then halve them.
2. In a small saucepan, combine the vinegar, water, sugar, and salt. Bring to a boil, then reduce the heat and simmer until the sugar and salt have dissolved.
3. Place the thyme, garlic, mustard seeds, coriander seeds, and peppercorns in the bottom of the ball jar. Add the halved tomatoes on top.
4. Pour the hot vinegar mixture over the tomatoes, making sure to completely cover them.
5. Close the ball jar tightly and let it cool to room temperature. Once cooled, place the jar in the refrigerator for at least 24 hours before serving. The pickled tomatoes will keep in the refrigerator for up to 2 weeks. Enjoy!

"SUMMERTIME IN A JAR: PICKLED TOMATO AND ROSEMARY"

This recipe is a great way to preserve the flavors of summer and enjoy them all year round. The combination of juicy tomatoes and fragrant rosemary is a match made in heaven. These pickled tomatoes are delicious on their own or as a topping for sandwiches, salads, and more.

---

1 pound tomatoes, sliced into wedges
2 sprigs of fresh rosemary
1 cup white vinegar
1 cup water
1 tablespoon sugar
1 teaspoon salt
1 garlic clove, minced
1 ball jar with a lid

1. Wash the tomatoes and slice them into wedges.
2. In a small saucepan, combine the vinegar, water, sugar, salt, and garlic. Bring to a boil, stirring until the sugar and salt have dissolved.
3. Place the tomato wedges and rosemary sprigs in the ball jar.
4. Pour the hot vinegar mixture over the tomatoes, making sure to cover them completely.
5. Close the lid on the jar and let the tomatoes cool to room temperature.
6. Once cooled, store the jar in the refrigerator for at least 24 hours before serving. The pickled tomatoes will last for up to a month in the refrigerator. Enjoy!

"SUN-RIPENED PICKLED TOMATOES WITH OREGANO"

There's nothing quite like the taste of a sun-ripened tomato straight from the garden. But when tomato season is over, it can be hard to find that same level of flavor in store-bought tomatoes. That's where pickling comes in! By preserving the tomatoes in a mixture of vinegar and herbs, you can enjoy the taste of summer all year round. These pickled tomatoes are flavored with the fragrant addition of oregano, making them a perfect accompaniment to any Mediterranean-inspired dish.

2 pounds cherry or grape tomatoes

1 cup white vinegar

1 cup water

2 tablespoons sugar

2 teaspoons salt

4 cloves garlic, thinly sliced

4 sprigs oregano

2 teaspoons peppercorns

1. Wash the tomatoes and cut them in half.
2. In a small saucepan, combine the vinegar, water, sugar, and salt. Bring to a boil and stir until the sugar and salt have dissolved.
3. Place the tomatoes in a clean, sterilized ball jar. Add the garlic, oregano, and peppercorns.
4. Pour the hot vinegar mixture over the tomatoes, making sure to cover them completely.
5. Close the jar tightly and allow it to cool to room temperature.
6. Once cooled, place the jar in the refrigerator. The tomatoes will be ready to eat in about a week and will keep for up to 3 months in the refrigerator.

Enjoy your pickled tomatoes as a condiment for sandwiches, on top of salads, or as a topping for grilled meats. The oregano adds a fragrant, herbal flavor that pairs particularly well with lamb and chicken.

"GRANDMA'S FAMOUS PICKLED TOMATO AND ONION RELISH"

This recipe for pickled tomato and onion relish was passed down from my grandma and has been a family favorite for generations. It's the perfect condiment for hot dogs, burgers, and sandwiches, and it adds a tangy, zesty flavor to any dish. Plus, it's super easy to make and can be stored in a ball jar for months in the refrigerator.

---

2 cups diced tomatoes
1 cup diced onions
1 cup white vinegar
1/2 cup sugar
1 tablespoon pickling spice
1 teaspoon salt

1. Combine the tomatoes and onions in a large bowl.
2. In a small saucepan, bring the vinegar, sugar, pickling spice, and salt to a boil. Stir until the sugar is dissolved.
3. Pour the hot vinegar mixture over the tomatoes and onions. Stir to combine.
4. Transfer the relish to a ball jar and seal with a lid.
5. Let the relish cool to room temperature, then refrigerate for at least 24 hours before serving. This will allow the flavors to meld together and intensify.
6. The relish will keep for several months in the refrigerator. Enjoy!

"ZESTY PICKLED TOMATO AND GARLIC DELIGHT"

If you love the flavor of sun-ripened tomatoes and pungent garlic, then this recipe is for you! The combination of the two ingredients creates a tasty treat that can be enjoyed on its own or as a topping for sandwiches and salads. And the best part? It's super easy to make and can be stored in the pantry for months to come.

---

2 pounds ripe tomatoes, sliced

1 cup white vinegar

1 cup water

1 tablespoon sugar

1 tablespoon salt

1 teaspoon black peppercorns

4 cloves garlic, minced

2 bay leaves

1 ball jar with a lid

1. Wash the tomatoes and slice them into wedges. Place them in a bowl and set aside.
2. In a small saucepan, combine the vinegar, water, sugar, salt, peppercorns, minced garlic, and bay leaves. Bring the mixture to a boil, stirring occasionally.
3. Once the mixture comes to a boil, remove the pan from the heat.
4. Place the sliced tomatoes in the ball jar and pour the hot vinegar mixture over the top. Make sure the tomatoes are completely covered with the liquid.
5. Close the lid of the ball jar tightly and allow the pickled tomatoes and garlic to cool to room temperature.
6. Once cooled, store the ball jar in the pantry for up to 3 months. Serve chilled or at room temperature as a topping for sandwiches, salads, or as a snack on its own. Enjoy!

"SPICY PICKLED TOMATOES AND CHILIES"

These spicy pickled tomatoes and chilies are the perfect addition to any Mexican-inspired dish. They add a tangy kick to tacos, burritos, and even salads. Plus, they're super easy to make and can be stored in the fridge for up to a month.

---

1 pound cherry tomatoes, halved

1 cup white vinegar

1 cup water

2 tablespoons sugar

1 tablespoon salt

2 cloves garlic, minced

1 jalapeno pepper, sliced

1 teaspoon black peppercorns

1 teaspoon mustard seeds

1 teaspoon coriander seeds

1 teaspoon cumin seeds

1 bay leaf

1. In a small saucepan, combine the vinegar, water, sugar, and salt. Bring to a boil and stir until the sugar and salt have dissolved.

2. In a clean, sterilized ball jar, place the cherry tomatoes, garlic, jalapeno pepper, peppercorns, mustard seeds, coriander seeds, cumin seeds, and bay leaf.

3. Pour the hot vinegar mixture over the top of the vegetables, making sure to cover them completely.

4. Close the ball jar tightly and let it cool to room temperature.

5. Once cooled, store the pickled tomatoes and chilies in the fridge for at least a week before serving, to allow the flavors to meld. Enjoy!

"SPICY PICKLED TOMATOES WITH BLACK PEPPER"

These pickled tomatoes are the perfect addition to any sandwich or salad. The combination of sweet, tangy, and spicy flavors will give your meal an extra kick of flavor. Plus, the black pepper adds an extra layer of depth and warmth. These pickled tomatoes are easy to make and can be stored in the fridge for up to a month, making them a great pantry staple to have on hand.

1 pound cherry tomatoes
1 cup apple cider vinegar
1 cup water
1 tablespoon sugar
1 tablespoon salt
1 tablespoon black peppercorns
1 teaspoon red pepper flakes (optional)
2 cloves garlic, sliced
2 sprigs fresh dill
2 ball jars with lids

1. Wash the cherry tomatoes and slice them in half.
2. In a small saucepan, combine the vinegar, water, sugar, salt, black peppercorns, and red pepper flakes (if using). Bring the mixture to a boil, stirring until the sugar and salt have dissolved.
3. Divide the sliced tomatoes, garlic slices, and dill sprigs evenly between the two ball jars.
4. Carefully pour the hot vinegar mixture over the tomatoes, making sure to completely cover the tomatoes.
5. Seal the jars and let them cool to room temperature. Once cooled, store the jars in the fridge for at least 24 hours before serving to allow the flavors to fully develop.
6. Enjoy the pickled tomatoes on sandwiches, salads, or as a tasty snack!

"SUMMER IN A JAR: PICKLED TOMATO AND BASIL"

There's nothing quite like the taste of summer, and with this recipe, you can capture that flavor and enjoy it all year round. These pickled tomatoes are bursting with the flavors of ripe tomatoes and fresh basil, and they're the perfect addition to any salad or sandwich.

---

1 pint of cherry tomatoes, halved

2 cloves of garlic, minced

2 tablespoons of fresh basil, chopped

1 teaspoon of sugar

1 teaspoon of salt

1 cup of white vinegar

1 cup of water

1 ball jar

1. In a small saucepan, combine the vinegar, water, sugar, and salt. Bring the mixture to a boil, stirring until the sugar and salt have dissolved.

2. Place the cherry tomatoes, minced garlic, and chopped basil in the ball jar.

3. Pour the hot vinegar mixture over the tomatoes, making sure to cover them completely.

4. Let the jar cool to room temperature, then seal the jar and refrigerate for at least 24 hours before serving.

5. These pickled tomatoes will keep in the refrigerator for up to 1 month. Enjoy them on sandwiches, salads, or as a flavorful addition to any dish.

"EXPLOSIVELY FLAVORFUL PICKLED SWEET AND SOUR RED PEPPERS"

These pickled red peppers are a delicious and easy way to add some tang and sweetness to your dishes. They're perfect on sandwiches, in salads, or as a topping for pizza. The sweet and sour flavors come from a mixture of sugar, vinegar, and spices, and the peppers are left crisp and crunchy after being pickled. This recipe will show you how to make a batch of these tasty pickled peppers at home.

1 pound red bell peppers, thinly sliced

1 cup white vinegar

1 cup water

1/2 cup sugar

1 teaspoon salt

1/2 teaspoon black peppercorns

1/2 teaspoon mustard seeds

1/2 teaspoon coriander seeds

1/2 teaspoon fennel seeds

1. In a small saucepan, combine the vinegar, water, sugar, salt, peppercorns, mustard seeds, coriander seeds, and fennel seeds. Bring to a boil over medium heat, stirring until the sugar is dissolved.

2. Place the sliced red peppers in a clean, sterilized ball jar.

3. Pour the hot vinegar mixture over the peppers, making sure to cover them completely.

4. Tightly seal the jar and allow it to cool to room temperature.

5. Once cooled, store the jar in the refrigerator for at least 24 hours before serving to allow the flavors to meld together. The peppers will keep for up to 2 weeks in the refrigerator. Enjoy!

"FIESTA PICKLED RED ONIONS"

These pickled red onions add a burst of flavor to any dish and are a staple in Mexican cuisine. They're easy to make and only require a few simple ingredients. All you need is a ball jar and some patience as they need to sit in the fridge for at least a couple of hours before serving.

1 large red onion, thinly sliced
1 cup apple cider vinegar
1/2 cup sugar
1 tsp salt
1 tsp whole peppercorns
1 dried bay leaf

1. In a small saucepan, combine the vinegar, sugar, salt, peppercorns, and bay leaf. Bring to a boil, stirring until the sugar and salt have dissolved.
2. Place the sliced onion in a ball jar.
3. Pour the vinegar mixture over the onions, making sure they are fully submerged.
4. Let the jar sit at room temperature for at least 2 hours before transferring to the fridge.
5. The onions will be ready to eat after at least 2 hours, but they will taste even better if you let them sit in the fridge for a couple of days.
6. Serve the pickled onions on sandwiches, tacos, salads, or as a garnish for cocktails. Enjoy!

DELICIOUS STRAWBERRY JAM

This recipe for strawberry jam is a summertime favorite in our household. We love to spread it on toast, mix it into yogurt, or use it as a topping for ice cream. It's the perfect way to use up a bounty of fresh strawberries and enjoy their sweet flavor all year round.

---

4 cups strawberries, hulled and chopped

3 cups granulated sugar

1/4 cup lemon juice

2 tablespoons pectin

1. In a large saucepan, combine the strawberries, sugar, and lemon juice. Bring to a boil over medium heat, stirring constantly.

2. Once the mixture comes to a boil, add the pectin and continue stirring until it is fully dissolved.

3. Bring the mixture back to a boil and let it cook for 1-2 minutes, or until it reaches 220°F on a candy thermometer.

4. Remove the pan from the heat and ladle the jam into clean, sterilized ball jars.

5. Place the lid on the jars and let them cool to room temperature before storing in the refrigerator. The jam will keep for up to a month in the fridge.

SPICY PEPPERONCINI RECIPE

Pepperoncini peppers are a delicious and versatile ingredient that can be used in a variety of dishes. They have a mild to moderate heat level and a slight tangy flavor, making them a perfect addition to salads, sandwiches, or even as a topping for pizza. In this recipe, we will be preserving these peppers in a ball jar to enjoy all year round.

1 pound pepperoncini peppers

2 cups white vinegar

2 cups water

2 teaspoons salt

1 teaspoon sugar

2 cloves garlic, minced

1 teaspoon dried oregano

1. Start by sterilizing a large ball jar and its lid. You can do this by boiling them for 10 minutes in a pot of water, or by running them through a dishwasher on the high heat setting.
2. Wash the pepperoncini peppers and trim off any stems.
3. In a small saucepan, combine the vinegar, water, salt, sugar, minced garlic, and oregano. Bring to a boil and then reduce heat to a simmer.
4. Pack the pepperoncini peppers into the sterilized ball jar, leaving about 1 inch of headspace at the top.
5. Pour the hot vinegar mixture over the peppers, making sure to cover them completely. Tap the jar gently to remove any air bubbles.
6. Wipe the rim of the jar clean with a damp cloth and seal the lid tightly.
7. Place the jar in a boiling water bath for 10 minutes to process.
8. Once finished, carefully remove the jar from the water bath and allow to cool completely on the counter.
9. Store in a cool, dry place for up to one year. Enjoy these spicy pepperoncini peppers on sandwiches, salads, or as a topping for pizza.

SPICY PICKLED JALAPENOS

If you're a fan of spicy foods, these pickled jalapenos are sure to be a hit. They're the perfect topping for tacos, sandwiches, or any other dish that needs a little extra kick. We love to make a batch of these at the height of jalapeno season and enjoy them all year round.

1 pound jalapeno peppers, sliced into rings
1 cup white vinegar
1 cup water
1 tablespoon salt
1 tablespoon sugar
1 teaspoon garlic powder
1 teaspoon onion powder
1 teaspoon black peppercorns
1 teaspoon mustard seeds

1. In a large saucepan, combine the vinegar, water, salt, sugar, garlic powder, onion powder, peppercorns, and mustard seeds. Bring to a boil over medium heat.

2. Once the mixture comes to a boil, add the jalapeno slices and cook for 2-3 minutes, or until they are slightly softened.

3. Remove the pan from the heat and ladle the jalapenos and pickling liquid into clean, sterilized ball jars.

4. Place the lid on the jars and let them cool to room temperature before storing in the refrigerator. The pickled jalapenos will keep for up to a month in the fridge.

CPSIA information can be obtained
at www.ICGtesting.com
Printed in the USA
BVHW021945260323
660858BV00035B/196